THE
ELOQUENT INVESTOR

Facts, Quotations, and Useful Sayings About Wall Street

THOMAS RAYMOND

Disclosure. Nothing in this book constitutes or should be construed as either an offer to sell or the solicitation of an offer to buy any securities. In the United States, offers to sell and solicitations of offers to buy any securities may be made only by a prospectus (as defined in the Securities Act of 1933, as amended) delivered to the prospective purchasers. Similar regulations apply in other countries. This book contains various forward-looking statements based on the author's ideas, research, and beliefs. All forward-looking statements contained herein reflect solely the author's opinions about such future events and are subject to significant uncertainty. Actual events may differ materially from those described in such forward-looking statements.

Any Federal tax advice contained herein is not intended or written to be used, and cannot be used by you or any other person, for the purpose of avoiding any penalties that may be imposed by the Internal Revenue Code. This disclosure is made in accordance with the rules of Treasury Department Circular 230 governing standards of practice before the Internal Revenue Service. Any written statement contained herein relating to any Federal tax transaction or matter should not be used without first seeking counsel from a tax professional.

The Eloquent Investor is a registered service mark with the United States Patent and Trademark Office.

ISBN-13: 978-1499509144 (CreateSpace-Assigned)
ISBN-10: 1499509146

To my ever patient family – Kieren, Owen, and Garrett

TABLE OF CONTENTS

FOREWORD

S ome of the smartest money in the world have read and yet not understood the many investment tomes that Thomas Raymond has read
and understood – and translated for us – in the book you now hold in
your hands. I can't put it more directly than that.

Supercomputers or a staff of elite analysts could not interpret suc-
cessfully all the ideas Tom has examined and parsed for our enjoyment
in this book. Not only is he a lifelong student of investing, capital markets and the economy, but he is a teacher as well, teaching economics in
the evenings after tending to his clients all day.

I would surely impress you folks by saying I had read all the books
that Tom has read – but I haven't. Instead, he has done so for us – and
we reap the benefits.

Having just read *The Eloquent Investor*, Tom's first book, he makes a
compelling case that getting started in understanding and talking about
investing is easier than you might think. But we do not necessarily have
to listen to the whole album to appreciate the songs of Charlie Parker
– or the wisdom of Warren Buffett – but instead we listen to their individual songs or screeds.

This is what Tom has done – distilled down some of the most rec-
ognizable and indeed some of the more obscure expert wisdom in the
investment world. Then he gives real-life examples and explains what
the heck these "experts" really mean. What is the real life application?
Does this investment principle stand the test of time? Do I understand?
If not, how can I?

Tom and I first met because we attended the same high school,
Archmere Academy, in Claymont, Delaware, and he and my sister

graduated in the same class. We hit it off instantly. He went on to follow in his father's footsteps in the banking business; my sister Maggie Arvedlund did the same, she as a portfolio manager in private equity; I follow in their wake as a financial writer.

Tom shared the same kind of value-oriented, market-aware approach to investments that you might expect from a couple of – well – nerds. We have compared notes on all kinds of markets, including stocks and bonds (the proverbial "dogs and cats"), master limited partnerships, even investments in water, on which Tom has written convincingly is a new asset class in an entire white paper for his clients. I've learned much more from him than he from me – particularly when I needed ideas for *Barron's* magazine and for the *Philadelphia Inquirer* newspaper, where I work as a staff writer.

Tom's endless appetite for knowledge has been a significant inspiration for me to learn more about the financial markets, not just to whip off clever-sounding quotes, but to understand the philosophy.

Investment books typically come to print in two types: one is a collection of anecdotes and stories about high-fliers and masters of the universe, the other is full of equations. For example: When I first started out as a reporter in 1993, I was ordered to read Maniacs, Panics and Crashes by Charles Kindleberger, and *Memoirs of Extraordinary Popular Delusions and the Madness of Crowds* by Charles Mackay, as well as Graham & Dodd's classic on financial statement analysis. I also read *Liar's Poker* and several other books that sounded like fiction.

Most investors are mentored by seasoned professionals, to paraphrase Edison: "Market genius is one percent mathematics, ninety-nine percent experience." Tom's book fuses both, and in a natural way that is patient with readers such as myself. We, the readers, are the kind of people who want to appear to know what we're talking about – but we don't have the time to deconstruct the themes. Tom had the idea, the time (when not co-parenting two children) and the writing ability.

Tom's book represents a slightly new form of financial text because it tears apart the truisms about finance which we hear, but it's as if the speaker chats in Greek or Albanian. The language is entirely foreign to us. He explains in plain speech. And instead of a tiresome "beat the market at its own game" piece of work, this book pretends none of that. It is a refreshing departure from the traditional, a way to understand how different players think and approach the market from all angles.

Speaking of supercomputers, mine is calling out to me, reminding me to get back to my work as a writer, so I will end this way: If you are looking to enhance your business-related opportunities by reading this book, it's a good way to go because you will be conversant in market-speak. I wish this book had been around when I got started over 20 years ago.

Erin Arvedlund
Philadelphia, Pennsylvania, 2014

INTRODUCTION

Most people are infatuated with quotations, adages, facts, and aphorisms. Just think about how often sayings are used in speeches, lectures, pitches, and general conversation. We hear them on the radio and remember the ones we've read. Frankly, we really don't care where they came from. Shamed political figures, authors with dependency issues, and convicted felons all serve as legitimate sources. What's behind this addiction? The answer resides in the old adage that 'It's not what you say, but how you say it.' That's why I've written *The Eloquent Investor*. This is a collection of contemporary and classic quotations, quick facts, and aphorisms assembled to help you convey your message in a polished, more persuasive style.

Our fascination with quotations starts with their ability to make us more effective messengers. It's no secret that brilliance is a desirable trait, and quotations convey intelligence. They offer evidence that the user is well-read, hence, well-informed. Quotations also carry credibility. Incorporating a quotation in a presentation or speech demonstrates that you have a command of the topic, which in turn boosts the audience's confidence in your authority.

Brilliance is rare, but brilliance and charm in an individual is even more elusive. Quotations can make a complex topic simple to understand. As such, a well-placed quotation can add polish and refinement to an already intellectually stimulating conversation. The quotation is an invaluable social currency that bestows upon the user a hint of eloquence within just a few short seconds.

Like it or not, people have short attention spans: first impressions matter. We live in a sound-bite society, which makes quotations, adages, facts, and aphorisms have an even greater value. If you subscribe to the *Blink* and *Gut Feelings* school of thought, a lot is at stake with your opening remarks. Thus, a few short quotations or facts may be all you need to shape someone's perception of you.

Nowhere is our obsession with quotations more obvious than in the investing world. The investing business is a purveyor of intellectual capital. It sells words and thoughts, more so than tangible items. The quotation makes anyone a more effective messenger, but it offers even more value to the investment practitioner. The stakes are often high in the industry, as competition is abundant and potential clients may only have a limited window to hear what there is to say. This places a premium on the *right* words and thoughts.

The Eloquent Investor will be useful for people outside the investment profession as well. Imagine that you're with a group of individuals whom you desperately want to impress. The topic du jour is investment, or an adjacent subject, and you are on the outside looking in. You feel deflated because you don't have a working knowledge of this topic. Panic sets in: the opportunity is fleeting and you have nothing of substance to add. But, if you have read *The Eloquent Investor,* you will know just what to say at that moment.

The Eloquent Investor provides a treasure trove of quotations, adages, facts, and aphorisms that are easy to absorb and can stand on their own. The content in *The Eloquent Investor* arms readers so that they can leave the impression that they have a scholarly investment pedigree. There are also some longer quotations that you may find rich with detail; these provide an even deeper understanding of a given topic. This collection should provide value if you want to be a more powerful speaker, a sort of Ronald Reagan, the Great Communicator, on Wall Street.

I have included a supporting narrative when necessary. As the economist Alfred Marshall once said, "In common use almost every word has many shades of meaning, and therefore needs to be interpreted by the context."[1] Context accompanies the quotations to make the book flow more seamlessly and help limit any ambiguity. You will see quotations

---

1   *The Principles of Economics* (1890)

from a diverse set of individuals outside the investing realm, from Karl Marx to Mike Tyson, and even William Shakespeare. Although it is somewhat self-indulgent, I have also editorialized and added some practical guidance. *The Eloquent Investor* covers a lot of investment related ground, including taxes, frontier markets, and Black Swans. Some topics are polarizing, and you'll see content on both sides of the debate. This approach was designed to be illuminating, not prescriptive. This book should be a refreshing change of pace in a sea of opinionated media. Theoretically, with *The Eloquent Investor* in hand, you should be able to parachute into just about any investment related conversation and hold your own.

In preparing *The Eloquent Investor*, I've perused hundreds of books and countless articles. Given everyone's busy schedule, it's impossible for most people to read or reread the classics as well as news and commentary on every topic. This book provides a concise and organized summary of useful information from years of commentary. In short, a lifetime of reading is now in the palm of your hand.

The Eloquent Investor isn't a textbook, but it may provide you with the beginning framework for a successful investment plan. Like most things in life, it's necessary to develop a blueprint before execution. The following content might serve as that foundation. Keep in mind the words commonly credited to Benjamin Franklin: "An investment in knowledge always pays the best interest."

CORE PRINCIPLES

The track record for investors is generally underwhelming. In fact, this generation's average investor's portfolio has failed to keep pace with popular stock and bond indices, or even the value of the run-of-the-mill home. There are a few reasons for this and the one we will tackle right out of the gates is *rigor*. After seeing these woeful results in the chart below, it shouldn't come as too much of a surprise that many people spend more time researching a kitchen appliance than they do an investment. At some level, conducting an exhaustive review of the menu of refrigerators makes sense. Yet, while refrigerators come with warranties and receipts, investments do not. A poor investment can create irrecoverable financial and emotional hardship. Despite the potential downside, investors too often cannot resist the temptation to make an investment after finding out about the majestic return attained by someone else. Unfortunately, the past is not investable. Further, the average investor too often gets swayed by a convincing sound bite with quick profits presumed to be right around the corner. Successful investing is like most challenging ventures in life: it requires passion, focus, and commitment. As Warren Buffett said, "investing is simple – but not easy…."

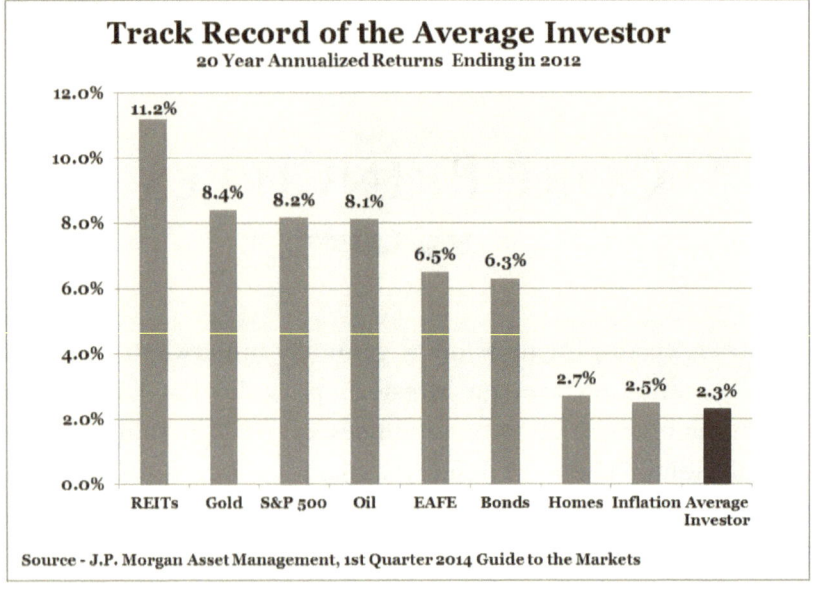

Track Record of the Average Investor
20 Year Annualized Returns Ending in 2012

Source - J.P. Morgan Asset Management, 1st Quarter 2014 Guide to the Markets

"Great investors tend to have a 'screw loose,' pursuing the game not for profit, but for sport." – David F. Swensen, chief investment officer of the Yale endowment, as quoted in Sebastian Mallaby's *More Money Than God* (2010)

> *Confucianism* promotes the thinking that humans are capable of change, but a true metamorphosis does not come easily. The meritocratic teachings believe that true mastery of a subject is a long and arduous journey.

"Success is dependent on effort." – Sophocles, ancient Greek tragedian

"Wishing will not bring riches." – Napoleon Hill, *Think and Grow Rich* (1937)

"Energy and persistence conquer all things." – Benjamin Franklin, American inventor, statesman, and Founding Father

"Wherever you go, go with all your heart." – Confucius, ancient Chinese philosopher and politician

- ☞ "If there is no struggle, there is no progress." – Frederick Douglass, West India Emancipation speech (August 3rd, 1857)

- ☞ "You have to have your heart in the business and the business in your heart." – Thomas J. Watson, former chairman and CEO of IBM

- ☞ "People who are unable to motivate themselves must be content with mediocrity, no matter how impressive their other talents." – Andrew Carnegie, early 20th century industrialist and philanthropist

- ☞ "Persistence is the twin sister of excellence. One is a matter of quality; the other a matter of time." – Marabel Morgan, *The Electric Woman* (1985)

- ☞ "The difference between a successful person and others is not a lack of strength, not a lack of knowledge, but rather a lack of will." – attributed to Vince Lombardi, former NFL head coach

> Would you give your money to a stranger you met on the street? As you will learn, management is a key ingredient to success at a company. You should research the management of a company as well as you can before you invest. Otherwise, you're basically giving your money to a stranger. Do your due diligence.

- ☞ "The art of investment has one characteristic that is not generally appreciated. A creditable, if unspectacular, result can be achieved by the layperson with a minimum of effort and capability; but to improve this easily attainable standard requires much application and more than a trace of wisdom." – Benjamin Graham, *The Intelligent Investor* (1949)

- ☞ "It's not supposed to be easy. Anyone who finds it easy is stupid." – Charlie Munger, Vice-Chairman of Berkshire Hathaway (2012)

- ☞ "But all things excellent are as difficult as they are rare." – Benedict de Spinoza, *Ethics* (1677)

- ☞ "No one who can rise before dawn three hundred sixty days a year fails to make his family rich." – Chinese proverb

- ☞ "Technique is noticed most markedly in the case of those who have not mastered it." – Leon Trotsky, *Literature and Revolution* (1924)

A 1990 study called *Expert Performance and Deliberate Practice* by psychology Professor K. Anders Ericsson concluded that elite performers need 10,000 hours of measured practice to achieve greatness. So read, read, and read. Reading is exercise for the mind and investing is a sport of intellect. Devoting 417 continuous, uninterrupted days (10,000 hours) to investment research may not be practical, but hopefully gives some sense for the rigor needed to be a successful investor. In short, have an insatiable appetite for knowledge....

- ☞ "I have said that in my whole life, I have known no wise person, over a broad subject matter who didn't read all the time – none, zero." – Charlie Munger, Berkshire Hathaway Annual Meeting (2003)

- ☞ "Reading maketh a full man, conference a ready man, and writing an exact man." – Francis Bacon, *Of Studies* (1597)

- ☞ "One's first step in wisdom is to question everything – and one's last is to come to terms with everything." – Georg Cristoph Lichtenberg, 18th century German scientist and satirist

- "The wisest mind has something yet to learn." – George Santayana, Spanish philosopher and novelist

- "Knowledge has to be improved, challenged, and increased constantly, or it vanishes." – Peter Drucker, management icon

> The capacity of the brain is astounding. In fact, on a per unit basis, it emits more energy than the sun (Chaisson, April 5, 2010). We all have this tremendous potential to learn just waiting to be unleashed.

- "Man is still the most extraordinary computer of all." – John F. Kennedy, 35th president of the United States, remarks upon presenting the NASA Distinguished Service Medal to astronaut L. Gordon Cooper at the White House, Washington, D.C. (May 21st, 1963)

- "And this I believe: that the free, exploring mind of the individual human is the most valuable thing in the world." – John Steinbeck, *East of Eden* (1952)

- "The person who stops studying merely because they have finished school is forever hopelessly doomed to mediocrity, no matter what their calling." – Napoleon Hill, *Think and Grow Rich* (1937)

The stakes are high; higher than that of an ill-fated appliance purchase. Therefore, immerse yourself with information related to a given investment. Read voraciously, stress test your thesis, and ask others for input all in an attempt to build a thoughtful mosaic of information that will help you make the most informed decision possible. George Bernard Shaw once supposedly said, "few people think more than two or three times a year." Hopefully, you can prove him wrong....

- "You have to know what you own, and why you own it." – attributed to Peter Lynch, former portfolio manager for the Fidelity Magellan fund

- "He will risk half his fortune in the stock market with less reflection that he devotes to the selection of a medium-priced automobile." – Edwin LeFevre, *Reminiscences of a Stock Operator* (1923)

- "It is a capital mistake to theorize before one has data. Insensibly one begins to twist facts to suit theories, instead of theories to suit facts." – Arthur Conan Doyle, "A Scandal in Bohemia" (1891)

Pillar one is rigor. Pillar two is **humility**. Frankly, it's not such a bad thing to have your teeth kicked in, as you don't want an investing ego. That can breed overconfidence, which can lead to complacency and lack of preparedness. Further, mistakes will happen. It's inevitable. All investors stub their toe, even the greats like Warren Buffett. Yet, each failure is a learning lesson in disguise. A critical tenet of investing success is to learn from your mistakes....

- "To kill an error is as good a service as, and sometimes even better than, the establishing of a new truth or fact." – Charles Darwin, *More Letters of Charles Darwin (Volume 2)*, letter to A.S. Wilson (March 5th, 1879)

- "In the business world, everyone is paid in two coins: cash and experience. Take the experience first; the cash will come later." – Harold Geneen, former president of ITT Corporation

- "Failure is the condiment that gives success its flavor." – Truman Capote, American author

☞ "A life spent making mistakes is not only more honorable, but more useful than a life spent doing nothing." – George Bernard Shaw, 19ᵗʰ century Irish playwright and co-founder of London School of Economics

Malcolm Gladwell popularized this 10,000 hour threshold 28 years later in his book *Outliers: The Story of Success.* He would highlight the Beatles, in the eyes of many the best rock band ever, and their tireless approach to showcase this concept of how consistent practice can lead to masterful results.

☞ "Experience is the name everyone gives to their mistakes." – Oscar Wilde, *Lady Windermere's Fan* (1892)

☞ "Failure is a trickster with a keen sense of irony and cunning. It takes great delight in tripping one up when success is almost within reach." – Napoleon Hill, *Think and Grow Rich* (1937)

☞ "A moral being is one who is capable of reflecting on his past actions and their motives – of approving of some and disapproving of others." – Charles Darwin, *The Descent of Man, and Selection in Relation to Sex* (1871)

☞ "The Mistake family is so large that there is always one of them around when you want to see what you can do in the fool-play line." – Edwin LeFevre, *Reminiscences of a Stock Operator* (1923)

☞ "Once we realize that imperfect understanding is the human condition there is no shame in being wrong, only in failing to correct our mistakes." – George Soros, chairman of Soros Investment Management and philanthropist

☞ "We shall not grow wiser before we learn that much that we have done was very foolish." – Friedrich August von Hayek, *The Road to Serfdom* (1944)

Mistakes, if viewed appropriately, are quite valuable. Use them as a learning mechanism; self-reflection can be an invaluable habit to adopt. Otherwise, investing can be an unnecessarily expensive exercise....

Keep a journal. Many investment heavyweights do. On a regular basis they write down their investment theses and later grade themselves on their predictions. This helps illuminate their missteps: it's hard to get better if you don't know what you're doing wrong. A feedback mechanism is an indispensable part of the learning process.

☞ "The game taught me the game. And it didn't spare me rod while teaching." – Edwin LeFevre, *Reminiscences of a Stock Operator* (1923)

☞ "Experience is a hard teacher because she gives the test first, the lesson afterwards." – Vern Law, former pitcher for the Pittsburgh Pirates

You should also study the mistakes of others. This is a less costly form of tuition, but perhaps of even greater value, as this will help you avoid making some of these same mistakes, yourself....

☞ "History does not repeat itself, but it does rhyme." – commonly attributed to Mark Twain, American author and humorist

☞ "When it comes to market history, there are only two choices: trading with awareness of it, trading in ignorance of it." – Brett Steenbarger, stock trader and professor

☞ "Study the past, if you would divine the future." – Confucius, ancient Chinese philosopher and politician

- "The charm of history and its enigmatic lesson consist in the fact that, from age to age, nothing changes and yet everything is completely different." – Aldous Huxley, *The Devils of Loudun* (1952)

- "Those who cannot remember the past are condemned to repeat it." – George Santayana, *Reason in Common Sense* (1905)

- "The only thing new in this world is the history you don't know." – Harry S. Truman, as quoted in *Plain Speaking: An Oral Biography of Harry S Truman* (1974)

Many profitable investment formulas have an expiration date. The problem with the investment space is that there are too many smart-minded, well-resourced capitalists chasing after that golden goose. If a way to mint money has been unearthed, it will be sure to attract imitators and thereby dilute future profits. It's not impossible to have an investing edge with a moat around it, but it is surely difficult. Therefore, you need to be ready to evolve. To put it another way: don't be stubborn and closed-minded. The exact circumstances of the past will likely not be repeated in the future. Markets and economies are dynamic and one must be willing to adapt and not continue to fight the battles of yesterday.

Changing your opinion on something can be excruciatingly difficult. Some people would rather have a root canal than change their stance on a subject, irrespective of any new facts or developments. The impediments to change are likely of the reputational genre. One perhaps doesn't want to appear unpredictable or fickle. These are really flimsy, shortsighted reasons, especially if you know that you are right. Don't be an unbending dogmatist, as having the right opinions will over time build reputational equity and prove more conducive to generating financial gain….

- "When my information changes, I alter my conclusions. What do you do, sir?"– John Maynard Keynes, as quoted in *The Keynes Centenary* (1983)

   ✆ "The reasonable man adapts himself to the world: the unreasonable one persists in adapting the world to himself. Therefore, all progress depends on the unreasonable man." – George Bernard Shaw, *Maxims for Revolutionists* (1903)

   ✆ "Loyalty to ideas is not a good thing for traders, scientists – or anyone." – Nassim Taleb, *Fooled by Randomness* (2004)

   ✆ "Merely having an open mind is nothing. The object of opening the mind, as of opening the mouth, is to shut it again on something solid." – G.K. Chesterton, English literary critic, novelist, and theologian

   ✆ "There are two ways to be fooled. One is to believe what isn't true; the other is to refuse to believe what is true." – Søren Kierkegaard, considered the first existentialist philosopher

   ✆ "A foolish consistency is the hobgoblin of little minds." – Ralph Waldo Emerson, *Self-Reliance* (1841)

   ✆ "A man should look for what is, and not what he thinks it should be." – commonly attributed to Albert Einstein, German-born physicist whose name is name synonymous with genius

   ✆ "To improve is to change; to be perfect is to change often." – Winston Churchill, House of Commons (June 23rd, 1925)

   ✆ "Some men never seem to grow old. Always active in thought, always ready to adopt new ideas, they are never chargeable with foggyism. Satisfied, yet ever dissatisfied, settled, yet ever unsettled, they always enjoy the best of what is, are the first to find the best of what will be." – William Shakespeare, foremost dramatist of the English language

- "When you are through changing, you're through." – Bruce Barton, *The Man Nobody Knows* (1925)

- "You can't just keep doing what works one time, because everything around you is always changing. To succeed, you have to stay out in front of that change." – Sam Walton, *Sam Walton: Made in America* (1992)

- "It is quite true what philosophy says; that life must be understood backwards. But then one forgets the other principle: that it must be lived forwards." – Søren Kierkegaard, *Journals IV A* (1843)

- "Change before you have to." – title of book by pastor Rob Ketterling (2012)

- "a point of inflection marks the moment when the same forces that have worked in particular way for a long time begin to operate in a different and frequently unfamiliar direction. After passing through a point of inflection, the world no longer obeys the same rules it has been obeying." – Peter L. Bernstein, "Points of Inflection: Investment Management Tomorrow," *Financial Analysts Journal* (July/August 2003)

- "When one door closes, another opens. But we often look so regretfully upon the closed door that we don't see the one that has opened for us." – commonly attributed to Alexander Graham Bell, considered the inventor of the telephone

- "A good player plays where the puck is. A great player plays where the puck is going to be." – Wayne Gretzky, Hall of Fame inductee of the National Hockey League

  ❦ "The dogmas of the quiet past, are inadequate to the stormy present. The occasion is piled high with difficulty, and we must rise – with the occasion. As our case is new, so we must think anew, and act anew." – Abraham Lincoln, annual message to Congress (December 1st, 1862)

  ❦ "He who rejects change is the architect of decay. The only human institution that rejects change is the cemetery." – Harold Wilson, speech to Consultative Assembly of the Council of Europe (January 23rd, 1967)

Most everyone is proven right if he or she waits long enough, but that doesn't make ignorance a productive strategy. You need a little empathy to factor in what others are doing, as your buy or sell activity alone will likely not influence the performance of an investment. Warren Buffett, Carl Icahn, and a small group of other elite investors can move markets. The rest of us are just minnows swimming in an ocean with nobody noticing or caring if you buy or sell a security. Instead, it will be the collective action of many that dictate the investment's future....

  ❦ "Professional investment may be likened to those newspaper competitions in which the competitors have to pick out the six prettiest faces from a hundred photographs, the prize being awarded to the competitor whose choice most nearly corresponds to the average preferences of the competitors as a whole, so that each competitor has to pick, not those faces that the competitor finds prettiest, but those which he thinks likeliest to catch the fancy of the other competitors, all of whom are looking at the problem from the same point of view." – John Maynard Keynes, *The General Theory of Employment, Interest, and Money* (1936)

The third key tenet is being ***dispassionate***. Your emotions are a double-edged sword. As you will read later in the behavioral finance section, we have a host of primal instincts that can be counterproductive to investment results. At the same time, emotional decision making by others can create opportunities for the self-aware to capitalize. Investing isn't personal. Treat it as a business – a ruthless one at that. Your investments aren't your friends, and you're not married to them, so act accordingly....

- ☞ "the tape is not chivalrous and moreover does not reward loyalty." - Edwin LeFevre, *Reminiscences of a Stock Operator* (1923)

- ☞ "The stock doesn't know you own it." – George Goodman (aka Adam Smith), *The Money Game* (1968)

Investing can test your emotional fortitude, and you need to be prepared for the cyclical nature of the markets and economy, as well as their vagaries. There will be bull markets and bear markets, bubbles, recessions, recoveries, expansions, periods of economic vibrancy and despondency. Then wash, rinse, repeat. More will be covered later, but the markets and economy can be unpredictable and rarely move in a linear manner. This may seem like an obvious preamble to investing. However, while many of these economic and market conditions are temporary, they are often treated as permanent....

- ☞ "You get recessions, you have stock market declines. If you don't understand that's going to happen, then you're not ready, you won't do well in the markets." – attributed to Peter Lynch

A common Wall Street maxim is that "Bull markets don't die of old age." They persist until economic conditions deteriorate or valuations become detached from reality.

- ☞ "Cycles always prevail eventually. Nothing goes in one direction forever. Trees don't grow to the sky. Few things go to zero. And there's little that's as dangerous for investor health as insistence on extrapolating today's events into the future." – Howard Marks, *The Most Important Thing: Uncommon Sense for the Thoughtful Investor* (2011)

- "There is an end to everything, to good things as well." – attributed to Geoffrey Chaucer, father of English literature

- "Change is the investor's only certainty." – T. Rowe Price, Jr., founder of eponymous investment firm

- "Bull markets are born in pessimism, rise on skepticism and die from optimism." – Sir John Templeton, legendary investor, businessman, and philanthropist

- "Frankly, we cannot imagine a stock market of the future in which there will never be any serious losses, and in which, every tyro will be guaranteed a large profit on his stock purchases." – Benjamin Graham, *The Intelligent Investor* (1949)

- "Profit margins are probably the most mean-reverting series in finance, and if profit margins do not mean-revert, then something has gone badly wrong with capitalism. If high profits do not attract competition, there is something wrong with the system and it is not functioning properly." – Jeremy Grantham, co-founder and chief investment strategist of Grantham Mayo van Otterloo (2006)

- "Markets are constantly in a state of uncertainty and flux and money is made by discounting the obvious and betting on the unexpected." – George Soros (2005)

Over any given short period of time (days, weeks, or even months) your returns can be ugly, and this can prove quite trying. This will likely happen as the markets can be irrational and maybe even a bit insane in the short run. Commitment and discipline may not deliver immediate results, but don't get frustrated and let your emotions get the best of you. Emotional investing rarely ends well.

These irrational market moments create opportunities for those who are emotionally prepared to capitalize. However, this is much easier said than done. In particular, creating wealth by buying low is very uncomfortable as we are predisposed to think that when investments fall in value they will continue their downward trajectory, as their flawed fundamentals have finally been exposed. For example, on March 9th, 2009 the S&P 500 established its low point, stemming from the unrelenting credit crisis. The economy was still close to cardiac arrest and fear was ubiquitous. In fact, in a *New York Times* interview that day, a hedge fund manager advocated the purchase of guns, as social upheaval was thought to be right around the corner.[2] Most people were rationalizing reasons to sell stocks, and the popular perception was that the S&P would continue to establish new lows. Portfolio risk was seen as radioactive, and the social pressures to sell low and exit equities were enormous. Yet, the market was screamingly cheap (more on stock valuations later) and for the dispassionate investor it was the chance of a lifetime....

- "Be ready when opportunity comes . . . . Luck is the time when preparation and opportunity meet."– attributed to both Roy Chapin Jr. and Pierre Elliot Trudeau

- "chance favors only the prepared mind." – Louis Pasteur, lecture at the University of Lille (December 7th, 1854)

- "The fortunate circumstances of our lives are generally found at last to be of our own procuring." Oliver Goldsmith, *The Vicar of Wakefield* (1766)

---

2   David K. Randall, "March 9, 2009: The Day Stocks Bottomed Out," *Forbes,* March 8, 2010.

☞ "I will study and get ready, and perhaps my chance will come." – Abraham Lincoln

☞ "Before everything else, getting ready is the secret of success." – Henry Ford, founder of Ford Motor Company and American industrialist

☞ "Remember that it is not the lawyer who knows the most law, but the one who best prepares the case, who wins." – Napoleon Hill, *Think and Grow Rich* (1937)

☞ "We should never lose an occasion. Opportunity is more powerful even than conquerors and prophets." – Benjamin Disraeli, *Tancred* (1847)

Remaining dispassionate in the way you approach the markets is a prerequisite for investment success. After that, it can get a bit more complicated. Unfortunately, there is no single universal formula for investment success, and what worked in the past may be rendered obsolete in the future. This shouldn't be inherently alarming. Instead, investing embraces creativity, as there are several different paths to the finish line of financial gain. For instance, you may excel at picking emerging market stocks or maybe you have a keen sense for the credit markets. The educated investor who adheres to the principle of rigor has few emotional attachments to any one of his or her various investments; your favorite investment should be the one that gives you the best risk-adjusted returns....

☞ "It does not matter whether the cat is black or white, only that it catches mice." – Deng Xiaoping, former Chinese leader from the late 1970's to the early 1990's

The next tenet is recognizing the ***value of time***. Employing a long-term perspective is an invaluable technique. For starters, it serves as a mechanism to prevent market timing. Market timing is the act of wholesale shifts in and out of assets. For example, hitting the abort button and liquidating your portfolio when you think the markets are headed south. Even if you do exhibit surgical precision on a trade like this, you still have to be right once more when you reverse it. To be sure, market timing is a seductive, but dangerous proposition. Just look at how the math works against you. If you had sat out the best four months over the past 20 years it would have cost two percent per annum to the S&P 500, or more than 48 percent on a cumulative basis. Further, recall the natural cyclicality of the economy and markets and the notion that most conditions are transitory. So when you think in terms of years, not weeks or days, you don't have to agonize over every single data point delivered to you courtesy of the 24/7 new environment. As such, a long-term perspective leads to a distinct investing advantage....

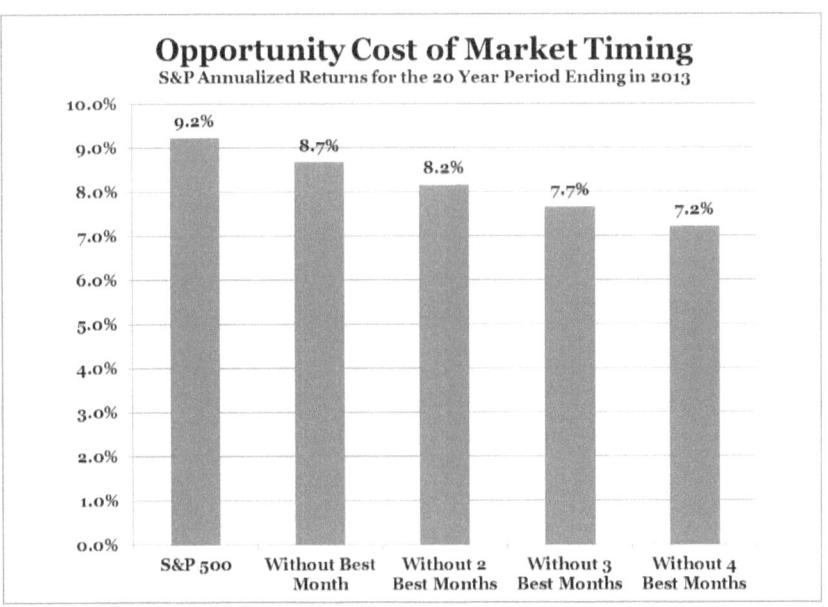

- "The average long-term experience in investing is never surprising, but the short-term experience is always surprising." – Charles Ellis, *Winning the Loser's Game* (2002)

- "Time is your friend. Impulse is your enemy." – John Bogle, founder of The Vanguard Group

- "When we own portions of outstanding businesses with outstanding managements, our favorite holding period is forever." – Warren Buffett, 1988 Letter to Shareholders

- "It never failed that during the dry years the people forgot the rich years, and during the wet years they lost all memory of the dry years." – John Steinbeck, *East of Eden* (1952)

- "Bottoms in the investment world don't end with four-year lows; they end with 10- or 15-year lows." – Jim Rogers, investment guru and author (more on him in the biography section at the end of the book)

The 24/7 news environment will lead you to believe that every economic data point is of critical importance. Most often, it's just bluster. The media wants you to pay constant attention, because this allows them to secure more advertising revenue. This point is worth repeating – your investing time horizon should be measured in years, not hours. In the short run (i.e. days, weeks, months), markets can be fueled by emotion and behave quite irrationally. Just remember that economies are like oil tankers: they don't change directions easily.

> In *Winning the Loser's Game*, Charles Ellis compares investing to a game of amateur tennis. The winner is not the one who hits the most elaborate shots but the one who commits the least amount of errors.

Time is your most generous companion during your investment voyage, not the talking heads on television. If you fancy yourself as a disciplined investor but you have a short-term time horizon, then you're a walking contradiction and a gambler. You're probably better off hitting the slot machine. Know that the house usually wins when you gamble, but, with the right level of discipline, you might have the edge when you invest....

More often than not, the front page news story is already priced into asset prices. What you should focus your energies on is the content found on page 20 or 21 (figuratively, not literally) to determine how or if that will impact future investment results.

> ⌘ "Investing should be more like watching paint dry or watching grass grow. If you want excitement, take $800 and go to Las Vegas." – Paul Samuelson, winner of Nobel Prize in Economic Sciences

> ⌘ "Time is Archimedes' lever in investing."[3] – Charles D. Ellis, *Winning the Loser's Game* (2002)

> ⌘ "Changing your position because of news is usually not a great idea." – Jim Leitner, Falcon Management, as quoted in *Inside the House of Money* by Steven Drobny (2006)

> ⌘ "Everywhere you turn you see Americans sacrifice their long-term interests for a short-term reward." – Michael Lewis, *Boomerang: Travels in the New Third World* (2012)

> ⌘ "A serious investor is not likely to believe that the day-to-day or even month-to-month fluctuations of the stock market make him richer or poorer." – Benjamin Graham, *The Intelligent Investor* (1949)

A long-term perspective serves as a device to help you resist the urge to speculate, even though speculation does offer the 'promise' of quick, easy profits. This can be just as sinister as market timing. Speculators often rely on *The Greater Fool Theory* as an exit strategy. It suggests that an

---

3 "Give me a lever long enough and a fulcrum on which to place it, and I shall move the world." – Archimedes, ancient Greek scientist, astronomer, and inventor

investment solely has merit based on the premise that you can sell to someone at an even higher price, irrespective of its intrinsic worth. In other words, speculation is investing devoid of rigorous research. Just know that the markets are not a get-rich-quick scheme and past performance alone is not a reason to buy something....

> Don't look. One of the best mechanisms to prevent short-term thinking is to resist the urge of viewing price quotes. You can drive yourself batty and make some avoidable mistakes by looking at price quotes on a too frequent basis (intra-day, daily, or even monthly). In fact, there are some top-notch asset managers that disallow their employees from looking at market quotes while they are at the office.

☞ "Speculation is an effort, probably unsuccessful, to turn a little money into a lot. Investment is an effort, which should be successful, to prevent a lot of money from becoming a little." – Fred Schwed, *Where Are the Customers' Yachts: or A Good Hard Look at Wall Street* (1940)

☞ "The market's not a very accommodating machine; it won't provide high returns just because you need them." – Peter L. Bernstein

☞ "when speculation has done its worst, two and two still make four." – Samuel Johnson, "The terrific diction ridiculed," from *The Idler* (1758)

☞ "There are two times in a man's life when he should not speculate – when he can't afford to and when he can." – Mark Twain, *Following the Equator* (1897)

☞ "October. This is one of the peculiarly dangerous months to speculate in stocks in. The others are July, January, September, April, November, May, March, June, December, August and February." – Mark Twain, *Pudd'nhead Wilson* (1894)

It seems pretty straightforward that speculating is perilous, just like smoking cigarettes or overloading on carbohydrates. Yet, we all still indulge in our vices from time to time, even though we know the warnings. Well, here's another warning – the future will hold a number of speculative frenzies that will entice you….

> ☞ "We find that whole communities suddenly fix their minds upon one object, and go mad in its pursuit; that millions of people become simultaneously impressed with one delusion, and run after it, till their attention is caught by some new folly more captivating than the first." – Charles Mackay, *Extraordinary Popular Delusions and the Madness of Crowds* (1841)

> ☞ "We learn from history that we do not learn from history" – Georg Wilhelm Friedrich Hegel, 19th century German philosopher

It may not be real estate, or technology stocks, or a precise replay of a past frenzy, but the temptation to speculate will come. What is also certain is that our financial memory banks tend to be ritualistically purged over time, and we can quickly lose sight of what can go wrong when speculation comes back en vogue. This opens the door for temptation. Further, the lure to participate is fueled by the stories of those lottery ticket winners who made a killing with little rigor applied. But don't let quick riches serve as a trap and have it overshadow the remote chances of it working. True, speculation can lead to financial gain, but this is certainly the exception and not the rule. Further, it's not for the faint of heart, and it's certainly not for investment business novices….

> ☞ "As a speculator you must embrace disorder and chaos." – Louis Bacon, founder Moore Capital Management

Market timing and speculation are high stakes forms of investment turnover. Sometimes you might feel compelled to do something, anything, to improve the chances of investment success. That's a flawed way of thinking. Sometimes inaction is the best investment action. Boring is good. This is true even for industry professionals.

There is a lot of evidence that shows an inverse relationship between turnover and peer group performance for professional asset managers in just about all asset classes (bonds, large cap stocks, etc.). Investment practitioners and non-practitioners both benefit from simply sitting tight.

Despite patience being an investment virtue, turnover has reached alarming heights. Consider that in 1957, the average investor had an average holding period of eight years (13 percent annual turnover) as measured by activity on the New York Stock Exchange.[4] Now average turnover is around 100 percent (one year holding period), which is a level not seen since the high margin days preceding the Great Depression.

Turnover levels have been on a steady incline since the mid-1970's and have rather ironic beginnings. On May 1st, 1975, the Securities and Exchange Commission issued an edict to unwind the fixed high cost commission structure. Costs plummeted as designed. For example, Charles Schwab charged $60 per trade in 1998 and now charges less than $10 for an online trade. This reduction of costs, while intended to help the average investor, may have perversely done a disservice as it paved the way for more frictionless trading.

> It rarely pays off to switch from lane to lane while driving. If your standing does improve, it tends to be a fleeting victory. The same goes for investing. A steady approach will often yield the best results.

There are a variety of other contributing factors to this new turnover paradigm beyond costs. You can point your finger at the decimalization of stock prices in 2000 and 2001, the adoption of electronic trading networks, and the rise of hedge funds. Yet, it should come as little surprise that the velocity of transactions has reached new heights during the information age. We have news streaming at all times from all directions. The benefit is that investors are empowered with more data than ever. The

---

4 Alex Dumortier, "Best Practices for Long-Term Investors in a Microsecond Market," *The Motley Fool*, September 14, 2012.

downside is that this information also creates that many more *reasons* to implement a trade. Regrettably, this more conducive trading environment has not resulted in improved investment performance (recall the past 20-year average investor returns)....

- "sometimes twiddling your thumbs is the least malignant activity." – Barton Biggs, *Diary of a Hedgehog* (2012)

- "Do not confuse motion and progress. A rocking horse keeps moving but does not make any progress." – Alfred A. Montapert, author of *The Supreme Philosophy of Man: The Laws of Life* (1977)

- "Most institutional investors feel compelled to swing at almost every pitch and forgo batting selectivity for frequency." – attributed to Seth Klarman, author and founder of Baupost Group

- "Long-term consistency trumps short-term intensity." – Bruce Lee, martial arts legend

- "One man's staying power is another man's foolish lack of discipline." – Anonymous

- "For investors as a whole, returns decrease as motion increases." – Warren Buffett, 2005 Letter to Shareholders

- "The most treasured asset in investment management is a steady hand at the tiller." – Robert Arnott, Chairman and Chief Executive of Research Affiliates, LLC (more on him in the biography section)

- "It was never my thinking that made the big money for me. It was always the sitting. Got that? My sitting tight!" – Edwin LeFevre, *Reminiscences of a Stock Operator* (1923)

☞ "Sometimes knowing when *not* to fight is just as important to a general's success as knowing *how* to fight." – Bill O'Reilly and Martin Dugard, *Killing Lincoln: The Shocking Assassination that Changed America Forever* (2011)

Unfortunately, it is all too common to hear investors select a company because of a single variable. "I love its product." "The CEO is brilliant." In reality, these well-known aspects of a business are likely already factored into the price of the company. Further, they can be fleeting: CEOs depart, products get recalled or rendered obsolete. Betting on a single trait of a company may prove profitable. However, those results may very well be due to luck.

There are a lot of lucky coin flippers out there. However, try not to confuse luck with skill, which can lead to unwarranted overconfidence and set the stage for failure. In fact, according to work by Professor Barr Rosenberg, a 70 year observation window is necessary in order to conclusively determine if superior investment results are derived from luck or skill[5]. Long story short, one or two successful trades should be placed in the proper perspective....

☞ "And an isolated piece of information, even though it normally counsels us correctly, can lead us to clearly stupid mistakes – mistakes that, when exploited by clever others, leave us looking silly or worse." – Robert B. Cialdini, Ph.D., *Influence: The Psychology of Persuasion* (2006)

☞ "If a man has tossed a coin 'heads' four times in succession, which do you think he is more likely to toss the fifth time, heads or tails? (If you think he is more likely to toss either heads or tails, look into the interior-decorating game.)" – Fred Schwed, *Where Are the Customers' Yachts: or A Good Hard Look at Wall Street* (1940)

---

5 Charles Ellis, *Winning the Loser's Game* (New York: McGraw-Hill, 2002).

- "You don't feel thirty percent smarter when the stock goes up by thirty percent, so when the stock goes down you shouldn't feel thirty percent dumber." – Jeff Bezos, as quoted in *The Everything Store: Jeff Bezos and the Age of Amazon* by Brad Stone (2013)

Luck does happen. Heck, there is whole casino industry built upon this concept. Frankly, sometimes it does help to be lucky....

- "Every once in a while, someone makes a risky bet on an improbable or uncertain outcome and ends up looking like a genius. But we should recognize that it happened because of luck and boldness, not skill." – Howard Marks, co-founder and CEO of Oaktree Capital Management, LLC (more on him in biography section)

- "Although men flatter themselves with their great actions, they are not so often the result of a great design as of chance." – François de La Rochefoucauld, 17th century French author

- "I returned, and saw under the sun, that the race is not to the swift, nor the battle to the strong, neither yet bread to the wise, nor yet riches to men of understanding, nor yet favour to men of skill; but time and chance happeneth to them all." – Ecclesiastes 9:11, Oxford King James Version

- "Even a stopped clock gives the right time twice a day." – Proverb

- "Getting rich takes hard work, a passion for what you do and luck." – Leon Cooperman, Chairman and CEO of Omega Advisors, Inc.

- "If there's 10,000 people looking at the stocks and trying to pick winners, one in 10,000 is going to score, by chance alone, a great

coup, and that's all that's going on. It's a game, it's a chance oper-ation, and people think they are doing something purposeful .
. . but they're really not." – Merton Miller, Nobel Laureate and Professor of Economics, University of Chicago, Transcript of the PBS Nova Special, *The Trillion Dollar Bet* (2000)

In parting, if you don't have the requisite time or interest, then don't be afraid to ask for help....

☞ "Follow an expert." – Virgil, ancient Roman poet

OVERTIME....

Heeding Virgil's Advice

There are a few poorly hatched home improvement projects that are vivid reminders that I am not an expert in many aspects of life. It's just not in the cards that we will be great at everything. Therefore, be pragmatic with the 10,000 hour threshold as it relates to investing. Achieving expert status is a steep hurdle and may not be achievable, at least not in the short-term. Therefore, seeking the counsel of a seasoned professional shouldn't be considered a sign of weakness. On the contrary, it shows humility and a dash of wisdom.

If you find yourself heeding Virgil's advice on the investment front, there are fortunately plenty of fantastic financial advisors and consultants to assist the non-experts out there. Unfortunately, there are also some not so good ones. Thus, the search process for an expert needs to be exhaustive and thorough. The CFA Institute is a good place to start if you are looking for a road map to guide you through the selection process. The CFA Institute is not a broker, dealer, or financial advice firm. Thus, it has no dog in the race. Moreover, part of its mission is to advance ethical behavior in the field of finance. Thus, it offers objective, uncompensated guidance in the quest for an expert.[6]

You'll probably hear different counsel from different people, but my first series of questions when interviewing a financial expert would address our alignment of interests. An advisor needs to be intelligent, but more importantly you want one who works for you, not against you. For starters, ask how they are compensated. If it's a commission structure (variable fees) they are incentivized to trade in your portfolio (i.e. high turnover) in order to generate commissions on each trade. That may be in their best interest, but probably not yours.

---

6 Go to http://www.cfainstitute.org/learning/investor/Documents/selecting_investment_services_provider.pdf for more details.

Market Timing Revisited

There are many cautionary tales on the ills of market timing that you wouldn't even imagine. At the risk of being overbearing, here are some more numbers that show its dangers. In the last 20 years, ending in 2013, cash (US 3 Month T Bill) outperformed the S&P 500 five times. In other words, you have a 25 percent chance of hitting the abort button during times of market turbulence and going to cash as a tactical maneuver and it being a profitable endeavor. This probability figure might be a bit generous as you also need pinpoint precision when you want to re-enter the stock market. The same message goes for fixed income, though with slightly better odds: according to the Barclays Aggregate Intermediate Index, cash outperformed fixed income in six calendar years during this same stretch. The math shows that when you try to get cute and meddle with your investments, the results can get ugly. Thus, stick with the odds and maintain a disciplined approach.

ECONOMICS

"The economy, stupid." – Bill Clinton 1992 presidential campaign credo

You don't need to be a detective to know that the economy, our financial ecosystem, plays a meaningful role with investment results. In fact, over longer periods, earnings per share growth of the S&P 500 (earnings are the lifeblood of stocks) should exhibit a high degree of positive correlation with that of nominal gross domestic product (GDP) growth. So, as the economy goes, so should corporate profits. Therefore, at least when it comes to stocks, your odds of investment success improve when an economy is accelerating, compared to when it is decelerating. This much is simple, but the economy is far more complex, which is at the root of why economics is a divisive subject. With so many different inputs into the economic engine, there are a corresponding amount of ideas and opinions. Further, conjecture is plentiful, because unlike other sciences, you cannot conduct experiments for an economy in a laboratory to test a hypothesis. That also means that the facts counter to the hypothesis will never be known. Further muddying the waters is the likelihood that the growth equation for one

GDP is the most conventional measure of economic growth. GDP has four main inputs: consumption (consumer spending), business investment, government spending, and net exports. In the United States, consumer spending represents roughly 70 percent of GDP.

GNP (Gross National Product) is similar to GDP, but it accounts for the production of a citizen even if it occurs outside his or her respective home country.

country may not be valid for another. As such, there is no one reliable formula to deliver economic growth....

⊕ "No one can pinpoint the precise mix of reasons why nations grow, or fail to grow. There is no magic formula, only a long list of known ingredients: allow the free-market flow of goods, money, and people; encourage savings, and make sure banks are funneling the money into productive investments; impose the rule of law and protect property rights; stabilize the economy with low budget and trade deficits; keep inflation in check; open doors to foreign capital, particularly when the capital comes with technology as part of the bargain; build better roads and schools; feed the children, and so on." – Ruchir Sharma, *Breakout Nations: In Pursuit of the Next Economic Miracles* (2012)

Economics obviously has a monetary element to it. However, human behavior and acting in one's self-interest are interwoven and vital aspects of commerce and general economics. Incentives are profoundly influential to any economic regime. Consider that the lack of the *right* incentives proved to be the fatal flaw with communism. This hybrid economic and political regime strived for financial homogeneity for all except for a few elite that oversaw the masses. The everyday laborer was compensated to fill government dictated quotas. That's it. There was limited upside for ingenuity or innovation, which is what an economy needs to catapult itself forward....

⊕ "The rich only select from the heap what is most precious and agreeable. They consume little more than the poor, and in spite of their natural selfishness and rapacity...they divide with the poor the produce of all their improvements. They are led by an *invisible hand* to make nearly the same distribution of the necessaries of life, which would have been made, had the earth been divided into equal portions among all its inhabitants, and thus without intending it, without knowing it, advance the interest of the society, and afford means to the multiplication of the species." – Adam Smith, *The Theory of Moral Sentiments* (1759)

Economics are an inescapable aspect of the world around us that intertwines us all. In fact, as economists will tell you "My spending is your income, and your spending is my income." We all contribute to the economic machine, whether we know it or not….

☞ "Every man thus lives by exchanging, or becomes, in some measure, a merchant, and the society itself grows to be what is properly a commercial society." – Adam Smith, *An Inquiry into the Nature and Causes of the Wealth of Nations* (1776)

☞ "An economy is simply the sum of the transactions that make it up. A transaction is a simple thing. Because there are a lot of them, the economy looks more complex than it really is. If instead of looking at it from the top down, we look at it from the transaction up, it is much easier to understand." – Ray Dalio, *How the Economic Machine Works* (2013)

Another defining characteristic is that economies are naturally cyclical. The pendulum continually swings back and forth with the euphoric boom at one end and the harrowing bust at the other. The darkest period in the economic cycle is a depression. It is the most sinister and woefully despondent form of economic bust, one that can take years to play out and is characterized by elevated unemployment, rampant bank failures, and a severe curtailment in general commerce. Desperate times call for desperate measures, which further increases the social and financial impacts of depressions. Forced and unpopular budget cuts can

The impact of macroeconomic forces explains one-half of a typical stock's annual performance. This number has risen 60 percent over the past six years, according to a June 2012 Morgan Stanley research report.

rip at the fabric of family units and incite criminal behavior for the Main Streeter to merely make ends meet. Unsurprisingly, even just the word 'depression' can send shivers down an economist's spine....

> ☞ "a chronic condition of subnormal activity for a considerable period without any marked tendency either towards recovery or towards complete collapse." – John Maynard Keynes, *The General Theory of Employment, Interest and Money* (1936)

Recessions are a less-menacing version of depressions that still, nonetheless, inflict hardships. Chronic and elevated unemployment are defining characteristics of a recession. Whether high unemployment is voluntary (inertia or reliance on government safety nets) or involuntary (due to a deterioration of the economy) is a matter of debate. This also shines some light on the interplay between politics and economics. Our elected officials are always trying to devise ways to optimize the economic machine. They want to put in place the right incentives via legislation, tax policy, foreign policy, etc.... Yet, these can have unintended consequences. Specifically, they can end up subsidizing people to not work and simply sit at home. That's legislation and incentives run amok, and it's a major source of friction in political circles.

Scholars, along with politicians, seem to focus more on the 'bust,' as compared to the 'boom.' In particular, what is the role of the government during challenging economic periods? The debate rages between two economic ideologies: Keynesian and Austrian. In an overly simplistic sense, the Austrian school believes in economic Darwinism. Translated, this means that an economy will have a more self-sustaining rebound if it lets the excesses and mal-investment be cleansed from the system. It's a Darwinian economic regime where the bad actors need to face consequences for their poor decision-making. Let's think about this more broadly. A world without repercussions would surely have more bank robberies and much longer lines at Dairy Queen. Thus, the Austrian ideology has some innate logic. However, the political process can sometimes interfere with this, as austerity is hardly popular....

⌖ "The 'boom,' then, is actually a period of wasteful misinvestment. It is a time when errors are made. The 'crisis' arrives when the consumers come to reestablish their desired proportions. The 'depression' is actually the process by which the economy adjusts to the wastes and errors of the boom, and reestablished efficient services of consumer desires." – Murray Rothbard, *America's Great Depression* (1963)

⌖ "Being an Austrian economist today is tantamount to holding libertarian economic beliefs. Indeed, a deep skepticism of government intervention in the economy – especially in the monetary system – is a pillar of the Austrian school." – Nouriel Roubini and Stephen Mihm, *Crisis Economics: A Crash Course in the Future of Finance* (2011)

⌖ "Liquidate labor, liquidate stocks, liquidate farmers, liquidate real estate . . . It will purge the rottenness out of the system. High costs of living and high living will come down. People will work harder, live a moral life. Values will be adjusted, and enterprising people will pick up from less competent people." – Andrew Mellon, famed American banker and industrialist

⌖ "Capitalism . . . is by nature a form or method of economic change and not only never is but never can be stationary . . . . The fundamental impulse that sets and keeps the capitalist engine in motion comes from the new consumers' goods, the new methods of production or transportation, the new markets, the new forms of industrial organization that capitalist enterprise creates . . . The opening up of new markets, foreign or domestic, and the organizational development from the craft shop and factory to such concerns as U.S. Steel illustrate the same process of industrial mutation . . . that incessantly revolutionizes the economic structure from within, incessantly destroying the old one, incessantly creating a new one. This process of *Creative Destruction* is the essential fact about capitalism. It is what capitalism consists in and what every capitalist concern has got to live in." – Joseph Schumpeter, *Capitalism, Socialism and Democracy* (1942)

⌘ "Creative destruction lies at the heart of a prospering capitalist society, and because well-connected incumbents have everything to gain from the established order, they are the enemies of capitalism." – Ruchir Sharma, *Breakout Nations: In Pursuit of the Next Economic Miracles* (2012)

Keynesians believe that the government should help smooth out the business cycle by providing stimulus. The Keynesian school often cites the entrance of the United States into World War II, and the accompanying surge in government spending, as the cure for the Great Depression. In fact, they would advocate doing just about anything to boost aggregate demand (ex. digging a ditch for the sake of digging a ditch) even if this stimulative technique appeared a questionable way to spend taxpayer dollars. However, as the government employs and ultimately stuffs the wallets of its citizenry it can spark discretionary spending and consumer confidence. This would then ignite a positive feedback loop that would be an economic launching pad. Further, tax receipts would eventually increase as the economy mends. Thus, the tax dollars used to pay the ditch diggers would ideally and effectively be merely a loan paid back in time with interest ....

⌘ "There can be no greater error then in supposing that capital is increased by non-consumption." – David Ricardo, *The Principles of Political Economy and Taxation* (1821)

⌘ "The boom, not the slump, is the time for austerity at the Treasury." – John Maynard Keynes

⌘ "the evidence is stronger than it has been ever been that fiscal policy matters – that fiscal stimulus helps the economy add jobs, and that reducing the budget deficit lowers growth at least in the near term. And yet, this evidence does not seem to be getting through to the legislative process." – Christina Romer, "What Do We Know About the Effects of Fiscal Policy? Separating Evidence from Ideology" (November 7th, 2011)

Even in times of fiscal deficits when a government's expenses exceed its revenues (i.e. borrowing on top on borrowing), the Keynesian argument remains undeterred....

☞ "In a depressed economy, budget deficits don't compete with the private sector for funds, and hence don't lead to soaring interest rates. The government is simply finding a use for the private sector's excess savings, that is, the excess of what it wants to save over what it is willing to invest." – Paul Krugman, *End This Depression Now!* (2012)

☞ "Reagan proved that deficits don't matter." – Dick Cheney, former Vice President of the United States (2002)

Deficit spending, or spending money you don't have, can rather curiously be a mechanism to help stabilize a shaky economy. When an economy is at a precipice, some say that the basic rules of the road don't apply, such as recklessly binging on debt. This school of thought views curing severe economic ailments in the same light as a military conflict....

☞ "in war times no one dreamed of balancing a budget. Fortunately we can borrow." – Henry Stimson, former Secretary of State under Herbert Hoover

Economies do head to the emergency room from time-to-time. It's an unavoidable part of the business cycle. However, the deficit spending prescription for an ailing economy has it skeptics. For starters, a nation will erode the value of their currency and invite inflation, amongst other considerations....

☞ "I do not think you can spend yourself rich." – George Humphrey, *The Congressional Record* (January 17th, 1957)

☞ "If a country falls into a military conflict, a deep slump, or other crisis, the Keynesian model immediately comes to the forefront: maintain spending at all costs, even if it means deficit financing. The misleading notion that consumer spending, rather than saving, capital formation, and technology drives the economy, is still very much in vogue in the halls of government and in financial circles." – Mark Skousen, *The Big Three in Economics: Adam Smith, Karl Marx, and John Maynard Keynes* (2007)

☞ "The Keynesian multiplier theory rests on the assumption that a dollar of government deficit spending can produce more than a dollar of total economic output after all secondary effects are taken into account. The multiplier is the Bigfoot of economics – something that many assume exists but is rarely, if ever, seen." – James Rickards, *Currency Wars: The Making of the Next Global Crisis* (2011)

☞ "The grand Keynesian myth is that you can spend money and thereby increase demand. And it's a myth because Congress does not have a vault of money to distribute in the economy. Every dollar Congress injects into the economy must first be taxed or borrowed out of the economy. You're not creating new demand, you're just transferring it from one group of people to another." – Brian Riedl, Heritage Foundation (February 3rd, 2009)

☞ "The idea that if you take a dollar out of the economy and then — from somebody who earned it, either through debt, or through taxes — and give it to somebody who's politically connected, that there are more dollars around, that if you stand on one side of the lake and put a bucket into the lake, and walk around to the other side in front of the TV cameras, pour the bucket back into the lake and announce you're stimulating the lake to great depths." – Grover Norquist, founder and president of Americans for Tax Reform

As you may infer, the Keynesians and Austrians have different thoughts on both the cause and prescription for the Great Depression in the United States. The Keynesians think the government did too little to help resuscitate aggregate demand. The Austrians felt that the government did too much, which prolonged the slump. Yet another hypothesis portrays a timid Federal Reserve (more on this in the next chapter) as the real villain....

☞ "All told, from July 1929 to March 1933, the money stock in the United States fell by one-third, and over two-thirds of the decline came after England's departure from the gold standard. Had the money stock been kept from declining, as it clearly could and should have been, the contraction would have both shorter and far milder." – Milton Friedman, *Capitalism and Freedom* (1962)

There is a human, social element to economics as well. In particular, there is the troubling matter of income inequality, or the growing wealth and income gap between the 'haves' and 'have nots'. Consider that the average pay for chief executives was 296 times that of the average worker in 2013 according to the Economic Policy Institute.

The *Gini Coefficient* is a measure of income equality in a country. A coefficient of zero represents perfect equality, and a coefficient of one expresses maximum inequality. China and the United States have the 30th and 41st highest Gini readings (out of 137 countries), respectively, according to data from the Central Intelligence Agency.

Yes, you read that number correctly. Further, it's a number on the rise as compensation for the grand pooba is up from 131 times relative to the worker bees in 1993 and 36 times in 1976.[7] Inequality deprives many of opportunity simply because they happened to be born into a situation of lesser financial means. Further, it does not put only the individual at a disadvantage. It deprives the world of potential doctors, inventors, and leaders. It also is a source of friction and jealousy, as the top ten percent earners in the United States own roughly 90 percent of all liquid financial assets. Predictably, there has been no shortage of rhetoric on this worrisome financial divide....

- "There is no doubt that income inequality is the single biggest threat to social stability around the world, whether it is in the United States, the European periphery, or China." – Kenneth Rogoff, "Technology and Inequality" (June 20th, 2011)

- "We can either have democracy in this country or we can have great wealth concentrated in the hands of the few, but we can't have both." – Louis Brandeis, justice of the U.S. Supreme Court from 1916 - 1939

- "All animals are equal, but some animals are more equal than others." – George Orwell, *Animal Farm* (1945)

The unequal distribution of wealth has plagued this country for much longer than one might think....

- "Sixty years ago there were no great fortunes in America, few large fortunes, no poverty. Now there is some poverty (though only in a few places can it be called pauperism), many large fortunes, and a greater number of gigantic fortunes than any other country in the world." – James Bryce, Viscount Bryce, *The American Commonwealth* (1894)

---

7 Morton Mintz, "Will Congress Reform Wretched Executive Excess?" *The Nation*, February 4, 2007.

More on this later, but the current political divide in the United States has much to do with how to solve this vexing issue....

ⓐ "There are two ideas of government. There are those who believe that, if you will only legislate to make the well-to-do prosperous, their prosperity will leak through on those below. The Democratic idea, however has been that if you legislate to make the masses prosperous, their prosperity will find its way up through every class which rests upon them." – William Jennings Bryan, "Cross of Gold" Speech at the Democratic National Convention (July 9th 1896)

The income inequality issue is a messy one. It seems to have kicked into a higher gear with this recent wave of globalization. Labor, particularly blue collar, waged jobs, can be shipped overseas with much more ease now than three or four decades ago. The end result has been stubbornly high unemployment in America.

The other inherent message is that economics should not be thought of as strictly a matter of dollars and cents....

ⓐ "Yet the gross national product does not allow for the health of our children, the quality of their education, or the joy of their play. It does not include the beauty of our poetry or the strength of our marriages; the intelligence of our public debate or the integrity of our public officials. It measures neither our wit nor our courage; neither our wisdom nor our learning; neither our compassion nor our devotion to our country; it measures everything, in short, except that which makes life worthwhile. And it tells us everything about America except why we are proud that we are Americans." – Robert F. Kennedy, Address at University of Kansas (March 18th, 1968)

Conventional economic measures, like GDP or GNP, fail to properly capture intangible factors, which have immense value. For instance, integrity and trust are said to be the invisible infrastructure for an economy....

    ⚭ "The real value of integrity is not personal; it's collective. It's the underpinning for all our commercial relationships. We are heirs to a huge stock of integrity, built up over centuries and visible in every aspect of our economy. It's a shared asset that makes us wealthy." – Anna Bernasek, *The Economics of Integrity* (2010)

    ⚭ "[Trust is] the most cherished and valuable commodity in the work environment." – Brad Anderson, CEO of Best Buy

    ⚭ "A man I do not trust could not get money from me on all the bonds of Christendom." – J.P. Morgan, turn of the 20th century financier, banker, and philanthropist (1912)

    ⚭ "Integrity without knowledge is weak and useless, and knowledge without integrity is dangerous and dreadful." – Samuel Johnson, *The History of Rasselas, Prince of Abissinia* (1759)

    ⚭ "Trust, like money, is a crucial lubricant for the economy." – Dan Ariely, *Predictably Irrational* (2009)

    ⚭ "Trust takes years to build, seconds to break, and forever to repair." - Anonymous

The word 'economics' conjures images of dollars and cents. However, economies are really a patchwork of financial and non-financial incentives alike, including social and moral ones. What deserves more focus is that what underpins an economy is trust. This is the basic glue for commerce, as no one wants to get swindled when conducting business. We tend to feel an innate suspicion toward business counterparties, as money can surely be corrosive. It has the ability to taint the behavior of even the most upstanding individuals. Sadly, integrity and personal economics are far too often in conflict....

- ☞ "It is difficult to get a man to understand something when his salary depends upon his not understanding it!" – Upton Sinclair, *I, Candidate for Governor: And How I Got Licked* (1935)

- ☞ "The lack of money is the root of all evil." – attributed to Mark Twain as well as George Bernard Shaw

- ☞ "No complaint, however, is more common than that of the scarcity of money." – Adam Smith, *An Inquiry into the Nature and Causes of the Wealth of Nations* (1776)

Following all this economic banter? Don't worry if you aren't, as there is a sect that challenges the broader utility of economics, along with its impact on investments....

- ☞ "Economics has never been a science – and it is even less now than a few years ago." – Paul Samuelson

- ☞ "The function of economics is to make astrology look respectable" – commonly attributed to John Kenneth Galbraith, but also to Ezra Solomon

- ☞ "Economics is extremely useful as a form of employment for economists." – attributed to John Kenneth Galbraith

It gets even worse: economists are critiqued for their general forecasting prowess, or lack thereof. Even Paul Krugman seems to think so. Yes, this is the same Krugman who won the Nobel Prize for Economics. He authored a column entitled "Why Most Economists' Predictions are Wrong" in 1998, which basically said that economists' projections have low hit rates, as they often miscalculate the impact of future technological advancements. As an aside I myself have taught economics, so this is all a bit humbling....

- ☞ "Of all the economists and strategists you follow, are any correct most of the time?" – Howard Marks, *The Most Important Thing: Uncommon Sense for the Thoughtful Investor* (2011)

- ☞ "If you hear a 'prominent' economist using the word 'equilibrium,' or 'normal distribution,' do not argue with him; just ignore him, or try to put a rat down his shirt." - Nassim Nicholas Taleb, *The Black Swan: The Impact of the Highly Improbable* (2007)

- ☞ "In economics, the majority is always wrong." – attributed to John Kenneth Galbraith

- ☞ "There are two types of forecasters; those who don't know and those who don't know they don't know." – John Kenneth Galbraith

- ☞ "It is a misfortune of the times that all of us must needs be amateur economists - including, and perhaps especially, the professionals." – Benjamin Graham, *World Commodities and World Currencies* (1944)

Their forecasting ability is not the only gripe against economists. They often carry conversations with pages of fine print. They seem programmed to obfuscate and hedge their projections with a litany of assumptions and caveats....

- ☞ "Give me a one-handed economist! All my economists say, 'On the one hand, on the other.'" – Harry Truman, 33rd President of the United States

⚙ "If all the economists were laid end to end, they'd never reach a conclusion" – attributed to George Bernard Shaw

And for good measure economists are also criticized for their pre-disposition to not be able to predict short-term events....

⚙ "This long run is a misleading guide to current affairs. In the long run we are all dead. Economists set themselves too easy, too useless a task if in tempestuous seasons they can only tell us that when the storm is long past the sea is flat again." – John Maynard Keynes, *A Tract on Monetary Reform* (1923)

It doesn't help in the quest for credibility when the former head of our Federal Reserve, which is tasked with helping to steer the United States economy, had one of the more epic forecasting misses On March 28th, 2007, right before the credit crisis really took hold, Ben Bernanke proclaimed....

⚙ "At this juncture, however, the impact on the broader economy and financial markets in the subprime market seems likely to be contained." (Before the Joint Economic Committee, U.S. Congress)

Still, economists are a captivating, intelligent group. Their thoughts undeniably will seep into our thinking, regardless of their track record....

⚙ "Practical men, who believe themselves to be quite exempt from any intellectual influences, are usually slaves to some defunct economist." – John Maynard Keynes, *The General Theory of Employment, Interest and Money* (1936)

Given the criticisms of economics it may be unsurprising to know about the *Bottom-Up* investing style. This type of investor proclaims that they are economy and industry agnostic. They just want good stocks, plain and simple, and the ebb and flow of the economy is just noise. The upside with this approach is that they don't have to concern themselves with the onslaught of never-ending economic data. However, it's a little pie in the sky, as no company is truly immune to the fortunes of the broader economy. I will admit that it is a noble endeavor, especially if you find yourself questioning the efficacy of economic forecasts....

    ☞ "If there is any relationship between economic development and stock prices that is predictable, it certainly has escaped my attention." – Bob Kirby, as quoted in *Capital: The Story of Long-Term Investment Excellence* by Charles Ellis (2004)

Some parting food for thought on economics. Economic growth is usually welcome with trumpets, cheers, and countless smiles. It is broadly considered a good thing as it consequently creates fatter wallets and more discretionary buying power to accumulate more 'stuff'. Savings accounts are flusher, and confidence abounds. Yet, economic growth does not magically appear. It comes as the result of ingenuity, productivity gains, and just plain old hard work. That means more time at the office and less time with family and friends. Not to mention, stress levels will go up, along with a long menu of potential health ailments. So, you'll have to decide: is economic growth *really* worth it?

OVERTIME...

Education: The Economic Fulcrum

South Korea is an economic marvel. In 1960, with just $82 GDP per capita, it ranked among the world's 25 poorest nations. Today their GDP per capita is more than $31k: compare to China's, which is less than $9k. The country's economic transformation occurred at a blistering pace. It took the United States and Great Britain at least a century to become industrialized nations. It took South Korea just a few decades. What's even more intriguing is that South Korea accomplished this feat in spite of being deprived of many natural resources, not to mention having a political agitator on its northern border. Its economic metamorphosis was carried on the back of the country's acclaimed and highly rigorous education system. Their economic model is one that effectively exports intellectual capital, with high-end multinationals, such as Samsung, Hyundai, and LG, as their vehicles to do so. Today's South Korea, an army of brainiacs, has found a way to succeed in a competitive global economy, and rather miraculously so, given a lack of built-in advantages.

As South Korea has shot up the global education rankings, the United States has slipped into

> According to the Department of Education, without a college education an individual in the bottom quintile of income earners only has an approximately five percent probability of transitioning to the top quintile income bracket.

> *Baumol's Cost Disease* is often cited as the villain behind the unbendable cost curve for education in the United States, along with health care. The concept is that productivity and cost containment opportunities are relatively scarcer in these labor-intensive fields. For instance, it would be pretty hard to replace doctors or teachers with robots, but it would save a few bucks.

mediocrity. Consider that in 2011, the Program for International Student Assessment ranked the United States 31st in math literacy among 15-year-old students, below the international average. In 2009, the United States was ranked 23rd. Curiously, the United States spends more per student than most countries, with only Denmark spending more on education as a percentage of GDP according to the OECD (Organisation for Economic Co-operation and Development). The result is a very underwhelming return on investment and a worrisome trend for our economic trajectory. All is not lost, since we still have many world-class schools, and places like Silicon Valley have a boundless ability to create and innovate. It's doubtful, though, that the answer alone is to divert more money to education. In fact, according to data from the Department of Education and Heritage Foundation, the real expenditures per pupil in the U.S. has increased by 49 percent between 1984 and 2004. Yet, something needs to be fixed, and the answers are above my pay grade. If South Korea is a harbinger of things to come, our standing as a future global economic power depends on improving our education deliverable.

Debts, Deficits, and the Laws of Financial Gravity

If you've been keeping track of what has transpired inside the D.C. beltway, then you're well aware that it is much easier to spend then save. For the past 40 years, the United States has averaged revenue (namely tax receipts) of 18 percent of GDP and expenditures (defense spending, entitlements, etc...) at 21 percent of GDP. The cumulative funding shortfall has led to a massive buildup in debt issuance. The national debt is now bigger than the entire United States economy - more than the annual GDP - and continues to grow. According to the Congressional Budget Office, the total gross federal debt is projected to grow to more than $20 trillion in 2018 and to more than $27 trillion by 2024. Furthermore, some estimates have the federal government's total unfunded liabilities exceeding $84 trillion and growing all the time. Sadly, there isn't enough capital on the planet to make good on these liabilities. Making matters worse is the rate debt is accumulating. Prior to the late 1980's, the United States had been practically self-sufficient in credit. Now we are beholden to the likes of China and Japan, which together held over $2.5 trillion of United States Treasury securities as of the end of 2013 according to the Treasury Department. In sum, the United States is the largest debtor nation in the history of mankind.

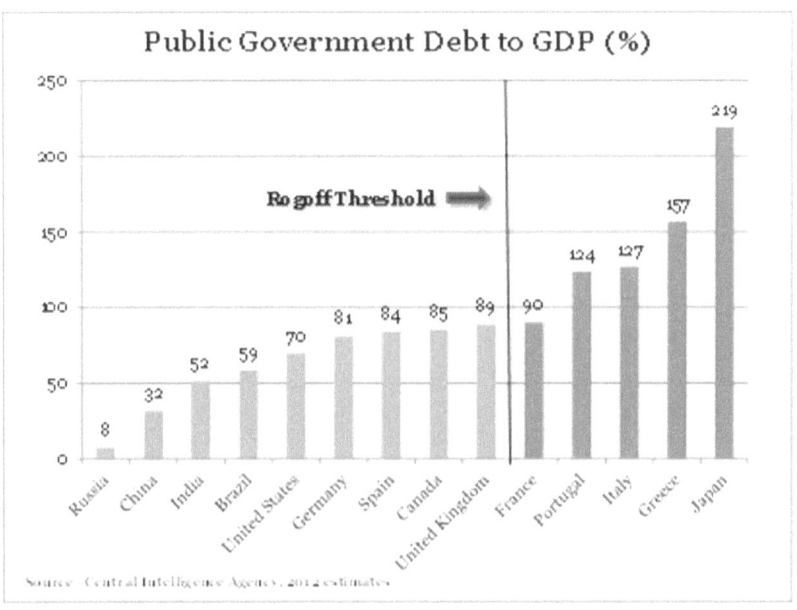

Thus far, the United States has gotten away without much of a slap on the wrist. As the supply of our debt has increased, prices still have yet to be adversely affected. Financial gravity has not yet occurred. However, we have crossed a worrisome threshold. A 90 percent debt to GDP ratio is considered an economic tipping point, according to the 2009 book *This Time is Different* by Kenneth Rogoff and Carmen Reinhart. At and above this level, median economic growth falls by at least one percent as more money is devoted to debt service than other more productive areas (i.e. education, infrastructure). Rogoff and Reinhart's book doesn't quite read like a Dan Brown novel, but it did invite a bit of drama. After its release, the supporting math to the authors' thesis was found to be flawed. The book's math may not have been perfect, but the inverse relationship between leverage and growth at the country level still has enduring logic.

We have seen this debt and spending narrative before. According to *Wagner's Law*, named after German economist Adolph Wagner, a nation's ascension to industrialized status will be accompanied by a rise in public expenditures (i.e. entitlements). The spending patterns of the United States have been somewhat predictable, but that shouldn't invite complacency.

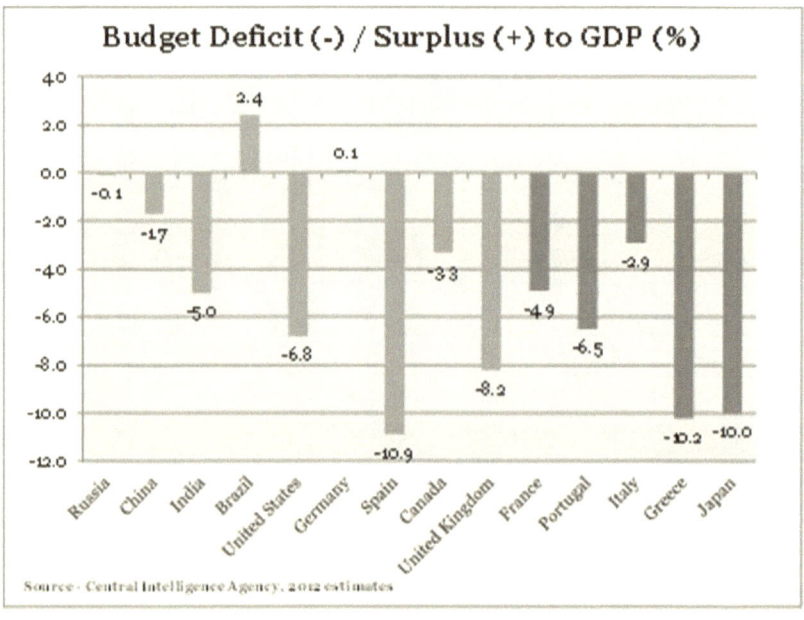

Data Dependent

Our Central Bank, the Federal Reserve, has become increasingly involved in steering the direction of the economy. It has injected an unprecedented amount of stimulus (zero bound interest rates and asset purchases) ever since the global credit crisis took hold. When the Federal Reserve (the Fed) wants to reverse course with its bold monetary actions is a matter of popular debate. The Fed decision makers promise to be data-dependent, or dispassionately reviewing the facts. If you could distill their focus down to one item, it would be unemployment, which has far-reaching tentacles. For starters, there is *Okun's Law.* This law suggests a relationship for which every one-percent increase in unemployment above its natural rate will translate into a two-percent reduction in a country's potential level of GDP. In addition, unemployment exacts a non-financial toll. It creates unnecessary anxiety on family units and can breed crime. The Fed knows this, and endeavors to get joblessness down to healthier levels before it puts an end to its unprecedented monetary stimulus.

Whenever I'm asked about the issue of joblessness, I tend to have Facebook in my response. Facebook has been transformative to the way we communicate with the world around us. It is the heart of the social media revolution and a testament to American ingenuity. The downside is that the company only employs roughly 6,000 people as of March 2014. These are mostly well-paying and highly desirable jobs. However, we will need thousands more Facebooks in order to put a dent in the population of 20 million or more Americans who are unemployed or underemployed (working in a job that does not fully utilize their skills). This is comparable to having everyone in the state of Florida (19.32 million people as of 2012) either jobless or looking for more satisfying employment. We are victims of our own success. Consider that in the 1990's the average startup had 7.6 employees. In 2011 that number had fallen to 4.7 employees, according to data from the Bureau of Labor Statistics. Facebook is a shining example of how innovative companies can do so much with so little. Unfortunately, Facebook also highlights how daunting the unemployment issue is in the United States, which the Fed knows all too well.

The Fed has received a gift though, courtesy of the energy industry. More on this later, but we now have a once unimaginable amount of gas and oil in this country. This helps keep a lid on costs for consumers and businesses alike, which keeps inflation in check. The Fed has a mandate of keeping inflation tame, and their aggressive policies do run the risk of igniting it. Hence, it knows it has a lot more policy maneuverability, since inflation isn't as much of a threat as it would have been prior to the domestic energy renaissance.

MONETARY POLICY

T he Federal Reserve is the independent Central Bank of the United States charged with governing monetary policy. Think of it as a bank for all banks. It has a dual mandate of keeping inflation under control and fostering long-term economic growth. It has a few weapons in its arsenal to help fulfill its mandate, notably control of the Federal Funds rate. The Fed also has more unconventional instruments it can utilize, including asset purchases. In the current environment, when the economy has been performing below potential, the Fed has been markedly aggressive and using all of the artillery at its disposal.

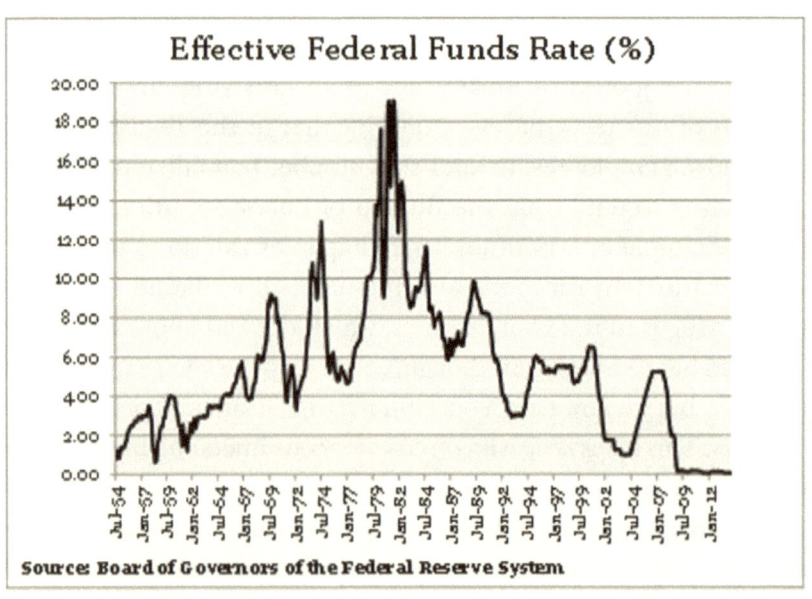

Source: Board of Governors of the Federal Reserve System

Make no mistake; the investment narrative over the past few years has been largely dictated by the role of monetary policy. The Fed, along with the actions of foreign Central Banks, has made credit cheap and liquidity abundant by keeping short-term interest rates near zero and making large scale asset purchases (commonly referred to as 'quantitative easing'). Generally speaking, these aggressive tactics proved helpful to the markets as the newly minted liquidity was a welcome visitor to many asset classes. However, their unprecedented and highly accommodative policy will end at some point, which makes 'Fed sensitivity' a theme to monitor closely. In other words, some corners of the global economy may be adversely affected when the monetary spigots are turned off. Notably emerging market equities languished in 2013, as they were deemed overly reliant on the Fed's soon to be unwound largesse. Yes, even the likes of India and Turkey are beholden to Fed policy. It is a bit surreal, but the Fed's influence is felt in all asset classes, with no geographic boundaries.

The Fed's aggressive stimulus efforts will end eventually, or 'normalize' if you prefer Wall Street jargon. Yet, it's 'how' not 'when' that is the more important question. That's because we got a whiff of what a disorderly exit looked like in the second quarter of 2013. That's when Ben Bernanke rather ambiguously announced that the Fed would be reversing course

> "A high degree of monetary accommodation remains warranted." – Janet Yellen, Congressional testimony (May 7th, 2014)

leaving the market with more questions than answers. The bellwether US Ten Year Treasury responded in kind as rates rose roughly one percent in less than two months, which was a weighty 63 percent move in relative terms. It wasn't just the credit markets that were roiled, as equities sold off and the real estate market almost ground to a halt. The market likes predictability, and Ben Bernanke misfired on delivering it. He, and his successor Janet Yellen, has since come out and offered more visibility on the Fed's 'tapering' efforts. It's a good thing that the Fed is keeping interest rates on a leash. Rates rising are not so sinister if consumers and investors have time to acclimate. The Fed is going to rein in the printing presses, but what's more important is that it should be an orderly flipping off of the 'on' button….

> Good news is bad news if you have an investment thesis tied to continued monetary support. As the economy mends, the likelihood of monetary support being withdrawn increases.
>
> Interestingly, the monetary policy story may just be heating up in other nations. Our Fed's aggressive approach wasn't perfect, but it was beneficial in some measure. Foreign Central Banks have already begun to imitate our Fed, which may keep this monetary policy 'dividend' in play even after Yellen et al reverse course.

ை "But the U.S. government has a technology, called a printing press (or, today, its electronic equivalent), that allows it to produce as many U.S. dollars as it wishes at essentially no cost." – Ben Bernanke, Before the National Economists Club, Washington, D.C. (November 21st, 2002)

ை "We have the power to deal with such an emergency by flooding the Street with money." – George L. Harrison, former New York Federal Reserve governor

While the Fed endeavors to bring more predictability to the economy, some argue the opposite has occurred. The critics will point to the erosion of the dollar. Since 1913, when the Federal Reserve System was born, the dollar has lost 96 percent of its value. In other words, $1.00 in 1913 would only be worth $.04 in 2013, according to the Bureau of Labor Statistics. The economy is surely not a shell of its 1913 self, as the drop in currency would imply. The rebuttal starts with the fact that wages have increased by a factor of twenty during this period. However, that seems like little consolation to the Fed critics….

ை "The stock of money, prices, and output was decidedly more unstable after the establishment of the Federal Reserve than before." – Milton Friedman, *Capitalism and Freedom* (1962)

Further, the series of asset bubbles that has occurred under the Fed's watch is another indictment. When you manipulate the cost of credit, you inject volatility into asset prices....

> ☞ "Since its inception in 1913, the Federal Reserve has been the perpetuator of asset bubbles. From the Fed-induced bubble of the 1920's that led to the Great Depression, to modern-day bubbles in NASDAQ and real estate, the Federal Reserve's manipulation of the cost of money has created a bubble economy." – Michael G. Pento, *The Coming Bond Market Collapse: How to Survive the Demise of the U.S. Debt Market* (2013)

The Federal Reserve's primary tool to influence the business cycle is the Fed Funds Rate. This rate has been zero-bound since 2008, which theoretically should stimulate the economy as it reduces the cost of credit and incentivizes risk taking. There are skeptics that wonder about the 'independent' decision-making surrounding their policy tools....

> ☞ "In the short run, a false prosperity takes root. Business expands. New construction is everywhere. People feel wealthier. This is why there is always such political pressure on the Fed to lower rates around election time: the prosperity comes in the short run, and the painful correction comes much later, well after people have cast their votes." – Ron Paul, *The Revolution: A Manifesto* (2008)

Here is an interesting cocktail party fact – J.P. Morgan, the de-facto Central Banker of his day, died in 1913. This was the same year that the Federal Reserve System came into existence.

The Fed can also conduct asset purchases, which has earned the dubious moniker of "money-printing." When the Fed buys assets, recently Treasuries and securitized mortgages, it simultaneously injects liquidity into the economy. This is another permutation of influencing interest rates, but, unlike the Fed Funds rate, it can help to reduce longer term rates. This helps reduce the cost of conventional mortgages and other types of credit that are based off certain longer maturity parts of the yield curve. As you would suspect, this helped ignite a refinance boom that helped put more money in consumers' pockets. Yet, asset purchases are a more aggressive monetary policy tool, as it runs the risk of creating unwanted inflation (too much money chasing too few goods). As such, it leads to more animated opinions....

- "How does taking money from people by selling bonds and giving the same amount of money back to people through fiscal spending create stimulus?" – Colm O'Shea, as quoted in *Hedge Fund Market Wizards* by Jack Schwager (2012)

- "The reason 'printing money' – actually, the Fed's purchase of assets with funds created by fiat, but close enough – can lead to inflation is that the credit expansion these Fed purchases set in motion leads to higher spending and higher demand." – Paul Krugman, *End This Depression Now!* (2012)

- "Our real incomes are best understood as the actual goods and services we ultimately consume, not the pieces of paper that help us do it. For if economic growth were as simple to generate as creating 'demand' out of thin air, the path to universal prosperity would be as simple as matching our unlimited human desire with a hefty printing press. Global history of inflationary collapse from China to Interwar Germany to Zimbabwe has shown that this approach truly is the worst of all macro folly. We can't consume our way to prosperity." – John Papola, "A Libertarian Take on Economic Faith, 'Facts' and Follies," *PBS Newshour* (April 4th, 2013)

- "Inflation is a more fundamental danger than speculative investment. Some countries seem to be in the unusual situation where they are trying to create inflation. They will come to regret that. People think they can manipulate the economy in a way that produces a little good inflation to go along with better economic activity. That's silly." – Paul Volcker, former Federal Reserve Chairman

This stimulus may alter the quantity of economic growth, but not necessarily the quality of it....

- "A rise in wages, from an alteration in the value of money, produces a general effect on price, and for that reason it produces no real effect whatever on profits." – David Ricardo

- "You can't change the carpenter into a nurse easily, and you can't change the mortgage broker into a computer expert in a manufacturing plant very easily. Eventually that stuff will sort itself out. People will be retrained and they'll find jobs in other industries. But monetary policy can't retrain people. Monetary policy can't fix those problems." – Charles Plosser, president of the Philadelphia Federal Reserve Bank (February 12th, 2011)

Our past Federal Reserve Chairman obviously disagrees....

- "Moreover, because stronger growth in each economy confers beneficial spillovers to trading partners, these policies are not "beggar-thy-neighbor" but rather are positive-sum, "enrich-thy-neighbor" actions." – Ben Bernanke, remarks at Department of Economics and STICERD, London (March 25th, 2013)

- "One myth out there is that what we're doing is printing money. We're not printing money." – Ben Bernanke, *60 Minutes* interview (December 3rd, 2010)

- "The money supply is not changing in any significant way. What we're doing is lowering interest rates by buying Treasury securities." – Ben Bernanke, from the same interview

Stimulus is what the Fed does, both injecting and siphoning it out of the economy. They have the task of limiting the extremes of the business cycle, which includes removing their stimulus before the economy overheats....

- "Take away the punch bowl just as the party gets going." – William McChesney Martin, chair of the Fed from 1951 to 1970

Speculation comes with the program when unprecedented actions are put into motion by the Federal Reserve. This is experimental policy that could play out in a number of ways. While we hope for the best, there are clearly risks....

- "We are still learning about the efficacy and appropriate management of these alternative tools .... One disadvantage of asset purchases relative to conventional monetary policy is that we have much less experience in judging the economic effects of this policy instrument, which makes it challenging to determine the appropriate quantity and pace of purchases and to communicate the policy response to the public." – Ben Bernanke, At the Revisiting Monetary Policy in a Low-Inflation Environment Conference, Federal Reserve Bank of Boston (October 15th, 2010)

POLITICS

"Politics is not the art of the possible. It consists in choosing between the disastrous and the unpalatable." – John Kenneth Galbraith, letter to JFK (March 2nd, 1962)

Legislation, rhetoric, and even inaction that emanates from government chambers shapes the world around us and influences investment results. Governments write the rules, but, more importantly, they can change them. Thus, that next political chess move can re-write the future narrative for companies, industries, and even the broader economy. It's no secret that governments can and will meddle in the economy and markets, which investors need to be prepared for....

- ☞ "we exist in a financial universe that is subject to massive gravitational pulls from states. States tug at us. States bend us. And, tirelessly, states seek to determine our orbits." – Mohsin Hamid, *How to Get Filthy Rich in Rising Asia* (2013)

- ☞ "As business becomes more heavily regulated, business decisions are based more on compliance with governmental edicts than on profit-making." – Ludwig Von Mises

One way to think about it: the more you hear about politics, the more volatile the environment is for investing and vice versa. This is because markets covet predictability, which is in short supply when governments have a more visible activist agenda. Also, the reality is that politics hits the news wire when there is something troubling afoot. This could be saber-rattling by a dictator from afar, but increasingly the more impact-ful news is coming from the D.C. beltway (Congressional term limits anyone?). The increase of partisan politics has frustrated the populous and held the business community hostage far too often. Investors have to manage the impact of the incessant tug-of-war between the sparring factions. At the root of the friction is the level and scope of government involvement. In the pro-democracy, limited government corner....

- "There's a clear cause and effect here that is as neat and pre-dictable as a law of physics: as government expands, liberty con-tracts." – Ronald Reagan, Farewell Address (January 12th, 1989)

- "The natural progress of things is for liberty to yield and gov-ernment to gain ground." – Thomas Jefferson, letter to Edward Carrington (May 27th, 1788)

- "Civilization is the progress of a society towards privacy. The sav-age's whole existence is public, ruled by the laws of his tribe. Civilization is the process of setting man free from men." – Ayn Rand, *The Fountainhead* (1943)

- "The state can be and has often been in the course of history the main source of mischief and disaster." – Ludwig Von Mises, *Omnipotent Government: The Rise of the Total State and Total War* (1944)

- "If [a businessman] makes a mistake, *he* suffers the consequences; if he fails, *he* takes the loss....If [a bureaucrat] makes a mistake, *you* suffer the consequences; if he fails, he passes the loss on to *you*, in the form of heavier taxes." – Ayn Rand, *The Ayn Rand Letter*

- "Government's view of the economy could be summed up in a few short phrases: If it moves, tax it. If it keeps moving, regulate it. And if it stops moving, subsidize it." – Ronald Reagan (August 15th, 1986)

☞ "It seems to me that socialists today can preserve their position in academic economics merely by the pretense that the differences are entirely moral questions about which science cannot decide." – Friedrich August von Hayek, 20th century Austrian economist

> In *The Republic*, Plato suggested that government followed a predictable evolution. Aristocracy is followed by timocracy, oligarchy, democracy, until it ultimately degenerates into tyranny.

☞ "Where the people fear the government you have tyranny. Where the government fears the people you have liberty." – John Basil Barnhill, "Indictment of Socialism" (1914)

☞ "Big government is the only institution that is touted as the solution to its own failures. If there is a major national security breach because some government agency didn't do its job, the immediate response is to give the agency more power. It's as if, at the height of the Enron scandals, people concluded that the problem was that Ken Lay didn't have enough authority." – W. James Antle III, *Devouring Freedom: Can Big Government Ever be Stopped?* (2013)

> The best stock market returns tend to occur when the Executive Office, the House, and the Senate are not controlled by one party. Thus, political gridlock is typically a good thing for investors as there is predictability (new legislation is scarce).

☞ "History, in general, only informs us what bad government is." – Thomas Jefferson, letter to John Norvell (June 14th, 1807)

- "Socialism is a philosophy of failure, the creed of ignorance, and the gospel of envy." – Winston Churchill

- "Freedom has many difficulties and democracy is not perfect, but we have never had to put a wall up to keep our people in, to prevent them from leaving us." – John F. Kennedy, Berlin speech (June 28th, 1963)

- "It is the highest impertinence and presumption, therefore, in kings and ministers to pretend to watch over the economy of private people, and to restrain their expense, either by sumptuary laws, or by prohibiting the importation of foreign luxuries. They are themselves always, and without any exception, the greatest spendthrifts in the society. Let them look well after their own expense, and they may safely trust private people with theirs. If their own extravagance does not ruin the state, that of the subject never will." – Adam Smith, *An Inquiry into the Nature and Causes of the Wealth of Nations* (1776)

This belief that government involvement does more harm than good may arise from an unflattering view of legislators and the legislative process….

- "there is no distinctly American criminal class except Congress." – Mark Twain, *Pudd'nhead Wilson's New Calendar* (1894)

- "The most exciting thing you encounter in government is competence, because it's so rare."

A love for democracy is not a universal sentiment. As Alexander Hamilton said in a 1788 speech, "It has been observed that a pure democracy if it were practicable would be the most perfect government. Experience has proved that no position is more false than this. The ancient democracies in which the people themselves deliberated never possessed one good feature of government. Their very character was tyranny; their figure deformity."

– Daniel Patrick Moynihan, former New York senator (March 1ˢᵗ, 1976)

- "There's never been a good government." – attributed to Emma Goldman, Russian-born American activist and writer

- "Giving money and power to government is like giving whiskey and car keys to teenage boys." – P.J. O'Rourke, *Parliament of Whores* (1991)

- "One of the greatest delusions in the world is the hope that the evils in this world are to be cured by legislation." – Thomas B. Reed, Speaker of the House from 1889-1891 and 1895-1899

- "One has to be a lowbrow, a bit of a murderer, to be a politician, ready and willing to see people sacrificed, slaughtered, for the sake of an idea, whether a good one or a bad one." – Henry Miller, interview in *Writers at Work* (1963)

- "politics is more concerned with the pursuit of power than the pursuit of truth." – George Soros, *The New Paradigm for Financial Markets: The Credit Crisis of 2008 and What It Means* (2008)

- "Emotion, fear, guilt, and racism: that's how you do a bill in Washington." – Senator Alan Simpson

Free-market capitalism is economic Darwinism. It's an ideology, and often said in the same breath with democracy….

- "Free market capitalism is the best path to prosperity." – Larry Kudlow, economist and former television anchor

- "History suggests that capitalism is a necessary condition for political freedom." – Milton Friedman

Socialist establishments, much to the chagrin of those in the small government corner, persist because they offer 'free' goodies to their respective citizens. Those who benefit, in turn, cast the ballot that keeps these subsidies going. It's a bit of an extractive regime, as it often taxes the well-to-do to pay for these social programs or entitlements, like education or medical assistance, to those of lesser means. This is very uncapitalist as you surmise. It's all well and good until, of course, the bill arrives....

- ☞ "There is an inverse relationship between reliance on the state and self-reliance." – William F. Buckley, Jr., American author and commentator

- ☞ "A government that robs Peter to pay Paul can always depend on the support of Paul." – George Bernard Shaw, *Everybody's Political What's What?* (1944)

- ☞ "Socialist governments traditionally do make a financial mess. They always run out of other people's money. It's quite a characteristic of them."—Margaret Thatcher, interview on Thames Television's *This Week* (1976)

The government has been behind many significant innovations, such as GPS, lithium batteries, and the airbag. Despite the messages from the capitalist camp, the government has some success wearing their venture capitalist hat.

Capitalists just want government to get out of the way of the private sector and its productive capacity. We know that meddling (i.e. high turnover) with portfolios does not typically lead to investment success. The same line of thinking can be applied to governments trying to involve themselves with the economy and our daily lives....

- "The great advances of civilization, whether in architecture or painting, in science or literature, in industry or agriculture, have never come from centralized government. Columbus did not set out to seek a new route to China in response to a majority directive of a parliament…." – Milton Friedman, *Capitalism and Freedom* (1962)

- "Even the polio vaccine was primarily developed by a private group, the National Foundation for Infant Paralysis, President Roosevelt personally provided the seed money – it's interesting that even a sitting president chose the private sector for such a task – and the foundation then raised the money and conducted the drug trials." – Steven Levitt & Stephen Dubner, *SuperFreakonomics* (2011)

- "Governments have no right to interfere with the pursuits of individuals, as guaranteed by those general laws, by offering encouragements and granting privileges to any particular class of industry, or any select bodies of man, inasmuch as all classes of industry and all men are equally important to the general welfare, and all equally entitled to protection. Whenever a Government assumes the power of discriminating between the different classes of the community, it becomes, in effect, the arbiter of their prosperity, and exercises a power not contemplated by any intelligent people in delegating their sovereignty to their rulers." – William Leggett, 19th century American poet and journalist

Regardless of your political affiliation, you should understand that capitalism, or any economic chassis for that matter, will encounter traffic on occasion. Rarely does any economy or economic regime move in a straight line….

- "Capitalism without failure is like religion without sin. It doesn't work." – Allan H. Meltzer, American economist and professor at Carnegie Mellon University

൚ "Instability is an inherent and inescapable flaw of capitalism." –
Hyman Minsky, American economist

൚ "Capitalism without bankruptcy is like Christianity without hell."
– Frank Borman, Eastern Airlines chief

൚ "A private free-enterprise economy, it is said, is inherently unstable." – Milton Friedman, *Capitalism and Freedom* (1962)

൚ "Economic progress, in capitalist society, means turmoil." –
Joseph Schumpeter, *Capitalism, Socialism, and Democracy* (1942)

A capitalist system is a meritocracy. Proponents will say it creates
an incentive system that encourages entrepreneurism. Capitalist constituents are financially motivated to innovate and success will deliver
spillover benefits to the broader economy. However, to the victor go the
spoils in this competition-based economic scheme, and this can breed
income inequality. In the eyes of some this is not a virtuous characteristic, and they believe that, if taken to an extreme, this will lead to a polarized society of the woefully poor and the famously rich. Inequality also
provides ammunition for those in the anti-capitalism, big government
corner, which even includes the Pope....

൚ "Capitalism inevitably and by virtue of the very logic of its civilization creates, educates and subsidizes a vested interest in social
unrest." – Joseph Schumpeter, *Capitalism, Socialism and Democracy*
(1942)

൚ "Some people continue to defend trickle-down theories which
assume that economic growth, encouraged by a free market, will
inevitably succeed in bringing about greater justice and inclusiveness in the world. This opinion, which has never been confirmed
by the facts, expresses a crude and naive trust in the goodness of
those wielding economic power and in the sacralized workings

of the prevailing economic system." – Pope Francis, *Evangelii Gaudium* (November 24th, 2013)

☞ "Capitalism knows only one color: that color is green; all else is necessarily subservient to it, hence, race, gender and ethnicity cannot be considered within it." – Thomas Sowell, *The Thomas Sowell Reader* (2011)

☞ "The meaning of peace is the absence of opposition to socialism." – Karl Marx, 19th century philosopher, economist, and revolutionary socialist

☞ "one of the necessary accompaniments of capitalism in a democracy is political corruption." – Upton Sinclair, *The Jungle* (1920)

☞ "The trouble with capitalism is capitalists. They're too damn greedy." – Herbert Hoover, 31st president of the United States, remark to columnist Mark Sullivan (1929)

☞ "Prosperity ends in a crisis. The era of optimism dies in the crisis, but in dying it gives birth to an era of pessimism. This new era is born, not an infant, but a giant." – Arthur C. Pigou, English economist (1877-1959), as quoted in *Business Cycles* by Wesley Clair Mitchell (1913)

There are more balanced ways of looking at these economic ideologies....

☞ "The inherent vice of capitalism is the unequal sharing of blessings. The inherent virtue of socialism is the equal sharing of miseries." – Winston Churchill (1945)

☞ "Capitalism undoubtedly has certain boils and blotches upon it, but has it as many as government? Has it as many as marriage?

Has it as many as religion? I doubt it. It is the only basic institution of modern man that shows any genuine health and vigor."
– Henry Louis Mencken, American journalist and intellect

The same for these seemingly divergent political ideologies....

☞ "For it is very clear, that in fundamental theory socialism and democracy are almost if not quite one and the same. They both rest at bottom upon the absolute right of the community to determine its own destiny and that of its members . . . . The difference between democracy and socialism is not an essential difference, but only a practical difference – is a difference of organization and policy, not a difference of primary motive." – Woodrow Wilson, unpublished essay (1887)

☞ "Democracy does not guarantee equality of conditions — it only guarantees equality of opportunity." – Irving Kristol, *Two Cheers for Capitalism* (1978)

The last stop in Plato's political cycle was tyranny, with fascism serving as an obvious example. Fascism is a revolutionary force born out of contempt for the establishment. The resulting dictatorial political regime is characterized by leadership with a close-to-zero tolerance for disagreement from the citizenry. It has an unenviable track record due to the consequent upheaval brought on by its signature faces of Benito Mussolini, Francisco Franco, and, of course, Adolf Hitler....

☞ "[Fascism is] capitalism plus murder." – Upton Sinclair, *I, Candidate for Governor: And How I Got Licked* (1935)

Unsurprisingly, fascism didn't last in Spain, Italy, or Germany. This goes to show that empires and political regimes, like economies, are not constants. Yet, this is true even irrespective of these particular results. This is surely subject to debate, but many see the United States in the midst of a metamorphosis from a state that once embodied capitalist and democratic principles to more of a socialist state....

- ☞ "in the end, more than they wanted freedom, the Athenians wanted security. Yet they lost everything – security, comfort, and freedom. This was because they wanted not to give to society, but for society to give to them. The freedom they were seeking was freedom from responsibility. It is no wonder, then, that they ceased to be free." – Margaret Thatcher, *The Moral Foundations of Society* (1995)

- ☞ "It may be observed, that provinces amid the vicissitudes to which they are subject, pass from order into confusion, and afterward recur to a state of order again; for the nature of mundane affairs not allowing them to continue in an even course, when they have arrived at their greatest perfection, they soon begin to decline. In the same manner, having been reduced by disorder, and sunk to their utmost state of depression, unable to descend lower, they, of necessity, reascend; and thus from good they gradually decline to evil, and from evil again return to good. The reason is, that valor produces peace; peace, repose; repose, disorder; disorder, ruin; so from disorder order springs; from order virtue, and from this, glory and good fortune." – Niccolò Machiavelli, *Florentine Histories* (1532)

Socialist regimes are in part defined by redistribution of taxpayer revenues from those at higher income levels to those of lesser means. Fiscal (federal government) stimulus is often the shelter or perspective legislatures use to rationalize this controversial reshuffling of money amongst their constituency. This is a much-debated political maneuver that can exude quite a bit of emotion (money has that effect). On one hand, it can be an antidote to what ails the economy during turbulent periods....

☞ "If the patient has a life-threatening infection and you have powerful antibiotics available, why not use them?" – Barton Biggs, *Diary of a Hedgehog* (2012)

> Joseph Stalin, infamous leader of the USSR, is believed to have once said, "Those who cast the votes decide nothing. Those who count the votes decide everything."

Stimulus is designed to provide a much-needed jolt to an ailing economy. Yet, there is precedent for fiscal stimulus not living up to expectations, and the parties who put it into motion are often chided for this. This is a somewhat flimsy critique, as most things in life do not play out exactly as planned. Also difficult is the matter of coming off of this economic sugar high. We all know dieting is tough. It's an even tougher task for our elected officials, as withholding the economic cookie jar from voters can put their employment in jeopardy....

☞ "The only things that are permanent are those which are temporary." – Washington D.C. motto

☞ "The haste with which spending programs are approved is not matched by an equal haste to repeal them or eliminate them." – Milton Friedman, *Capitalism and Freedom* (1962)

☞ "The fact that government programs have not worked is no excuse for those in government not to act." – Dan Coats, former GOP House Budget Committee chairman, as quoted in *Devouring Freedom: Can Big Government Ever Be Stopped?* by W. James Antle, III (2013)

Protectionist policies, which fall under the fiscal stimulus umbrella, are designed to give a boost to a country that is underperforming on the global economic stage. The primary intent is to improve the appeal of domestically-produced goods from a pricing standpoint, with the corresponding effect of making imports more expensive. The increased demand for domestic goods would lead to employment gains and provide a general B-12 shot to an economy struggling to keep pace with foreign competition.

Protectionist tactics come in a variety of forms, like tariffs and levies on imported products. Increasingly, these tactics have included currency devaluations, which appear less offensive than an overt mark-up of a foreign good. Their appearance is rather predictable. When massive trade imbalances are brewing, protectionist policies gain traction in order to harmonize a country's imports and exports. Yet, irrespective of how enacted, protectionism is a bit of a dirty word due to its blemished track record: it invites domestic inflation and foreign retaliation....

Do deliberate attempts to reduce the value of a currency work? The evidence is spotty. For instance, the US dollar has been on a rather steady decline since the end of the gold standard. During roughly the same time, the US manufacturing base has fallen from 20 percent of the US economy in 1980 to 12 percent in 2012. Manufacturers would conceivably benefit the most from a cheaper currency, however, as it improves exporting prospects.

⌘ "Indeed, policies designed to promote domestic export industries – so-called beggar-thy-neighbor policies such as competitive currency devaluations, import tariffs, and/or export subsidies – risk unleashing a wave of destructive protectionism." – Dennis C. Blair, U.S. Director of National Intelligence, testimony before Senate Committee on Intelligence (February 2009)

⌘ "Higher input costs are not the only downside of devaluation. A bigger immediate concern may be the competitive, tit-for-tat devaluations." – James Rickards, *Currency Wars: The Making of the Next Global Crisis* (2011)

- "tariffs do foster monopoly." – Milton Friedman, *Capitalism and Freedom* (1962)

- "Protectionism will do little to create jobs; and if foreigners retaliate, we will surely lose jobs." – Alan Greenspan, At the Greater Omaha Chamber of Commerce 2004 Annual Meeting (February 20th, 2004)

By many accounts, The Smoot-Hawley Tariff Act, protectionist legislation designed to protect the United States farming industry and curb an economic decline, made the Depression of the 1930's, well, 'Great'. "That Act intensified nationalism all over the world," according to Thomas Lamont, the top lieutenant to J.P. Morgan at Morgan Bank....

- "The philosophy of protectionism is a philosophy of war." – Ludwig Von Mises, *Human Action, The Scholar's Edition* (1949)

PORTFOLIO CONSTRUCTION

A sset allocation, or your mix of stocks, bonds, cash, and other classes, is arguably the most important decision to make *prior* to breaking ground on your portfolio. 'Prior' is the operative word in the preceding sentence. The whole concept is very similar to building a home. For instance, deciding you want to add a sunroom or fourth bedroom halfway through the construction process will be a costly adjustment. Likewise, figuring out you have too much stock exposure in your portfolio during a market correction and hitting the eject button will likely be a pricy mistake. You want to build a portfolio with your eyes as wide open as possible. The thoughtful investor will prepare for all sorts of different scenarios before actually putting real money to work.

> Strategic asset allocation explains roughly 90 percent of a portfolio's variability of returns over time, with shorter duration tactical asset allocation decisions (typically two years or less) and security selection representing the majority of the residual ten percent. – Roger G. Ibbotson and Paul D. Kaplan, "Does Asset Allocation Policy Explain 40, 90, or 100 Percent of Performance?" (2000)

There is no perfect science in determining the right asset allocation mix for you. I always suggest starting off with a very conservative portfolio and (if appropriate) growing into a more risky one after experiencing a few ups and downs in the markets. Fortunately, there are also some time-tested rules of the road for building a portfolio. In particular, your asset class positioning is a function of your ability (ex. time horizon, liquidity needs) and willingness (i.e. mental fortitude to withstand volatility) to take risk. For instance, a long time horizon and a limited need for liquidity alike are factors that give you a greater ability to take risk. A greater ability to take risk allows you to invest in more volatile investments, like stocks, which typically have a greater upside compared to bonds and cash. However, your willingness to incur risk is controlling. If the volatility associated with equities gives you indigestion, then a more conservative portfolio orientation is appropriate. This is because you should limit the likelihood of emotions driving investment decisions, which can happen at the worst possible times (this is covered in more detail in the behavioral finance section)....

- ☞ "I think that the first thing is you should have a strategic asset allocation mix that assumes that you don't know what the future is going to hold." – Ray Dalio, founder of Bridgewater Associates

- ☞ "Any security specific selection decision is preceded, either implicitly or explicitly, by an asset allocation decision." – Scott Lummer and Mark Riepe, *The Role of Asset Allocation in Portfolio Management* (1994)

The concept of portfolio construction is analogous to constructing a home. You wouldn't just tell an architect to build you a home without providing any guidance. With regard to your investments, you need to thoughtfully develop a blueprint that includes your wants, needs, vulnerabilities, and concerns. More importantly, once in place, you need to stay true to your plan, even during times of market turbulence....

- ☞ "Strategy without tactics is the slowest route to victory. Tactics without strategy is the noise before defeat." –attributed to Sun Tzu, though likely apocryphal

- ☞ "Weapons change, but strategy remains strategy, on the New York Stock Exchange as on the battlefield." – Edwin LeFevre, *Reminiscences of a Stock Operator* (1923)

- "A good portfolio is more than a long list of good stocks and bonds. It is a balanced whole, providing the investor with protections and opportunities with respect to a wide range of contingencies." – Harry Markowitz, *Portfolio Selection: Efficient Diversification of Investments* (1959)

- "The will to win is important, but the will to prepare is vital." – Joe Paterno, former head football coach at Penn State

- "Forewarned, forearmed; to be prepared is half the victory." – Miguel de Cervantes, *Don Quixote* (1615)

- "I am prepared for the worst, but hope for the best." – Benjamin Disraeli, British Prime Minister

- "It is a doctrine of war not to assume the enemy will not come, but rather to rely on one's readiness to meet him; not to presume that he will not attack, but rather to make one's self invincible." – Sun Tzu, *The Art of War* (6th century BC)

- "By failing to prepare, you are preparing to fail." – Benjamin Franklin

- "The skillful commander takes up a position so he cannot be defeated . . . . Thus, a victorious army wins its victories before the battle." – Sun Tzu, *The Art of War* (6th century BC)

- "Stock market post-mortems don't pay dividends." – Edwin LeFevre, *Reminiscences of a Stock Operator* (1923)

Rarely does the market or economy play out precisely as expected. That makes portfolio construction all the more valuable, particularly when it comes to managing emotions. Adherence to an investment blueprint can help you avoid self-inflicted wounds when you're tempted to do something counter-productive with your finances....

- ☞ "It is easier to resist at the beginning than at the end." – Leonardo da Vinci, foremost figure of the Italian Renaissance

- ☞ "If you have trouble imaging a 20 percent loss in the stock market, you shouldn't be in stocks." – John Bogle, founder of The Vanguard Group

- ☞ "To be in the game, you have to endure the pain." – George Soros

- ☞ "Trends can reverse for no apparent reason with incredible celerity." – Barton Biggs, *Diary of a Hedgehog* (2012)

Keep in mind, investing blueprints are rarely one size fits all. Risk tolerances, liquidity needs, and time horizons will all vary....

- ☞ "Investors come in a unit of one." – Anonymous

- ☞ "Don't compare your path with anybody else's. Your path is unique to you." – Ram Dass, American spiritual leader and author

Asset Class	Minimum Weighting	Strategic Target	Maximum Weighting
Equities	55%	65%	75%
Fixed Income	20%	30%	40%
Cash	0%	5%	10%

Once you establish a thoughtful investment, as an investor, you need to follow through. Regimented rebalancing, or selling your winners and buying more of your losers, can require an adjustment in your holdings. Consider the following illustrative investment policy, which establishes asset class ranges that serve as automatic triggers. For instance, adherence to this would mean methodically selling equities if they exceeded 75 percent of your portfolio and redeploying the proceeds into fixed income or cash. Generally speaking, when an asset class hits the high end of a range it typically indicates that it has become expensive and vice versa. Therefore, you have some math to help you buy low and sell high. Further, failing to adhere to an investment policy should be looked at as another permutation of market timing. As discussed, that roulette-esque approach can shift the odds out of your favor, and it's entirely avoidable.

It's important to have a sound financial plan that addresses cash flow requirements, taxes, and transfer of assets at death. For instance, try to put tax unfriendly investments, like high yield bonds, into tax friendly entities, like an IRA. You also want to consider engaging a lawyer or estate planner to make sure at death your wealth transfers seamlessly to your desired heirs. In short, misplaced assets and poor planning can overshadow and undermine an otherwise sound investment strategy. To end this section, here are two adages (the second is one of my own) to keep you on the right track as you hash out your financial plan:

1. "There's asset allocation, and then there's asset location."
2. "You should construct your financial blueprint to synergistically and effectively manage wealth vertically (across generations) and horizontally (across entities)."

BUSINESS SUCCESS

usiness success is a decidedly vague and relative term. It can mean commanding the highest share, or one of the highest, of a given market. On the other hand, some companies may define business success by healthy profitability metrics, such as revenues or margins, despite not having a top share in a given market....

    ☞ "Happiness is a positive cash flow." – title of the book by Fred Adler, venture capitalist

Some companies might define success by the quality of their product, irrespective of their financials. Then there is the trick of maintaining success, which can be accomplished in a variety of ways. What is clear, however, is that good businesses can serve as good investment opportunities....

    ☞ "Over the long term, it's hard for a stock to earn a much better return than the business which underlies it earns. If the business earns six percent on capital over forty years and you hold it for that forty years, you're not going to make much different than a six percent return – even if you originally buy it at a huge discount. Conversely, if a business earns

> This might be a bit confusing, but a good business can be a bad investment if the price paid is excessive. This notion becomes a bit more intuitive if applied in other facets of life. For instance, you may love a house, but you'll probably fall out of love rather quickly if you paid an inordinate premium for it.

eighteen percent on capital over twenty or thirty years, even if you pay an expensive looking price, you'll end up with one hell of a result." – Charlie Munger

☞ "If a business does well, the stock eventually follows." – Warren Buffett

There is not one single blueprint for businesses to follow, which presents challenges for investors that covet a formulaic way of looking at things. Yet, a good business does not have to be truly original....

☞ "Google did not come up with the first search engine. Apple did not invent the MP3 player. Chipotle did not invent the first burrito. But they figured out how to get stuff done – how to get it in the hands of people." – Khanjan Mehta, founding director of the Humanitarian Engineering and Social Entrepreneurship Program at Penn State

☞ "Good artists borrow, great artists steal." – attributed to Pablo Picasso, as well as T. S. Eliot

Ideas are the indispensable foundation of a business. However, there is a lot more involved to getting a business off the ground. You have to develop a business plan, hire staff, engage vendors, develop infrastructure, among other countless tasks. The savvy investor shouldn't solely invest in ideas, which are rarely in short supply. Ideas are fundamentally worthless when they are not actionable and without someone passionate and motivated to act upon them. It takes a person with a unique DNA to throw themselves at an idea and actually be able to monetize it. This rare breed has to be, collectively, amazingly undeterred, freakishly creative, and exceptionally intelligent....

☞ "Action is the foundational key to all success." – Pablo Picasso, artist and pioneer of Cubism

- "Vision without execution is a hallucination." – attributed to both Henry Ford and Thomas Edison

- "If you want to increase your success rate, double your failure rate." – attributed to Thomas J. Watson, Sr.

- "In the modern world of business, it is useless to be a creative, original thinker unless you can also sell what you create." – David Ogilvy, considered the father of advertising

Be willing to invest in those who dream big, as many successful brand names were founded by people who did just that....

- "I think it is often easier to make progress on mega-ambitious dreams. I know that sounds completely nuts. But, since no one else is crazy enough to do it, you have little competition." – Larry Page, co-founder of Google

- "If I had asked people what they wanted, they would have said faster horses." – commonly attributed to Henry Ford

> As one of my undergraduate professors told me, "Remember, you are always selling." Sales aren't just to customers. You sell ideas, concepts, and your capabilities.

- "Ideas shape the course of history." – attributed to John Maynard Keynes

- "The best way to predict the future is to invent it!" – Alan Kay, American computer scientist

- "Those who dare to fail miserably can achieve greatly." – John F. Kennedy

The type of disruptive innovation that has changed the world around us does not come about seamlessly. It can certainly have interesting and even humbling beginnings....

- "If anybody laughs at your idea, view it as a sign of potential success!" – Jim Rogers, *A Gift to My Children: A Father's Lessons for Life and Investing* (2009)

- "If you're not failing every now and again, it's a sign you're not doing anything very innovative." – Woody Allen, American director, actor, and screenwriter

- "Thomas Edison 'failed' 10,000 times before he perfected the incandescent light bulb." – Napoleon Hill, *Think and Grow Rich* (1937)

A business can thrive by having the 'best' products (like Apple), but also by being the least expensive. For instance, Vanguard has become an asset management behemoth due to its menu of low-cost investment solutions. Even for the low-cost provider, a focus on product quality is needed....

- "People forget how fast you did a job – but they remember how well you did it." – Howard W. Newton, 20th century American advertising executive and author

- "Quality means doing it right when no one is looking." – attributed to Henry Ford

- "It is quality rather than quantity that matters." – Seneca the Younger, *Epistulae Morales ad Lucilium* (c. 65 AD)

@ "Quality is how well our product works in relation to the custom-er's need." – Ken Blanchard and Sheldon Bowles, *Raving Fans* (1993)

@ "Fast is fine, but accuracy is everything." – Xenophon, ancient Greek historian and author

@ "Be a yardstick of quality. Some people aren't used to an envi-ronment where excellence is expected." – Steve Jobs, co-founder of Apple Inc.

There are various other elements key to business success, including good management (more on this later) and optimization of customer prices. You don't want to price a product too low, as you would be leaving money on the table. Nor do you want to price it too high as this makes the cost prohibitive to consumers. Further, high profit margins, which can accompany high prices, are a magnet for competition….

@ "Get costs down by better management. Get the prices down to the buying power." – Henry Ford, as quoted in *American Icon* by Bryce Hoffman (2013)

Management is just one layer of a business structure. There are a few different answers to the appropriate organizational structure. Many businesses employ tens of thousands, but a boutique approach may be more conducive to success. In *The Tipping Point* (2002), Malcolm Gladwell speaks of the *Rule of 150*, and states that once an organization exceeds 150 members, the quality of its relationships begin to erode. Small companies don't have the war chests and economies of scale of large organizations, but they have the advantage of being more stealthy and nimble….

@ "Small companies have huge competitive advantages. They are uncluttered, simple, informal. They thrive on passion and ridicule bureaucracy. Small companies grow on good ideas – regardless of their source. They need everyone, involve everyone, and reward or remove people based on their contribution to winning. Small companies dream big dreams and set the bar high – increments and fractions don't interest them." – Jack Welch, former General Electric CEO (read more about him in the biography section)

One essential aspect of an organization is its efficiency in effectively delivering the product to the customer. It can be one product or several. Diversity of products may help a business immunize itself from the vagaries of customer interest and the ebb and flow of the business cycle. My advice? You don't want to be good at just one thing, as you run the risk of your product becoming commoditized or obsolete.

While product diversification has several benefits, it also has its own set of risks....

⛆ "If you spend life trying to be good at everything, you will never be great at anything. While society encourages us to be well-rounded, this approach inadvertently breeds mediocrity." – Tom Rath and Barry Conchie, *Strengths Based Leadership* (2009)

⛆ Those who chase off in too many directions suffer by diffusing their energies and diminishing their performance."

There are five ways management can use a company's free cash to help enhance shareholder value:

1. Pay dividends
2. Offer share buybacks, but not if it is done to mainly offset the exercising of options for management
3. Pursue M&A, but be leery of the mega cap transaction (think AOL/Time Warner). Sometimes a company's eyes can be bigger than their stomach.
4. Pay down debt
5. Make capital expenditures

     – Peter Drucker, *The Five Most Important Questions You Will Ever Ask About Your Organization* (2008)

⚉ "If you try to please everybody, somebody's not going to like it." – Donald Rumsfeld, *Rumsfeld Rules* (1974)

⚉ "I don't know the key to success, but the key to failure is trying to please everybody." – Bill Cosby, American comedian and actor

⚉ "When you're number four or five in a market, when number one sneezes, you get pneumonia. When you're number one, you control your destiny. The number fours keep merging; they have difficult times. That's not the same if you're number four, and that's your only businesses. Then you have to find strategic ways to get stronger." - Jack Welch, Business Today (February 1995)

Either way, a good business should make efforts to avoid stagnation and feverishly try to understand the latest consumer desires. "We have always done it this way" is a dangerous mentality. Think of how the emergence of Amazon played a role in driving Borders and Circuit City out of business, or the unfortunate buggy whip or 8-track cassette businesses that perished for stubbornly failing to adapt. This train of thought was cemented in academia in 1960 when Theodore Levitt introduced the *Marketing Myopia* concept. Levitt's seminal work encouraged an outward view of the marketplace to determine customer wants, not what the business insists on providing. For instance, many seasoned 'oil' companies have been looking to rebrand themselves as more multi-faceted, more environmentally conscious 'energy' companies. The consumer has spoken - oil slicks out, renewable energy in....

⚉ "Business success is less a function of grandiose predictions than it is a result of being able to respond rapidly to real changes as they occur." – Jack Welch, *Jack: Straight from the Gut* (2003)

☞ "I don't worry about it 'cause I know it's inevitable. Companies come and go. And the companies that are, you know, the shiniest and most important of any era, you wait a few decades and they're gone." – Jeff Bezos, CEO of Amazon, *60 Minutes* interview (December 7th, 2013)

Good management is a typical pre-condition for a good business, and there exists a positive correlation between strong management and above-average equity returns for the respective company.…

☞ "Every business is manmade. It is a result of individuals. It reflects the personalities and the business philosophy of the founders and those who have directed its affairs throughout its existence. If you want to have an understanding of any business, it is important to know the background of the people who started it and directed its past and the hopes and ambitions of those who are planning its future." – Thomas Rowe Price, Jr.

When it comes to effective management, Peter Drucker (more on him in the biography section) delivers a bounty of sage advice. Here is a sampling from his 1967 management classic *The Effective Executive*.…

☞ "Executives are not paid for doing things they like to do. They are paid for getting the right things done."

☞ "Effective executives build on strengths . . . . They do not start out with things they cannot do."

☞ "Effective executives know that their subordinates are paid to perform and not to please their superiors."

☞ "While the others complain about their ability to do anything, the effective executives go ahead and do."

Of course, there are others who know a thing or two about good management....

- "Getting the right people in the right jobs is a lot more important than developing a strategy." – Jack Welch, *Jack: Straight from the Gut* (2003)

- "All of the great leaders have had one characteristic in common: it was the willingness to confront unequivocally the major anxiety of their people in their time. This, and not much else, is the essence of leadership." – John Kenneth Galbraith

- "The conventional definition of management is getting work done through people, but real management is developing people through work." – Agha Hasan Abedi, Bank of Credit Commerce International founder

- "Hire people who are better than you are, then leave them to get on with it. Look for people who will aim for the remarkable, who will not settle for the routine." – David Ogilvy

- "When a management with a reputation for brilliance tackles a business with a reputation for bad economics, it is the reputation of the business that remains intact." – Warren Buffett, as quoted in *The Wall Street Journal* (December 10th, 2009)

- "Good management is the art of making problems so interesting and their solutions so constructive that everyone wants to get to work and deal with them." – Paul Hawken, environmentalist, entrepreneur, and author

- "Management is nothing more than motivating other people." – Lee Iacocca, former Chrysler chairman and Ford president

- "Efficient leaders lead by encouraging, not by trying to instill fear in the hearts of their followers." – Napoleon Hill, *Think and Grow Rich* (1937)

- "Make your top managers rich and they will make you rich." – attributed to Robert H. Johnson, former Wyoming state senator

- "If you pick the right people and give them the opportunity to spread their wings –and put compensation as a carrier behind it – you almost don't have to manage them." – Jack Welch

- "Good management consists in showing average people how to do the work of superior people." – attributed to John D. Rockefeller

- "A good manager is a man who isn't worried about his own career but rather the careers of those who work for him." – H. S. Mackenzie Burns, former president of Shell Oil Company

- "Withhold not good from them to whom it is due, when it is in the power of thine hand to do it." - Proverbs 3:27, Oxford King James Version

As you may be able to infer, it's the quality of management that matters most, not the quantity....

- "Reduce the layers of management. They put distance between the top of an organization and the customers." – Donald Rumsfeld, *Rumsfeld Rules* (1974)

Good management teams are never a constant, which lends itself to investing in businesses that can essentially run themselves....

- "I try to buy stock in businesses that are so wonderful that an idiot can run them. Because sooner or later, one will." – Warren Buffett

Management and leadership are not synonymous. Good managers know how to operate and fine-tune a business. They keep expenses in check, hire and fire employees, along with other basic blocking and tackling. The differentiating factor is that leaders inspire their employees. They instill a sense of purpose up and down the organization. They place equal value on even the smallest of contributions, which makes everyone feel that they are vital to the success of the business. Leaders recast times of turbulence as moments of great opportunity, which can help carry a business in times of adversity. All told, leaders can make a good company a great one....

- "Effective leadership is not about making speeches or being liked; leadership is defined by results not attributes." – Peter Drucker

- "Management is doing things right; leadership is doing the right things." – Peter Drucker

- "A leader is best when people barely know that he exists, not so good when people obey and acclaim him, worst when they despise him. Fail to honor people, they fail to honor you." - Lao Tzu, *Tao Te Ching* (6th century BC)

- "A leader is someone who can get things done through other people. They have to be able to do so knowingly, enthusiastically and effectively." – Warren Buffett

Good leaders tend to get the most out of people, but that can only take a business so far. There needs to be talent. For instance, Google is renowned for being a great company for a variety of reasons, but one of the more salient features is its talented work force. The company is incredibly exclusive when it comes to hiring employees. The point is that, in business, a junior varsity roster may able to compete against the varsity squad, though victories will likely be scarce.

Good leaders pick their employees wisely. Consider that Zappo's, the online retailer, offers $2k to job candidates to walk away during their onboarding process. Yes, $2k to *not* take an open job. They want to weed out potential employees who aren't fully committed to their pending new role in the company. It still may seem questionable to pay someone for nothing, but it's actually quite brilliant. Hiring the wrong person can be costly, due to an erosion of morale and productivity. It's not an insignificant mistake, as the cost of a bad hire is probably at least $25k[8]. This seems to make those $2k checks look like money well spent....

- "Here Lies A Man Who Knew How to Enlist in His Service Better Men Than Himself." – epitaph of Andrew Carnegie

- "People inspire you, or they drain you – pick them wisely." – Hans F. Hansen, entrepreneur and former soccer star

- "You're only as good as the people you hire." – attributed to Raymond Albert Kroc, McDonald's executive who made the company into the giant that it is today

- "A small team of A+ players can run circles around a giant team of B and C players." – Steve Jobs

Changing gears a bit: on a more micro-level, good managers should resist the temptation of frequent meetings....

- "Meetings are by definition a concession to deficient organization. For one either meets or one works. One cannot do both at the same time." – Peter Drucker, *The Effective Executive* (1967)

---

8 Mary Lorenz, "What's the True Cost of a Bad Hire?" *The Hiring Site*, December 16th, 2011.

☞ "People who enjoy meetings should not be in charge of anything." – Thomas Sowell

It's important for investors to identify companies where management has skin in the game. Investors should covet management teams that are also shareholders, as a mechanism to help ensure proper alignment of interests. This breakdown can be a costly one if you are not paying attention. While there isn't a formulaic way of determining the right amount of company stock to be held, you can find value in determining if insiders are adding to or subtracting from their stakes. In particular, if executives are selling, that could be a very telling vote of no confidence. For example, Kenneth Lay, the former CEO of Enron, sold 1.8 million shares of company stock between early 1999 and July 2001. Enron filed for bankruptcy in December 2001. Fortunately, share amounts and company stock transactions by the respective top brass are public information[9].

After the business is off the ground, maintaining success is also difficult. For instance, expense management can only get you so far. Remember:

☞ *You cannot cost cut in perpetuity. Eventually you cut bone.*

M&A can prove very telling. If a company is using its own stock as currency for an acquisition it may very well indicate that management thinks their company stock is overvalued.

There will also be the lure of inorganic growth tactics, such as merger and acquisitions (M&A), as an alternative to internally generated opportunities. Successful M&A blends both art and science....

☞ "Our business is really simple. When you look at a deal and its structure looks like an octopus or spider, just don't do it." – Timothy Sloan, former Wells Fargo CFO (March 3rd, 2011)

---

9 Data available at www.secform4.com

And being able to walk away from a deal is as valuable as identifying the right one to consummate. You don't want to own a company that does a deal just for the sake of it....

⌖ "What you decide not to do is probably more important than what you decide to do." – Tom Peters, management guru, as quoted in Daniel Pink's *Drive* (2009)

There is a dark side to M&A, as it often is a precursor to future expense reductions. M&A may as well give you a license to lay off staff. Also, there is innate skepticism about M&A and the motives behind it. They are involved transactions with large-scale fees for brokering them. They also provide a means to mask financial difficulties. As such, M&A needs to be closely scrutinized by investors....

⌖ "Mergers provided lucrative opportunities for accounting tricks." – Burton Malkiel, *A Random Walk Down Wall Street* (1973)

⌖ "Mergers and acquisitions – M&A – were the ultimate creature of Wall Street because win, lose, or draw, they produced fees: fees for advising, fees for divesting unwanted businesses, fees for lending money." – Bryan Burrough and John Helyar, *Barbarians at the Gate: The Fall of RJR Nabisco* (1989)

Stock splits are another tactic management can employ to attract investors. In a conventional stock split, additional shares are issued; this reduces the stock price, all else being equal. Splits are used to make the stock appear more of a bargain for investors. They aren't much of a growth strategy and don't alter the intrinsic worth of a company. Just remember....

Investors also need to be leery of excessive initial public offering (IPO) activity, which can flood the market with a new supply of equity that can weigh on future returns. This was the case in the late 1990's right before the tech bubble burst. Thus, when it comes to IPO's, you don't want to party like its 1999.

ⓐ "A pie doesn't grow through its slicing." – Wall Street maxim

ⓐ "If a stock which is not paying a dividend is split two for one, how much good does that do the stockholder? (If you think it does him any real good, come down and join our sales department, but steer clear of our trading department)." – Fred Schwed, *Where Are the Customers' Yachts: or A Good Hard Look at Wall Street* (1940)

While not a line on the balance sheet, corporate culture is of significant value. Culture can account for up to half of the difference in operating profit between two organizations in the same business, according to James Heskett.[10] Culture is the foundation, infrastructure, and most importantly the catapult for business success....

ⓐ "Culture eats strategy for breakfast." – commonly credited to Peter Drucker

> Sales are like calories for businesses. They will sputter without a recurring diet of them. It's no coincidence that individuals highly effective at the point of sale are some of the most coveted employees in any industry.

It goes without saying – the customers of a business determine its financial fortunes. No sales, no future. Yet, not all customers are created equal. On one hand, there are fickle customers with one foot out the door waiting for the next better or cheaper product. It is less than ideal to have a customer base predominantly comprised of them. Instead, you want *Raving Fans* (title of a book by Ken Blanchard and Sheldon Bowles) who are satisfied and fiercely loyal customers. The metamorphosis to Raving Fan status doesn't happen overnight for a business. It takes a long time and a history of understanding and executing on the client's

---

10 Sean Silverthorne, "The Profit Power of Corporate Culture," *Working Knowledge*, September 28, 2011.

precise wants and needs. This is the apex of customer status, as once they are there they can be a great referral source, without even being on the payroll. In fact, word-of-mouth is the primary factor behind 20 percent to 50 percent of all purchasing decisions[11]....

    ☞ "All production is for the purpose of ultimately satisfying a consumer." – John Maynard Keynes, *The General Theory of Employment, Interest and Money* (1936)

---

11 Jacques Bughin, et al. "A New Way to Measure Word-of-Mouth Marketing," *McKinsey & Company*, April 2010.

OVERTIME....

The Technology Life Cycle

It may be frustrating that you find youself coughing up well over $100 to get a new cell phone every few years, but this is indicative of how quickly change is ushered in with technology. Technologies often follow an *S-Curve* life-cycle pattern with four phases: research and development (R&D), ascent, maturity and decline. Profitability is negative in the R&D phase and peaks at the maturity phase. As many consumers can attest, the peak maturity phase now occurs rather quickly. This is *Moore's Law* in action. Named after Gordon Moore, a co-founder of Intel, the computing power of microchips is said to double approximately every two years. The rate of advancement in technology is fueled by pursuit of financial gain, but it also helps to have a lot of brilliant people in the field (think Silicon Valley). Consequently, we now accumulate information at a spectacular rate. In fact, the quantity of knowledge in certain scientific fields reportedly doubles every eighteen months, as compared to around every ten years before the advent of the internet. This 'tech library' has been a springboard for innovation. Unfortunately, this could mean fleeting profits for the more stagnant technology companies, which could also mean bad news for their respective investors. The upside to this rapid pace of innovation and obsolescence is that we can get our hands on new and improved consumer electronics seemingly all the time. This also means there is a window of opportunity for those next disruptive technology companies, which should excite many businessmen, investors, and hopefully consumers.

> *Kaizen* is a Japanese business mantra with the goal of continuous process improvement. If a part of a business is unproductive, it should be systematically eliminated. The Toyota production process helped popularize this concept.

ASSET CLASSES

Investors must understand there are different types of assets. The next couple of chapters will cover equities (stocks), fixed income (bonds), cash, real estate, commodities, and even art & collectibles. There is also a section devoted to alternative investments that do not meet the purist definition of an asset class. Instead, they are better thought of as vehicles to gain exposure to conventional asset classes. Each asset class has different risk factors and return potential. Muddying the waters even more is the fact that there is little homogeneity within asset classes. As such, there is no magic bullet for making an asset class investment decision.

If there is one common thread across the coming chapters it would be a recommendation to thoroughly examine valuations. All too often, asset classes are defined by the range of their historic price swings. For instance, bonds seem to be less risky than stocks because the pricing hasn't been as jittery in the past. There is some value to this approach for setting expectations of future returns. Further, some investors just may not be able to stomach the ups and downs of a more volatile asset class. Yet, volatility is better thought of not as a means, but an end. A harbinger for extreme volatility is paying a hefty premium for an asset, and investors really get burned if they aren't careful about cost. If you look back at history, the precipitous falls in the market (Ex. NASDAQ collapse, Japanese real estate bubble) were really the corrective process that naturally follows the appreciation of assets well beyond their fundamental worth. "Trees don't grow to the sky," as they say on Wall Street. Those hope-induced asset class valuations were destined to come back to Earth, and they eventually did. The preceding chapters of any market meltdown are characterized by optimism and complacency that can easily sneak up on you. Nothing, not even the core tenet of valuing time, can save you from grossly overpaying for an asset. In fact, had you bought the NASDAQ or Japanese real estate at peak pricing you would still be looking at losses even after more than a decade has lapsed. That's what makes astute attention to valuations so critical – it helps avoid over-paying for an investment and inviting unwelcome, potentially crippling asset class volatility.

The following chapters hit the salient characteristics and valuation tools for a variety of asset classes that should be of value to the eloquent investor.

EQUITIES

When people ask, "How did the market do?" they typically aren't referring to the recent returns of bonds or commodities. The question at hand is about public equities, a global opportunity set that exceeded $63 trillion as of November 2013, according to the World Federation of Exchanges. Within that expansive menu is potential, which gives rise to the lure of equities. Great fortunes have been made with seemingly little effort through the stock market. This is why equities are the center of gravity for investors and have such a mystique. True, equities can lead to riches, but the market is also littered with potential flops that can cause great hardship. In fact, from 1983 through 2000, close to 19 percent of the Russell 3000 Index lost 75 percent or worse, even during a back drop of the one the greatest bull market runs we have ever seen[12]. Stock investors need to know that industry disruptions and business failures will occur (courtesy of capitalism). Thus, in no uncertain terms, equities have a lot of inherent risk. They are complex beings with various factors influencing pricing. Yet, at their core they simply are a way to participate in the future earnings power of an underlying business....

> There are three main drivers of equity market returns: earnings growth, dividends, and P/E multiple changes.

☞ "I think you have to learn that there's a company behind every stock, and that there's only one real reason why stocks go up.

---

12 Melanie Faber and Eric Richardson, *The Ivy Portfolio* (Hoboken, NJ: Wiley, 2009).

Companies go from doing poorly to doing well or small companies grow to large companies." – attributed to Peter Lynch

Paul Samuelson once said that, "Wall Street indexes predicted nine out of the last five recessions." Maybe stocks aren't so forward looking after all.

A stock represents ownership interest in a company and a way to participate in their *future* earnings potential. The stock market has a long, colorful, and fascinating history, but that's somewhat irrelevant. You own stocks not for how they have performed, but how they will perform in the future. That's a seemingly subtle, but vitally important distinction, as a rear-view mirror analysis of a stock is far from ideal. There's a reason why the stock market is considered a forward-looking indicator. As they say on Wall Street, "Equities are a discounting mechanism that captures present and future information for a company."

Source - Yahoo! Finance. MSCI Russia Capped ETF (ticker ERUS) used as proxy.

The general long-term direction of the stock market is up. In fact, the price of the Dow Jones Industrial Average ascended roughly 17,420 percent (from 66 to 11,497) during the 20th century. However, you had to have been continuously invested to achieve that majestic gain, and that would certainly have been a bit difficult. One certainty with investing is that there will be turbulence from time-to-time that could cause you to lose sight of the stock market's innate trajectory. In fact, corrections (a decline of 10 percent of more) for the S&P 500 have occurred once every 11 months or so since 1928. At any given point in time there will be something that makes you uncomfortable. It could be military conflicts, coups, bankruptcies, poor earnings announcements, epidemics, commodity shortages, political scandals, etc. There will be other reasons for anxiety and they will all test your mettle. Of course certain companies could be adversely affected or even permanently impaired as a result of the aforementioned news item, but usually not the market at large, at least not for any extended period of time.

The 2014 Russian annexation of Crimea and subsequent threat of doing the same with the Ukraine is a vivid example of an exogenous shock and its fleeting impact to the stock market. Vladimir Putin's saber-rattling was front page news for days and sent the Russian stock market and currency into a tailspin. It was unsettling for us all and certainly uncomfortable for any one with Russian market exposures. As with all military episodes, anxiety was in surplus and the convenient action was to sell or avoid Russian equities. Russian markets are not exactly magnets for capital to begin with and consequently trade at very low valuation multiples. These events transformed this chronically cheap stock market into something screamingly cheap. In fact, the near 30 percent correction that ensued over the course of the first half of 2014 caused the market in its entirety to descend to a capitalization lower than that of Apple. The Russian stock market has it blemishes, in particular its energy concentration, but it's not worthless. For instance, Lukoil and Gazprom, two of the top constituents in the Russian market are global franchises with respectable earnings capacity. The skittish investor had every reason to run away after Putin took center stage. Yet, sanity prevailed as Putin eventually withdrew his troops from the Ukrainian border. Vulture investors also stabilized the market by swooping in to purchase Russian stocks trading at a fraction of their intrinsic worth, which came at a point in time of the global economic expansion when cheap assets were few and far between. The result was that, after hitting its low in mid-March when Crimea was annexed, the market catapulted to basically where it started at the beginning of 2014. In other words, if you blinked, you would have missed the erratic market response to Putin's antics. It was surely a rollercoaster story, but a financial loss was very much avoidable if you simply sat tight. The point is that there are always plenty of excuses to lose sight of the big picture, act on emotion, and engage in dangerous short-term thinking. The better way to think about these negative headlines is as temporary distractions that could cause you to drive off the road during your investment journey. While the market doesn't move in a straight line, don't ever forget that over the long-term the odds are in your favor with the stock market….

  ☞ "Historically, the stock market is like a gambling casino with the odds in your favor. Over the long pull, stocks are given something like nine and a half to ten percent compounded per year. The banks have probably given you something in the order of four to five." – Burton G. Malkiel, *20/20* interview (November 27th, 1992)

There are two general approaches to equity investing: growth and value. Value investors look to identify assets on sale, like Russian stocks when there is panic selling, with low prices compared to their earnings and other metrics, such as book value. However, there are no guarantees in the stock market, even if a company is trading at a markedly low valuation. A company may be trading at a discount for all the right reasons – it may simply be beyond repair. Hence, finding value stocks set for takeoff is easier said than done. Trying to avoid those aforementioned companies is the inherent challenge for value investors. There is plenty of upside, however, if executed correctly….

☞ "Value investors believe that stock prices depart from underlying value and that investors can achieve above-market returns by buying undervalued securities. To value investors the concept of indexing is at best silly and at worst quite hazardous. Warren Buffett has observed that 'in any sort of contest – financial, mental or physical – it's an enormous advantage to have opponents who have been taught that it's useless to even try.' I believe that over time value investors will outperform the market and that choosing to match it is both lazy and short sighted." – Seth Klarman, *Margin of Safety: Risk-Averse Value Investing Strategies for the Thoughtful Investor* (1991)

☞ "If you wish to reach the highest, begin at the lowest" – Publilius Syrus, ancient Syrian writer

☞ "As I've said many times, the real goal of active management is to buy things for less than they're worth." – Howard Marks, *The Most Important Thing: Uncommon Sense for the Thoughtful Investor* (2011)

☞ "Once you adopt a value-investment strategy, any other investment behavior starts to seem like gambling." – Seth Klarman, *Margin of Safety: Risk-Averse Value Investing Strategies for the Thoughtful Investor* (1991)

☞ "Long ago, Ben Graham taught me that 'Price is what you pay; value is what you get.' Whether we're talking about socks or stocks, I like buying quality merchandise when it is marked down." – Warren Buffett, 2008 Letter to Shareholders

The *Margin of Safety* concept, a pillar of value investing, was made famous by Warren Buffett and his mentor Benjamin Graham. It is the difference between the current price of a company and its intrinsic or liquidation value.

☞ "Valuation is the prime determinant of returns." — Anonymous

Value stocks are the underdog or comeback stories in the market. They are beaten-up companies trying to find ways to return to prominence and lure investors back. If they do, they have a very favorable asymmetry. With so much bad news baked into the price there is little downside, but tons of upside if the market starts to regain confidence in the company.

In a lot of cases value investors get paid as they wait. These companies tend to have relatively higher dividend yields (dividend divided by stock price) due to the mathematical boost from their low stock prices. Dividends aren't sure things, as they can be reduced or even eliminated by management. However, dividends can offer some level of comfort during uncertain times and double as a decent form of advertising for potential investors.

Corporations issue dividends as effectively a 'thank you' for owning their stock. They generally aren't particularly large dollar amounts, but they offer a steady, recurring form of income. They also paint a picture of a company's financials. You need earnings to pay dividends, after all! Therefore, dividends offer value beyond just the receipt of cash. *The tangible cash flow of dividends delivers a message about the level of integrity with a company's financials. Dividends keep managers honest....*

Value investing, compared to growth investing, is less tax-sensitive, because you look to buy cheap assets and systematically sell them as they become expensive (i.e. at a gain).

☞ "Like the 'life-rendering pelican,' [a corporation] feeds it shareholders upon dividends." – statement from *Commissioner of Internal Revenue v. First State Bank of Stratford* (1948)

❧ "Do you know, the only thing that gives me pleasure? It's to see my dividends coming in." – John D. Rockefeller, co-founder of Standard Oil and philanthropist

Value investors need to avoid buying assets just for the sake of their price; this tactic is otherwise known as avoiding the dreaded 'value trap'....

❧ "The greatest of all gifts is the power to estimate things at their true worth." – François de La Rochefoucauld, *Reflexions, ou Sentences et Maximes Morales* (1665)

My advice on how to avoid the value trap? Ask yourself this: is a low priced security cheap, or is it inexpensive? Cheap insinuates inferior quality, inexpensive means there is a price dislocation. If it's the former, the price is right.

Growth investors are a different breed. They mine their available opportunity set for industry darlings with accelerating, robust earnings. They are on the hunt for disruptive businesses like Apple or Google, and may even pay a premium to acquire them. Growth stocks typically recycle their earnings with a focus on business expansion initiatives (think iPods and Android smartphones). Growth companies will typically invest in technology and talent that will hopefully drive future earnings, as compared to issuing dividends. For instance, Google encourages its engineers to devote one day a week to side projects. This sanctioned time for innovation and R&D helped spawn Gmail and Google News. Another way to think about growth investing is these businesses want to reward their shareholders with a different kind of dividend....

❧ "Shareholders should be indifferent to a corporation's dividends policy because they reap the same benefit when the stock price increases to reflect undistributed earnings and they are free to generate 'homemade dividends' by strategically timed sales of stock." – Merton H. Miller and Franco Modigliani, "Dividend Policy, Growth, and the Valuation of Shares" (October 1961)

Growth investors can exhibit less price discipline than value investors....

  ☞ "I have never cared what something costs; I care what it's worth." – Ari Emanuel, co-CEO of William Morris Endeavor

  ☞ "It's far better to buy a wonderful company at a fair price than a fair company at a wonderful price." – Warren Buffett, 2009 Letter to Shareholders

Growth investing is predicated upon a continued acceleration of a company's earnings stream, which lends itself to some questionable arithmetic....

  ☞ "that discounting forecasted dividends at a uniform rate in perpetuity may lead to absurdities or paradoxes, since implied present value of infinity sometime result. 'We have not yet seen any growth stocks marketed at the price of infinity dollars per share,' they remark, 'but we shall hereafter be watching.'" – David Durand, "Growth Stocks and the Petersburg Paradox" (1957)

Growth and value investment styles both have merit. Regardless of the style you side with, it is important that you have an exit strategy. This concept may sound somewhat contradictory given that the core principles section espoused the merit of a buy and hold philosophy. Yet, the 'hold' part of that mantra is a relative misnomer. Circumstances change, valuations balloon, and companies evolve, which make the chances of a perpetual time horizon remote. An exit strategy shouldn't be in terms of days or weeks in most cases, but the sun does set on most businesses. Consider that the twelve constituents of the Dow Jones Industrial

Average at its launch in 1896, only General Electric remains. Granted, that metamorphosis was over a century in the making, but rest assured that the clock is ticking on the industry stand-outs of today. Even Jeff Bezos has said as much regarding Amazon, which has redefined basic commerce and is beloved by many. A helpful framework would be to establish sell signals based off stock prices or even valuation metrics (more on this soon). The bottom line is: do not enter an investment without some thought on how you intend to exit it....

- ☞ "A thing is worth only what someone else will pay for it" – Latin maxim

Moreover, timing and execution, just like in comedy, is critical for growth and value investors alike....

- ☞ "Opportunities are like sunrises. If you wait too long, you miss them." – William Arthur Ward, author and aphorist

- ☞ "Smart investing doesn't consist of buying good assets, but of buying assets well. This is a very, very important distinction that very, very few people understand." – Howard Marks, co-founder of Oaktree Capital Management

- ☞ "Do not wait. The timing will never be 'just right.'" – Napoleon Hill, *Think and Grow Rich* (1937)

- ☞ "Valuation is a poor timing mechanism. Value investors are often early." – Wall Street speak

- ☞ "Being early and right is a euphemism for being wrong." – more Wall Street speak

One's time horizon may be the determinative factor regarding which style is most appropriate for an investor....

> "Over the long term, value stocks appear to have outperformed growth stocks, but over some three month periods, boy have they gotten crushed. Over the long term, value stocks will outperform because growth stocks by definition are priced too expensively."– Jim Leitner, Falcon Management, as quoted in *Inside the House of Money* by Steven Drobny (2006)

> Over the 85 years ending in 2013, the S&P 500 had a positive calendar year return 61 times. In other words, the probability of the stock market being up in a given year is 72 percent. Those are pretty good odds for the patient and disciplined investor.

Patience is also of great importance. Good trades can take several years to cultivate. This is particularly true for value-minded investors. Stocks typically fall into the value bucket due to large swaths of investors issuing a referendum that the company is tarnished. An about-face in popular perception can be a lengthy and trying process. A company may cycle through a few management teams, misfire on a marketing strategy, or miscalculate on a customer trend. These misses will give you anxiety, but the ability to persevere, more often than not, will prove lucrative.

Also know that most corporations, particularly large enterprises,

> Market momentum can lead to worrisome conditions. According to a Wall Street Journal commentary contemporary to the Panic of 1907, "The worst and most dangerous feature in the view of Wall Street was the alarm among the public." (October 23rd, 1907)

make decisions with a multi-year time horizon. For instance, it typically takes around a decade for a pharmaceutical drug to go through all the phases of research and development before it can finally be approved by the Food and Drug Administration. A failed drug trial may be a lightning rod for bad press, and the stock price may very well head south. However, a large, diversified pharmaceutical company typically has a lot of factors influencing earnings – not just the results from a single drug trial.

A failure would certainly be disappointing, but this likely won't drive the company to insolvency. Don't take things out of context, as most companies won't be issuing a final verdict on its corporate health after only a few weeks or months, and neither should you.

When you invest in a large, diversified company, you should employ a time horizon similar to that of the business. Investors shouldn't rent businesses. Instead, you will do yourself a favor by having a mentality of owning stocks for the long haul. This helps prevent you from acting on the short-term vagaries of the market, with the added bonus of shifting the investment math in your favor. Since the markets have a general upward trajectory, the longer you hold an investment, the greater the chance it will generate good performance....

- "Time is the friend of the wonderful business, the enemy of the mediocre." – Warren Buffett, 1989 Letter to Shareholders

- "Why should the immediate opportunity set be the only one considered, when tomorrow's may well be considerably more fertile than today's?" – attributed to Seth Klarman

- "He that can have patience, can have what he will." – Benjamin Franklin, *Poor Richard's Almanack* (1736)

- "Patience is the fund investor's single most powerful ally." – Benjamin Graham, *The Intelligent Investor* (1949)

- "Patience is the companion of wisdom." – Augustine of Hippo, early Christian theologian and church father

- "Patience is a necessary ingredient of genius." – Benjamin Disraeli, *Contarini Fleming* (1832)

- "How poor are they that have not patience! What wound did ever heal but by degrees?" – William Shakespeare, *The Tragedy of Othello, the Moor of Venice* (c. 1603)

◈ "the market is not a *weighing machine*, on which the value of each issue is recorded by an exact and impersonal mechanism, in accordance with its specific qualities. Rather should we say that the market is a *voting machine*, whereon countless individuals register choices which are the product partly of reason and partly of emotion." – Benjamin Graham & David Dodd, *Security Analysis* (1934)

◈ "If investing is entertaining, if you're having fun, you're probably not making any money. Good investing is boring." – George Soros, as quoted in *Winning Investment Habits of Warren Buffett and George Soros* by Mark Tier (2006)

Perhaps best aligned with growth investors, momentum traders are another contingent in the equity markets. These traders look to ride a market trend without conducting intensive fundamental company research. These are the poker players of the market as they try to determine everyone's next move. There is money to be made employing this type of approach, as markets can be sometimes self-feeding, and predictably so....

> There are plenty of Wall Street adages to help defend a momentum based approach. "The trend is your friend" or "Ride your winners, sell your losers" are popular ones that you might have also heard at a craps table. This strategy has merit, but its preferred use should be to augment a more exhaustive fundamental analysis.

◈ "There are plenty of economic theories that believe that departure from a price level can cause further divergence and cause cascading feedback loops." – Nassim Taleb, *Fooled by Randomness* (2004)

◈ "There are times when the currents leading to wealth can manage to pull you along regardless of whether you kick and paddle in the opposite direction." – Mohsin Hamid, *How to Get Filthy Rich in Rising Asia* (2013)

☞ "and a rising tide lifts all boats." – John F. Kennedy, speech in Canton, Ohio (September 27th, 1960)

☞ "For purposes of easy explanation we will say that prices, like everything else, move along the line of least resistance." – Edwin LeFevre, *Reminiscences of a Stock Operator* (1923)

There are some quirky rules of thumb about stock market performance. For example, the win of a NFC team over an AFC team Super Bowl is said to be a favorable indicator for stocks and vice versa. Don't let these types of heuristics serve as a substitute for intensive research, though they do make for good cocktail party chatter.

☞ "I never argue with the tape. Getting sore at the market does not get you anywhere." – Edwin LeFevre, *Reminiscences of a Stock Operator* (1923)

Momentum-oriented investors are always forced to ponder the following....

☞ "A trend is a trend

But the question is, will it bend?
Will it alter its course
Through some unforeseen force
And come to a premature end...?"

\-   Sir Alec Cairncross, economic advisor to the UK government and founder of the Government Economic Service

George Soros uses the onset of acute back pain as a warning sign for his investments. Whether it is Hanes stock or back pain, your instincts, even if they are a bit quirky, can serve you quite well.

Where do you start the hunt for stock investments? Just look around. Good stock investments surround us. Peter Lynch once took notice of his wife's effusive praise of the L'eggs pantyhose line, conducted research, bought Hanes (parent company), and then reaped an estimated 600 percent return. These types of stories are more of the exception, but it shows that the equity hunting ground has few boundaries....

☞ "Ideas, he says, are only formed in their natural and normal surroundings; the promotion of the growth is effected by the enumerable impressions appealing to the senses which a young man receives daily in the workshop, the mine, the law court, the study, the builder's yard, the hospital; at the sight of tools, materials and operations; in the presence of customers, workers and labour, of work well or ill done, costly or lucrative." – M. Taine, as quoted in *The Crowd: A Study of the Popular Mind* by Gustave Le Bon (1896)

Remember that stock investing is a zero-sum game: someone wins and someone loses with every transaction. As such, they pose quite an irony....

☞ "One of the funny things about the stock market is that every time one person buys, another sells, and both think they are astute." – William Feather, 20th century American publisher and author, founder of *William Feather Magazine*

In parting, the fortunes of the stock market have a societal impact. Consider the following....

☞ "If we exaggerate the present and future value of the stock market, then as a society we may invest too much in business start-ups and expansions, and too little in infrastructure, education, and other forms of human capital. If we think the market is worth more than it really is, we may become complacent in funding our pension plans, in maintaining our savings rate, in legislating an improved Social Security system, and in providing other forms of social insurance." – Robert Shiller, *Irrational Exuberance* (2005)

OVERTIME....

Making Sense of Equity Risk

Investors have been analyzing stocks and their corresponding risk ever since the Dutch East India Corporation, formed in 1706, issued the first stock certificate. Perhaps the best place to start the analysis is with valuations, and trying to ascertain if they are rich or cheap. The most common valuation metric cited is the Price/Earnings (P/E) multiple. In essence, the P/E multiple is a measure of confidence of the future earnings power of a company. The higher the P/E, the greater the expectation for future earnings as compared to a stock with a lower P/E. Yet, the higher the P/E the more you are paying for the earnings stream of a company and vice versa. As such, the higher P/E represents a more expensive equity as compared to a lower P/E.

> You cannot have a P/E multiple for a company with negative earnings. Basic math will not allow it. That doesn't mean all negative earners are worthless. For instance, a company may have latent value in their balance sheet.

The average P/E (tailing 12 month earnings) for the S&P 500 since 1870 has been around 15 times earnings, or 15x, for short. High P/E's have a historic tendency to result in lower returns when compared to low P/E's. In other words, what goes up often must come down. From 1871 through 2008, there were 26 ten year-periods when the initial P/E was below ten. The result was that in 24 of the 26 periods the P/E multiple increased from that starting point and delivered an above average return in the process. During the same observation window, there were 22 instances of P/E multiples above 18. The result was that 82 percent of the time, the P/E multiples fell over the subsequent decade.

There are a number of factors that influence the P/E multiple. For starters, an unhealthy dose of inflation depresses multiples, as was the case in the 1970's. Also, higher interest rates tend to have a negative influence due to the cost of capital rising, along with the relative valuations of bonds and cash improving. Finally, higher dividend payouts have a positive influence. The overarching theme is that if confidence is high in the earnings capacity of a company and the economy, the multiple will be, too, and vice versa.

S&P 500 Normalized Price/Earnings

Source - Home Page of Robert Shiller

There are several different versions of the P/E multiple. The forward P/E utilizes projected earnings in the denominator. The criticism with this approach is that the forward P/E relies on earnings a company has not produced yet. Then there is the *Shiller P/E*, or normalized P/E, which uses ten years' worth of earnings (not applicable for recent IPO companies like Twitter or Facebook) in the denominator of the equation. The advantage is that you utilize a fairer depiction of a company's operating performance that limits extraordinary items impacting earnings. The line of demarcation for the Shiller P/E is 25x. Once above this level, which has occurred only a handful of times, the subsequent ten-year annualized real return is approximately 0.5 percent. This compares unfavorably to the long-term average of around seven to ten percent for equity market returns. Thus, while disconnects can persist for several years, the Shiller P/E will eventually exert a gravitational pull on equity prices.[13]

> Think of the emerging markets as where the United States was 60 or 70 years ago. These are countries brimming with economic potential and with short runways to take off from.

The *PEG Ratio* builds off the valuation-centric P/E multiple. It helps to standardize valuations per unit of growth. This metric divides a company's P/E multiple by its annual earnings per share growth. A lower PEG ratio is a more favorable reading for a company.

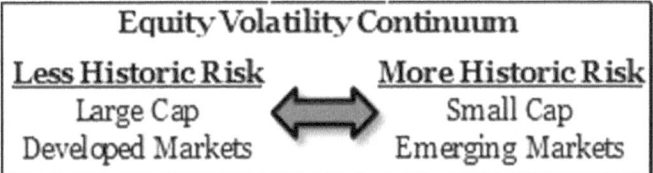

Finally, there are certain corners of the equity market that have historically exhibited higher amounts of volatility. Small companies ("Small Cap") are typically less proven entities, and have less reliable financials than larger companies ("Large Cap"), like General Electric or Exxon Mobil. This isn't always the case, and is very much a general comment. The same goes for stocks in emerging markets, such as companies headquartered in countries including India and Brazil. They tend to be more volatile than domestic business. Much like small cap, emerging market stocks aren't as widely followed as domestic stocks, and investors can have a quicker trigger finger if they don't like what they are seeing. That does not mean these stocks are categorically worse. Quite the contrary, as "rewarding investments tend to hide in dark corners, not in the glare

---

13 The index for the data consulted in the previous section can be found on Robert Shiller's website (http://www.econ.yale.edu/~shiller/data.htm).

of floodlights."[14] There can be a surplus of opportunities in these less efficient corners of the market for the skillful investor. It just means that the range of outcomes is broader, and the conservative investor must consider the added volatility as part of his or her decision.

Valuation Compass

Among the more interesting anomalies you will find are times when stocks trade below replacement costs. There are a few metrics that indicate when this might be the case. First off, *Tobin's Q* is the ratio between replacement costs and market value. If the ratio falls below 1.0, the stock market is considered inexpensive, and vice versa. There is also the Price/Book measure, and a reading below 1.0x indicates stocks on the inexpensive side. Yet, when these valuation anomalies occur, investors need to ask themselves: is the stock inexpensive (buy signal) or cheap (inferior quality)?

"For there is no sense in building up a new enterprise at a cost greater than that at which a similar existing enterprise can be purchased; whilst there is an inducement to spend on a new project what may seem an extravagant sum, if it can be floated off on the Stock Exchange at an immediate profit." – John Maynard Keynes, *The General Theory of Employment, Interest and Money* (1936)

A Price/Book reading below 1.0x is not an all-clear signal to buy, as it could mean the company may be imperiled and facing liquidation. Interestingly, there are instances where an entire index trades below book value, as was the case with the Japanese Nikkei 225 as recently as 2012, due to its multi-decade deflationary spiral. The Russian stock market also frequently trades below book value given the country's less-than-sterling reputation on the corporate governance front. The moral of the story is that your valuation compass may lead you to low Tobin's Q or Price/Book readings, but it does not necessarily mean the stock is poised for takeoff.

---

14 As quoted in the 2005 Yale Annual Report.

The Power of Dividends

The total return for equities comes from both dividends and price appreciation. Dividends lack the sizzle of 'growth', but their importance should not be understated. Consider that a $1 investment in U.S. stocks in 1900 would have grown to $198 by 2000, excluding dividends.[15] If dividends were reinvested, this portfolio would have grown to $16,797 during this same period. Dividends serve as a barometer of the issuing company's health and can help keep management honest. This, in some measure, has contributed to the track record of success for dividend-paying stocks. According to Robert D. Arnott's 2003 study "Dividends and the Three Dwarfs," five percent of the 7.9 percent annualized return over the past 200 years has come from dividends. These findings, Arnott claims, are "wildly at odds with conventional wisdom" that stock market returns are largely attributed to price appreciation.[16]

The recent trend to enhance shareholder value has de-emphasized cash dividends, as evidenced by payout ratios of roughly 35 percent, compared to the historic average of around 50 percent, for the S&P 500. Corporations have been emphasizing share buybacks and M&A as a more prominent means to drive a stock price. The verdict is still out, but don't let the recent trend cast doubt on the power of dividends.

Quick and Easy

The *Gordon Equation* offers a general, long-term (multi-year) expected equity return, albeit a crude one. It's simply the dividend yield plus expected earnings growth. 'Expected' is the operative word in the preceding sentence, since earnings expectations are always a garbage-in/garbage-out type of figure. Consensus earnings numbers are usually just a Google search away, but I would advise you round down these numbers as a matter of prudence. Earnings estimates tend to be on the more rosy side. The dividend yield for an index is easily ascertained

---

15 Elroy Dimson et al., *Credit Suisse Global Investment Returns Yearbook*, 2014.
16 *Financial Analysts Journal*, (Mar/Apr 2003)

and not subject to controversy (the S&P 500 yield has hovered around two percent for the past several years). Keep in mind that the historic annual return for the S&P 500 is in the neighborhood of eight to ten percent. In short: try to be practical with your earnings growth figure, and make sure it's not widely at odds with what equities have traditionally offered.

Stock buyback yields, or the amount of shares being repurchased by corporations in relation to the share amount outstanding, have been around two percent over the past few years for large cap, domestic companies.

The Gordon equation is a simple formula, and it can deliver an answer that materially deviates from actual equity results. This difference will often be due to the influence of fear and greed on market prices. Yet, this can lead to opportunities for the skillful, disciplined investor. If equities have a woeful result that falls decidedly below your Gordon answer, then it may be a buy signal, and the reverse is true as well. The Gordon equation is not perfect, but it may serve as a launching pad for determining your equity exposure.

FIXED INCOME

Stacked up next to stocks, fixed income (bonds) can be quite blah. Bonds are really just pieces of paper that spell out a contractual loan from one party to another. As an investor, you are often playing the role of a creditor, in which you lend money over a specified period and obtain an interest payment for relinquishing your rights to use the capital. Your financial fortunes are based on the borrower's ability to return the capital upon maturity and make interest payments in a timely manner. Also, bondholders are typically the first in line to get paid when an issuer enters into bankruptcy. This gives them a bit more security, compared to equities. This is also provides the technical underpinning to why bonds can be an anchor to volatility in a portfolio. However, this safety has a cost, since fixed income investors will generally not participate in the upside (profits) of the company as an equity investor would....

- ☞ "The shareholder [equity investor] is an adventurer in the corporate business; he takes the risk, and profits from success. The creditor, in compensation for not sharing the profits, is to be paid independently of the risk of success, and gets a right to dip into the capital when the payment date arrives." – *Commissioner v. O.P.P. Holding Corp.* (1935)

- ☞ "A pure equity investor – the shareholder – has voting rights and upside potential. A pure debt holder – the creditor – is an outsider with no prospect of sharing in the growth of the enterprise." – Stephen Schwarz and Daniel Lathrope, *Fundamentals of Corporate Taxation* (2012)

In part, due to their priority standing in a bankruptcy proceeding, bonds are generally considered conservative investments. However, the conventional thinking can be flawed. The innate problem with fixed income is that often the people you want to lend to do not want to borrow, and the people that want to borrow can be a crowd that you probably shouldn't be lending to....

☞ "Don't invest in bonds because you've heard bonds are conservative or for safety of either income or capital. Bond prices fluctuate nearly as much as stock prices do." – Charles D. Ellis, *Winning the Loser's Game* (2002)

Conventional fixed income is vulnerable during periods of unanticipated inflation. This is because inflation erodes the purchasing power of the interest payments (fixed amount) received. However, there are bonds that are re-priced, according to changes in the level of inflation (and deflation), notably Treasury Inflation Protected Securities (TIPS). The principal component of TIPS is reset according to the changes in the CPI-U inflation reading. Furthermore, during periods of inflation, the income component will increase commensurately because the rate is applied to the adjusted principal and vice versa. TIPS are an exception to the way inflation treats the bond market....

☞ "Every portfolio benefits from bonds; they provide a cushion when the stock market hits a rough patch. But avoiding stocks completely could mean your investment won't grow any faster than the rate of inflation." – Suze Orman, financial advisor, author, speaker, and television host

Compared to equities, corporate bond investors have a different overarching mission. Equity investors are more focused on earnings acceleration that should conceptually drive the stock price higher. On the other hand, corporate bond investors put more weight on avoiding earnings-impairments to ensure interest payments aren't in jeopardy.

The etymology of credit is from the Latin word *credere*, which means to believe or trust. The credit markets are predicated upon the belief or trust that lenders will be paid back in full within the time period specified. High-yield bonds, also known as junk debt, are one of the more risky corners of the asset class, with lenders having their doubts. Given the questionable finances of the junk debt issuers, the bonds are charged a higher interest rate, which is designed to compensate lenders for incurring a bit more credit risk. Most often, you want your bonds to be pretty boring. However, not all bonds are created equal. So for those looking for more excitement with their fixed income allocation, take a gander at high-yield, and remember:

⊂⊃ *High yield is the close cousin of equities in times of market adversity.*

But you should also keep in mind these other words of wisdom....

⊂⊃ "High-yield bonds are very rarely repaid from operating cash flow. They are refinanced." – Wilbur Ross, from an interview with Vyvyan Tenorio (August 31st, 2012)

⊂⊃ "More money has been lost reaching for yield than at the point of a gun." – Raymond DeVoe, Jr., investment analyst, as quoted in the Victoria, TX *Advocate* (February 22, 1995)

⊂⊃ "Buying a bond only for its yield is like getting married only for the sex. If the thing that attracted you in the first place dries up, you'll find yourself realizing there is nothing left" – Benjamin Graham, *The Intelligent Investor* (1949)

Government-issued debt is a controversial subject (you will read more about this in the Sovereign Debt Bubble section). There are obvious economic concerns, and moral ones, too, as future generations may have to foot the bill....

☞ "After all, government debt is simply a tax on future private-sector production with interest." – Michael G. Pento, *The Coming Bond Market Collapse: How to Survive the Demise of the U.S. Debt Market* (2013)

In this environment, with generationally low yields created by government and monetary authority activism, fixed income investing is more complicated. Bond prices look rather fragile, as they have been propped up by Central Bank purchases. In particular, government bonds have historically been a portfolio instrument used to soften the

As of April 2014, there are only three U.S. companies with a pristine AAA credit rating: Johnson & Johnson, Exxon-Mobil, and Microsoft. This is the highest credit rating bestowed by the Standard & Poor's rating agency.

blow from potential financial accidents. Now, the opposite may be true, as well, since investors could conceivably flee en masse these 'flight to quality' investments when Central Banks start to lose their government bond appetite. Investors need to expand their boundaries when looking for income, because, with zero bound rates, we are in a global quest for predictable, safe yield.

Meddling with asset prices can set the stage for misallocation of capital, with worrisome outcomes. In fact, in March 2014, Richard Fisher, the Dallas Fed President, warned that the Federal Reserve's bond buying could be distorting the financial markets. The crux of the matter is that their interference alters incentives and corresponding behavior, which has a domino effect throughout the markets and economy. In particular, the Fed's suppression of cash and fixed income returns encourages investors to look for returns

In his 1987 book *Crisis and Leviathan,* Robert Higgs suggests that governmental involvement in society is merely a precursor for trouble, and ultimately leads to even more governmental involvement in order to correct the damage.

elsewhere, often in riskier asset classes. If we look back to the recent past, we see how artificially low yields on safe haven investments, like money markets, can upend an economy. You may recall that from the end of 2001 through November 2004, the effective Federal Funds rate was held below two percent, which helped drive many investors into real estate. Unfortunately, many people would buy real estate they couldn't afford. When the music stopped, we experienced one of the most severe market and economic contractions experienced in the past few generations. Monetary stimulus is like using artificial sweeteners. It may be convenient and helpful in the short-term, but they become hard to wean off and have latent, long-term risks that could prove ruinous....

⌗ "[Friedrich Hayek concluded that] artificially low interest rates not only cause investment to be artificially high, but also cause mal-investment... too much in long-term projects relative to short-term ones, and the boom turns into a bust. The way to avoid busts, is to avoid the booms that cause them." – Biography of Friedrich Hayek, from *The Concise Encyclopedia of Economics* (2008)

OVERTIME...

Yield-to-Best

B onds may be historically more conservative than equities, but this fact shouldn't make investors complacent. The core principle of rigor needs to apply to the analysis of bonds, as well. The starting point for analyzing bonds is typically their yield. Bond prices and yields (interest rates) move in opposite directions. Remember back to the seesaw image in your Finance 101 undergraduate course. As rates rise, the price of a bond will fall since it has to compensate for the reduced yield relative to newly issued securities, and vice versa. For some perspective, the average yield for the bellwether United States 10 Year Treasury bond for the 40 years ending in 2012 was 6.5 percent, with core inflation averaging 4.1 percent during the same time period. As of July 2014, the 10 Year bond has a yield of approximately 2.5 percent. Hence, these low yields should prove cautionary when assessing the valuations of fixed income.

Yields for fixed income will be a function of the prevailing interest rate environment and the creditworthiness of the issuer. Bonds from a more speculative issuer will carry a higher yield, while those from a more creditworthy issuer will carry a lower yield. However, if a bond defaults, or fails to make an interest of principal payment, it does not mean that all is lost. The recovery rate will ultimately determine the merits of a fixed income investment if there is a default. For instance, since the Civil War, the recovery rate for defaulted general obligation municipal bonds is 100 percent, which means there

> Fixed income mutual funds offer diversification and professional management. However, unlike owning an individual bond, fixed income funds don't have a specified, amortizing maturity, which may prove harmful in a rising rate environment.

was no permanent loss of capital.[17][18] However, the past may not be a prologue, as holders of Detroit bonds will tell you: Detroit defaulted on its general obligation debt on October 1ˢᵗ, 2013 and a full recovery is not expected.

The expected return for individual bonds is fairly predictable, assuming the issuer does not become insolvent. If you hold a bond to maturity, the return will be the *Yield-to-Maturity*, which is a number available at the time of purchase. There will be volatility along the way, but an investor's fortune is generally predetermined. The one caveat is if the bond carries a call feature, which gives the issuer the ability to retire the debt early. The bond issuer will generally only exercise this feature in a declining rate environment, as it could re-issue debt at a lower cost. This is not a favorable development for the bondholder, as they would lose a coupon that could not be replicated in the lower rate environment, all else equal. Therefore, the most conservative way to forecast bonds is the *Yield-to-Worst*, which incorporates the impact of bonds being called. Since it accounts for call features, the yield-to-worst may be the best way of gauging future performance.

Municipal Bond Myth Busting

Municipal bonds are a valuable financing tool for states, cities, towns, and even universities. However, you should know that they are not 'tax-free,' despite the fact that they are frequently described that way. For starters, the appreciation from municipal bonds is subject to capital gains taxation. Also, the interest component can be taxable, as the Supreme Court case of *South Carolina v. Baker* removed any constitutional impediments to taxing municipal income. There is a lot of speculation that the interest tax exemption will be curtailed, at least for individuals in the top tax

---

17 General obligation municipals are backed by the taxing power of their respective jurisdiction, as opposed to revenue from a service or project (ex. toll booth, water system).

18 "Fitch Provides Municipal Default and Recovery Expectations by Sector," *Business Wire*, January 10, 2007.

brackets. However, this has failed to gain any real legislative traction, at least for the time being. Municipals are still tax-friendly investments, but you shouldn't subscribe to the myth that they are tax immune.

Politicians popularize another myth that impacts the municipal market. All states, except for Vermont, have some sort of balanced budget provision, which means revenues and expenses need to be brought into harmony, typically on an annual basis. This is a positive for the creditworthiness of state issued municipal bonds. It is also a sound bite you hear on the campaign trail. Governors will tout how heroic of a feat it is to balance their respective state's budget. Don't be fooled: this is something they *have* to do.

Preferred Stock: Not Quite Stocks, Not Quite Bonds

Preferred stocks are hybrid instruments that blend elements of equities and fixed income. They typically carry a generous interest rate, like bonds, but also exhibit a stock-like volatility that can be unnerving. Notably, the Bank of America Merrill Lynch preferred stock index fell close to 25 percent in 2008, which seems outside the acceptable range of returns for many conservative investors. Preferred stocks are still a rarely visited hunting ground for investors, in part due to the industry concentration. The financial sector provides roughly 80 percent of the issuance in the $450 billion space, with REITs and utilities making up most of the residual. Given the sector's role in the global credit crisis, financials still have a cloud of anxiety over them. Yet, an investment area ignored due to ideology or politics typically creates opportunity, and preferred stocks are no exception. In fact, you could argue that preferred stocks offer a non-investment grade yield for investment grade quality. The space is comprised of recognizable, large financial conglomerates that have, hopefully, very little risk of insolvency.

The preferred narrative has gotten a little more interesting as of late. The financial sector's presence in the preferred universe stems from the fact that Trust Preferred Securities (TruPS), which reside just below bonds in terms of seniority, has been granted Tier 1 capital treatment.[19] Tier 1 capital is the primary measure of a bank's financial strength in the eyes of regulators. Consequently, it behooves banks to meet certain thresholds for Tier 1 capital. However, Trust Preferred Tier 1 status will be phased out over time as the result of new regulations, such as the Basel Accords. Without Tier 1 status, many United States banks have been calling their preferreds, since they are becoming expensive forms of capital. There are still some European TruPS outstanding, but the ones of the better-capitalized domestic banks are now near extinction. This call cycle has shrunk the amount of net supply of preferreds, and also served to change the character of the preferred ecosystem.

Preferred stocks are far from riskless. They often have undefined or perpetual maturities, absent an issuer exercising a call feature. This makes them vulnerable in times of rising rates, as they tend to have fixed rates (recall the seesaw image of rates and prices). However, if the slope of the yield curve increases, it may prove beneficial to preferred stocks. Since preferreds are largely issued by financial companies, including commercial banks which typically have an expanding net interest margin (assets are long maturity, liabilities are shorter term), the risk of a negative credit event (i.e. default) should diminish. When it comes to assessing preferreds, *how* rates rise or fall should be just as important to you as *how much*.

---

19 Seniority refers to the ordering of investors within the capital structure. The positioning plays a role in determining the recovery amount in a bankruptcy process, as the more senior investors get paid first, while more junior ones are paid later. Accordingly, senior investments typically pose less risk than junior investments.

CASH

C ash is king or cash is trash depending on whom you ask and when you ask them. The "cash is king" camp will tell you that it can serve as dry powder for future investment, particularly during times of market stress. Cash has rather invaluable *Optionality*, if you prefer technical jargon. It is as liquid as it gets, and when there are market fire sales you will need convenient capital to pounce on these opportunities. On the other hand, cash (savings accounts, money markets), in-and-of itself, typically delivers a return right on top of the rate of inflation. In other words, your purchasing power when holding cash remains largely unchanged. Thus, I can say in no uncertain terms that a portfolio that only holds cash will not lead to spectacular riches....

> ☞ "How many millionaires do you know who have become wealthy by investing in savings accounts? I rest my case." – Robert G. Allen, founder of the Enlightened Wealth Institute

Cash may not turn you into a tycoon, but it won't leave you destitute, either. Cash has merit as an insurance policy, and a pretty darn good one at that. Unlike a conventional insurance policy, however, cash doesn't have a maturity date, or come with the burden of recurring premium payments. It may not be the most glamorous investment, or one that you will brag about at cocktail parties, but it's a no-fuss asset. Also, when those unexpected liabilities hit, you will be glad you have cash on hand....

☞ "There are three faithful friends, an old wife, an old dog, and ready money." – Benjamin Franklin, *Poor Richard's Almanack* (1738)

☞ "How little you know about the age you live in if you think that honey is sweeter than cash in hand." – Ovid, ancient Roman poet

☞ "Ready money works great cures." – French proverb

☞ "This is perhaps the oldest, easiest, and most underrated source of tail risk protection. If one is worried about systemic illiquidity events or drawdown risks, then what better way to help than keeping some dry powder in the form of cash – the most liquid of all assets." – James Montier, "A Value Investor's Perspective on Tail Risk Protection: An Ode to the Joy of Cash" (June 2011)

OVERTIME....

Risky Cash

Money market funds, in investing parlance, are used interchangeably with cash. Yet, unlike the cash in your pocket, they are interest bearing, as they are invested in short duration assets, mainly loans to municipalities, corporations, and even the government. Money markets, first formed in 1971, have a history characterized by stability with a SEC endorsed net asset value (NAV) of an even $1.00 that rarely budges. Then 2008 and the global credit crisis came along. This is when the Reserve Primary Fund 'broke the buck' when its net asset value fell to $.97, that is, below $1.00, the day after Lehman Brothers filed for bankruptcy and sent shock waves across the money market complex. This $3.5 billion fund would be liquidated with an ultimate recovery rate of $.99. This loss might seem miniscule, but the recovery was not immediate, and investors had to cope with some unanticipated illiquidity, demonstrative that the renowned safe haven of 'cash' still carries risk.

There was the 2008 wake-up call, but the impregnability of money markets is now even more suspect courtesy of a July 2014 SEC edict. Institutional prime and institutional money market funds, which are those used by large dollar clientele, will now have their net asset values float in accordance with investor interest. The SEC's motive is well captured in the classic Louis Brandeis quotation of "sunlight is said to be the best of disinfectants". The SEC wanted to create transparency in certain pockets of the money market space to prevent funds from creating a false façade of price stability cloaked by the $1.00 NAV. Money markets may be thought of cash, but they are not bulletproof: capital loss is a possibility, albeit a remote one, and thanks to the SEC this sleepy space has now been awaken again.

REAL ESTATE

There are a number of different paths to invest in real estate, whether through rental properties, land ownership, or property development. Further, real estate opportunities are rarely similar with each having their own considerations and corresponding risks. Yet, at the surface, real estate is strikingly similar in a way. Despite the varied paths for real estate investors to pursue, all are unified by the potential for outsized profit and a corresponding unbridled enthusiasm that has characterized the asset class for generations....

- "Buy land, they're not making any more of it." – attributed to both Mark Twain and Will Rogers

- "[Landlords] grow richer, as it were, in their sleep, without working, risking, or economizing." – John Stuart Mill, *Principles Of Political Economy* (1848)

- "if . . . you [buy land], you need do nothing more. You may sit down and smoke your pipe; you may lie around like the lazzaroni of Naples or the leperos of Mexico; you may go into a ballroom, or down a hole in the ground and without doing one stroke of work, without adding one iota of the wealth of the community, in ten years you will be rich." – Henry George, *Progress and Poverty* (1879)

- "The best investment on Earth is earth." – Louis Glickman, real estate investor and philanthropist

- "It's tangible, it's solid, it's beautiful. It's artistic, from my stand-point, and I just love real estate." – Donald Trump

- "Now, one thing I tell everyone is learn about real estate. Repeat after me: real estate provides the highest returns, the greatest values and the least risk." – Armstrong Williams, American political commentator, columnist, and radio show host

- "Buy real estate in areas where the path exists . . . and buy more real estate where there is no path, but you can create your own." – David Waronker, American real estate investor

- "Now I would give a thousand furlongs of sea for an acre of barren ground." – William Shakespeare, *The Tempest* (c. 1610-1611)

- "It is quite true that land monopoly is not the only monopoly which exists, but it is by far the greatest of monopolies – it is a perpetual monopoly, and it is the mother of all other forms of monopoly." – Winston Churchill, speech at King's Theatre in Edinburgh (July 17th, 1909)

- "Real estate is an imperishable asset, ever increasing in value. It is the most solid security that human ingenuity has devised. It is the basis of all security and about the only indestructible security." – Russell Sage, 19th century politician and railroad executive

Real estate can be a tool for riches, but you have to buy it at the right time and the right price. Residential real estate pricing should generally appreciate at the same rate as real wage growth – the more you earn, the more you can spend on a house. However, there are other forces that can impact pricing. For instance, demand can organically increase through increased immigration levels. Without commensurate new supply, a flood of new buyers can drive prices higher. Demand can also grow inorganically (and temporarily) due to leverage. As we saw in the buildup of the housing bubble, cheap and abundant credit can trigger a buying binge. Like fine wines, not all vintage years are created equal with real estate. Had you purchased a home from 2006 through 2008 you may be having some buyer's remorse. However, the corrective process with prices led to some terrific buying opportunities from 2009 through 2012. In some cases, the value of real estate at its nadir fell below replacement costs. The value of a home can't go to zero. There is value in the land, lumber, pipes, etc. needed to build a home. Thus, when home prices really get bludgeoned, an arbitrage opportunity may exist – the parts are greater than the sum. The moral of the story is that prices for real estate can be quite disconnected from reality. For the smart investor, these dislocations can become the basis for wealth creation....

- "Every person who invests in well-selected real estate in a growing section of a prosperous community adopts the surest and safest method of becoming independent, for real estate is the basis of all wealth." – Theodore Roosevelt, 26th president of the United States

- "Owning a home is a keystone of wealth – both financial affluence and emotional security." – Suze Orman, "Suze Orman's Twelve Steps to Wealth, Step Seven" (July 2003)

- "The major fortunes in America have been made in land." – John D. Rockefeller

- "Ninety percent of all millionaires become so through owning real estate. More money has been made in real estate than in all industrial investments combined. The wise young man or wage earner of today invests his money in real estate" – Andrew Carnegie

Real estate comes in all shapes and sizes, with varying risk and return profiles. For instance....

☞ "Commercial real estate always trails residential, and as residential growth flourishes, shopping centers flourish and service the communities, and jobs come out." – Johnny Isakson, United States Senator, interview with Ethan Hutten for the Macon, GA *Examiner* (January 13th, 2010)

Real estate can lead to riches, but can also plant the seeds for financial turmoil. Prior to the recent global credit crisis, the conventional thinking was that residential real estate pricing never declined. Unfortunately, many people were lured into buying homes they couldn't afford based on this false premise, along with other factors like low interest rates. Leverage was abundant, which made home ownership possible for those with otherwise inadequate means. There was also some questionable underwriting. In fact, one of the more dubious varieties of mortgages was the NINJA loan (No Income No Job No Assets). As we know, this did not end well. The U.S. housing market peaked in 2006, losing on average more than 30 percent before ultimately bottoming out in 2012. Real estate is not impervious from the ills of excessive leverage. Nor are the broader economy and other asset classes immune. You can almost set your watch to this. A study of the real estate market in developed economies by the Bank of International Settlements concluded that

The United States was not the lone participant in the real estate bubble that precipitated the global credit crisis in 2008-09. In fact, the U.S. bubble looked a bit tamer than corresponding bubbles in other countries. Here are some cumulative appreciation levels for home prices from 1997 through 2005:

- United States: 73 percent
- Australia: 114 percent
- Spain: 145 percent
- Dubai: 226 percent (from 2003 to 2007)

Source: Nouriel Roubini and Stephen Mihm, *Crisis Economics: A Crash Course in the Future of Finance*, (New York: Penguin, 2011).

housing prices tend to peak about two years after stock market peaks.[20] Long story short, the fortunes of the real estate market, good or bad, often extend into other markets, as well, and you should always do your best to buy prudently....

⊛ "Real estate cannot be lost or stolen, nor can it be carried away. Purchased with common sense, paid for in full, and managed with reasonable care, it is about the safest investment in the world." – Franklin D. Roosevelt, 32nd president of the United States

Some parting food for thought: real estate offers the basic need for food and shelter, unlike other asset classes. You can't house a family with gold or stock certificates. As such, there is an argument that other classes should have more of an upside, in order to compensate for their lack of utility compared to that offered by real estate. Perhaps this vital utility of real estate is not a bad place to start for the loyal real estate investor who wants to make their case for the asset class, but is unconvincing with sheer performance data.

---

20 Claudio Borio, "The financial cycle and macroeconomics: What have we learnt?" *Bank for International Settlements*, December 2012.

OVERTIME....

Interplay of Government and Real Estate

Popular perception portrays real estate as a virtuous investment on the tax front. This notion is largely shaped by the mortgage interest deduction on your primary residence. However, that's just the beginning. For instance, one of the few gifts in the United States Tax Code is the ability to rent out your property for 14 days or less without having to report the income on your tax return. Furthermore, the taxpayer can still deduct mortgage interest and property taxes during this period, but not depreciation or maintenance deductions.

The United States government has also chosen to facilitate the dream of home ownership, and there involvement is by no means insignificant. In 2013, through its real estate marionettes of Fannie Mae, Freddie Mac, and Federal Housing Administration (FHA), the government either bought or insured 90 percent of all mortgages in this country.[21] The government's tentacles in the real estate market are surely significant, as is their risk exposure. In particular, approximately 40 percent of them are explicitly guaranteed by the FHA, which requires a down payment of only 3.5 percent.[22] This comes at a time when many banks require an upfront payment of at least ten percent. The low FHA down payments seem to be hardly a conservative underwriting practice, and for the taxpayer, this is a legitimate gripe.

The government's reach in the real estate market goes beyond your primary residence or vacation home. Real Estate Investment Trusts, or REITs, are an exchange-traded means of gaining exposure to real estate assets. They are a creature of tax legislation in 1960 (Cigar Excise Tax Extension) and typically offer investors exposure to a diversified mix of

---

21 Bob Ivry, *The Seven Sins of Wall Street: Big Banks, Their Washington Lackeys, and the Next Financial Crisis* (New York: PublicAffairs, 2014).

22 Michael G. Pento, *The Coming Bond Market Collapse: How to Survive the Demise of the U.S. Debt Market* (Hoboken, NJ: Wiley, 2013).

properties with stock-like liquidity. Yet, unlike a traditional corporate structure, a REIT is not subject to income tax, as long as it distributes 90 percent of its taxable income to their respective shareholders and generates at least 75 percent of that income from mortgages, rents, and property sales. REIT's are capital-intensive businesses, and they thus require a healthy credit market. Hence, REIT's have their vulnerabilities, but they also give the everyday investor a way to easily participate in the fortunes of the real estate market, along with typically offering a decent yield, to boot.

REIT Mania

REITs have been around for decades in the United States, but it seems that the rest of the world only recently took notice. The REIT structure has been adopted in a number of forms outside of the U.S. during the past decade, with Hong Kong launching them in 2005 and Germany in 2007, among others. Each of these REIT adaptations has its own bells and whistles, but the end result has been that the value of public real estate market abroad exceeds that of the United States. As of December 31, 2013, the equity market capitalization of the U.S. REIT market (as measured by the FTSE NAREIT Equity REIT Index) totaled $541 billion and included 140 companies. The market capitalization for property securities on a global basis (as measured by the FTSE EPRA/NAREIT Developed Index) totaled $1.1 *trillion* at the end of December and included 309 companies.

This is a favorable development for investors, as is typically the case when there is an expanded menu. No longer are you limited to solely domestic opportunities. However, this also carries the burden of more homework. It may be best to farm out this analysis and pay an expert in international real estate a management fee, unless you have the time or means to conduct primary research of properties and operators for real estate companies in countries such as Australia, France, and Japan.

GOLD & CURRENCIES

Ah gold, that shiny precious metal. If only it was viewed so simply by the investment world. Gold is a chameleon of sorts. It possesses elements of both a commodity and a currency. Yet, there is little confusion that gold represents one of the more polarizing investments. As such, let's prepare you for both sides of the conversation with a sample of the type of remarks you may overhear during any number of auric discussions:

- "Gold pricing is predictably unpredictable."

- "Gold is the only incorruptible currency."

- "Gold is a form of disaster insurance."

- "Gold is a referendum on political and monetary sanity, or lack thereof."

Views on gold are often polarized. On one end of the spectrum, there is the camp that finds gold distasteful because it has no yield, no revenues, and no earnings capacity. It's just an ornament that contributes little to economic growth. As Warren Buffett famously pointed out, all the gold unearthed by man would only fill the infield of a baseball diamond, though it would command a value of

> Gold effectively has a negative yield. It generates no interest and dividends and has carrying costs associated with owning it.

roughly $7 trillion. Alternatively one could own seven Exxon Mobil's (NYSE:XOM), all of the farmland in the United States, and have about a trillion in cash to spare. That's some trade-off, as farmland, Exxon Mobil, and perhaps even cash (easier to transact with than gold) being more valuable economic cogs. Gold prices have corrected since 2012 when Buffett made this observation, but his underlying point still rings true.

There are two sides to every coin. Yet, sometimes when it comes to gold, it adheres to the old saying, "don't let the facts get in the way of a good story." For starters, gold has been considered a hedge against inflation. There are many different drivers of inflation, of course, but the gold bug is more concerned with inflation induced by the government printing more money. The supply of gold, on the other hand is rather constant – it's a precious metal for a reason. If a government flooded the economy with paper currency, the thinking is that investors would gravitate to the 'incorruptible currency' as something that would retain its purchasing power....

☘ "Money, like wine, must always be scarce." – Adam Smith, *An Inquiry into the Nature and Causes of the Wealth of Nations* (1776)

At times, this anti-printing press thesis makes money. For instance, gold's Gilded Age lasted from 2000 to 2011, when the spot price soared from just over $200/ounce to over $1,800/ounce. Life was good for the gold bugs, and especially so in 2009 and 2010, when gold was up roughly 24 percent and 29 percent, respectively. Central Banks were flooding the economy with money, and gold reacted predictably. Right? Sort of. During this same time period, the inflationists out there probably needed a glass of wine to lift their spirits as inflation (CPI-U) muddled along at a very benign clip of around two-and-a-half percent. Compare this to the United States' long-term average, north of three percent. Gold pricing went parabolic, but inflation certainly did not. That's gold for you. It can trade on perception, not reality. So, when someone says gold is a hedge against inflation, you now know the facts, but be polite and let them finish their story.

Gold is also used as a hedge against political and economic uncertainty. When fear grips the market, the cynics will latch on to that remote chance that we will head back to the economic Dark Ages when we transacted through barter, with paper currencies rendered useless. Then, gold would reassert itself as a preferred instrument of commerce. Sounds crazy, but fear can conjure up wild images....

☞ "Gold is a way of going long on fear, and it has been a pretty good way of going long on fear from time to time. But you really have to hope people become more afraid in a year or two years than they are now. And if they become more afraid you make money, if they become less afraid you lose money, but the gold itself doesn't produce anything." – Warren Buffett, as quoted in Wade Slome, "Here's What Warren Buffett Says About Gold and Commodities," *Wall Street Cheat Sheet* (March 8th, 2011)

Gold pricing can be volatile and should be looked at with humility. You don't want to invest great sums of money into anything that almost seems to have a mind of its own....

☞ "nobody really understands gold prices and I don't pretend to really understand them either." – Ben Bernanke, Senate Banking Committee testimony (July 18th, 2013)

The gold standard, which collateralized the United States currency with bullion, was officially ended on August 15th, 1971 by Richard Nixon, in order to, in his words....

☞ "protect the position of the American dollar as the pillar of monetary stability around the world."

Think of the gold standard as a governor on fiscal largesse. Exiting the gold standard offered our executive branch more fiscal maneuverability to alter the direction of our economy. It also meant that the U.S. dollar no longer had collateral supporting it, and the strategy of debasing your currency is a dubious one. It's effectively a zero-sum game. It may make exports more attractive, but your cost of imports goes up as well, which invites inflation. With a rather balanced sum of winners and losers, exiting the gold standard was met with mixed emotions....

☞ "In the absence of the gold standard, there is no way to protect savings from confiscation through inflation. There is no safe store of value." – Alan Greenspan, *Gold and Economic Freedom* (1966)

Gold is a volatile investment. Gold mining stocks are even more volatile, due to their operating leverage (gold mines are an expensive undertaking).

☞ "no great nation that abandoned the gold standard has remained a great nation." – Ronald Reagan, as quoted in Ron Paul's *End the Fed* (2009)

☞ "Since the world left the vestiges of the gold standard in 1971, the global economy has been set adrift. The technocrats keep assuring us that they can steer the economy much more efficiently than the 'obsolete' gold standard, and yet a continual series of crises suggest otherwise." – Robert Murphy, "Fiat Money and the Euro Crisis," *Mises Institute* (October 10th, 2011)

As much as many people would like to return to the gold standard, it's not practical. The use of the 'new' dollar is too entrenched in global commerce. Consider that, as of 2010, the US dollar represents 62 percent of all foreign exchange reserves, with the Euro, the closest competitor, at 26 percent, according to the International Monetary Fund. John Maynard Keynes seems well ahead of his time in the following quote....

⌾ "In truth, the gold standard is already a barbarous relic." – John Maynard Keynes, *A Tract on Monetary Reform (1923)*

More on this topic later, but gold does have characteristics of a commodity, and should be valued accordingly....

⌾ "Gold and silver, like other commodities, have an intrinsic value, which is not arbitrary, but is dependent on their scarcity, the quantity of labour bestowed in procuring them, and the value of the capital employed in the mines which produce them." – David Ricardo, *The High Price of Bullion* (1810)

Like most investments, gold should be analyzed on a relative basis. Unsurprisingly, gold's meteoric rise over the past decade (ending abruptly in 2013) occurred during a time of muted prospects for stocks, bonds, and cash.

⌾ "Gold and silver are no doubt subject to fluctuations, from the discovery of new and more abundant mines; but such discoveries are rare, and their effects, though powerful, are limited to periods of comparatively short duration." – David Ricardo, *On The Principles of Political Economy and Taxation* (1817)

Gold is often used as an outlet for frustrations with fiat currencies (paper money), like the U.S. dollar. Fiat currencies are those that a government has declared to be legal tender. In the United States, federally-backed paper currencies have been in circulation since 1861, when their use was first authorized by Congress. However, fiat currencies have no intrinsic value and don't need to be backed by reserves, which can get many gold bugs up in arms. Fiat currencies can be manipulated, and exiting the gold standard made such manipulation much easier....

⌾ "There's fool's gold – pyrite – and then there's fool's gold – gold owned by idiots willing to trade it for worthless dollars." – Jarod Kintz, *This Book Has No Title* (2012)

❧ "The demand for money is regulated entirely by its value, and its value by its quantity." – David Ricardo, *The Principles of Political Economy and Taxation* (1817)

❧ "All money is a matter of belief." – attributed to Adam Smith, 18ᵗʰ century philosopher and early figure of economic study

Currencies do have an impact investment results for investors with unhedged assets in foreign countries. In fact, a domestic investor with an appreciated foreign asset can still achieve a negative return if the respective foreign currency depreciates (domestic currency simultaneously strengthens), and the reverse is true as well. The return is eroded in this instance, as it would be costly to repatriate the asset given the diminished value of the foreign currency.

❧ "There is no historical precedent for a fiat currency that has succeeded in holding its value. Twenty percent [of 775 fiat currencies studied] failed through hyperinflation, twenty-one percent were destroyed by war, twelve percent destroyed by independence, twenty-four percent were monetarily reformed, and twenty-three percent are still in circulation approaching one of the other outcomes." – Mike Hewitt, "The Fate of Paper Money," *DollarDaze.org* (January 7th, 2009)

Currency movements can be quite random in the short-term. That may be more the case now than ever in this day and age of political and monetary activism. Governments have been intervening in the currency markets as a means to stabilize and/or ignite economic growth. You can devote countless hours to researching currencies, but it may yield little, as there is a cloud of unpredictability that hovers over them. Further, currencies can move violently, and investors can get whiplash. Consider the theatrics with Emerging Markets over the past two years. After faltering in 2013, they did an about-face in 2014, courtesy of, in part, some lever-pulling from central banks. For instance, the Brazilian Real fell 17 percent in 2013 relative to the U.S. dollar, stoking unhealthy inflation pressures for its citizenry. Brazil's Central Bank was forced to take decisive action in order to defend the currency, and embarked on a rate hiking campaign. Their benchmark rate started in 2013 below 8 percent and, as of July 2014, stands at 11 percent. The real responded accordingly and rose 5 percent for the first half of 2014, as interest rate hikes can give a currency a much-needed face-lift. It was a rather dizzying chain of events, but is sort of microcosm for the volatility currencies can exhibit. All things considered, a heavy dose of humility is in order when trying to play the direction of currencies….

☞ "Paper currency has hitherto been regarded with suspicion, as insecure." – John Beverly Robinson, *Economics of Liberty* (1916)

OVERTIME....

Gold Supply and Demand

There are only about 170,000 tons of gold known to man, with seventy-five percent of all the gold ever produced having been extracted after 1910. Gold is a precious metal for a reason, with supply increasing at a rather meager and consistent rate of around one to one-and-a-half percent each year. This narrative of gold supply is predictable, but the demand side of the ledger has a bit more sizzle. The majority of gold demand comes from jewelry consumption (53 percent), as well as certain technological, industrial, and dental (10 percent) applications.[23] Investment accounts for most of the remaining demand, with a growing interest from emerging markets, and this buying played a prime role in the most recent gold bull run. In fact, Central Banks (mainly those for emerging markets) globally bought more gold in 2012 than the previous 48 years combined. This buying helped these countries diversify their foreign exchange reserves away from the fiat offenders and helped drive the price of gold to the moon.

Emerging markets have been the marginal buyer of gold, so gauging their appetite for that shiny metal is important, as they will help shape future gold pricing. Their willingness to buy is a bit speculative, but they conceivably have the ability to do so. Note that gold comprises 10 percent of foreign exchange reserves for emerging markets, as compared to 36 percent for developed, according to the International Monetary Fund. Gold pricing is always a bit unpredictable, but we can say with some degree of confidence that going forward it will be a derivative on the emerging market growth story.

---

23 Louise Street, et al., "Gold Demand Trends: First Quarter 2014," *World Gold Council,* May 2014.

Fiat Frustrations

The frustrations with fiat currencies have reached a crescendo. Fiat currencies, by definition, have no supply constraints and can be issued at will. Supply has been on the rise in this day and age when 'money printing' is still in use to help resuscitate economies still dealing with the lingering effects of the global credit crisis. This is a convenient policy tool that can serve to inject liquidity into an economy, but it also serves to weaken the currency at the same time as the volume in circulation increases. The manipulation of fiat currencies has roots dating back decades. In particular, the United States has had an effectively weak dollar policy ever since it exited the gold standard, which collateralized the currency. Consider that an item priced at $0.25 in 1971, when the U.S. exited the gold standard, now costs roughly $1.44 today, according to the Bureau of Labor Statistics.

Gold had once been the primary outlet for frustrations with fiat currencies, but now it has some competition: Bitcoin. This digital currency with a fixed quantity (21 million unit ceiling), has gained significant interest since its 2009 launch, in large part due to the anti-fiat thesis. Bitcoins are created digitally through a process called 'mining,' which can be done by anyone with the technical knowledge and computing power to devote to it. Ironically enough, Bitcoin, like paper currencies, has no underlying collateral. This is somewhat appropriate, as the Bitcoin narrative is dizzying and often volatile. On any given day, this peer-to-peer payment system will be touted as a means for individuals to transact without financial institution fees. The next day, it will derive negative press for its use as a currency for illicit operations, like drug trafficking. As such, its future is subject to much speculation. Moreover, Bitcoin is freely priced and famously volatile, with single day movements of upwards of 40 percent. To put this in perspective, since 1899, the Dow Jones Industrial Average has had only ten instances of single-day price swings of ten percent or more. Large price swings should be expected as long as Bitcoin continues to lack a mature exchange for transactions and remains unregulated. All things considered, Bitcoin is not an advisable investment for conservative investors.

Alternative Investments (Hedge Funds and Private Capital)

Defined simply, 'hedge' (verb) means to offset risk. Unfortunately, when it comes to hedge funds, that's where the simplicity ends. Defining these unshackled investment vehicles in a few words poses a challenge, as the universe is decidedly eclectic. The expansive menu stems from the fact that they have no investment boundaries. For starters, unlike traditional investment solutions, a hedge fund can go both long (profit if a security appreciates) or short (profit if a security depreciates). Further, it can own liquid and illiquid investments, such as residential homes, along with quirky investments like weather derivatives and even the loan on Michael Jackson's Neverland Ranch. Hedge funds are also captained by a wide array of personalities. Some are introverts, some are media hounds, some brazen, some not. Sometimes hedge fund managers even have enough audacity and capital to take on (and defeat) Central Banks, as George Soros, the famed macro trader, did with the Bank of England. What is clear, however, when it comes to hedge funds, is that their innate independence, if deployed effectively, can make them the Swiss army knife in your investment tool kit....

☞ "I love a hedge, sir." – Henry Fielding, *Pasquin: A Dramatic Satire on the Times* (1736)

☞ "Prophesy as much as you like, but always hedge." – Oliver Wendell Holmes, "Bread and Newspaper" (1861)

One common thread of this very fragmented space is their notorious '2 and 20' fee structure (2 percent management fee and 20 percent incentive fee on positive performance), which makes them easy targets of the populist media.[24] That said, this fee structure does serve as a magnet for top talent....

☞ "Hedge funds are just a compensation structure." – Main Street adage

However, some of these paychecks are in the billions, and that presents some legitimate issues. Schoolteachers, military servicemen, and even doctors are compensated at just a fraction of what some of the hedge fund titans take home. Yes, these hedge funds are getting paid for being very good at what they do in a capitalist society. Further, they mostly have very knowledgeable investors paying the 2 and 20 who are not having their arms twisted to do so. Also, many brand names in the hedge fund space are even extremely philanthropic, and give back a lot of what they make. Yet, you can't help but scratch your head at what they take home at the end of the day, and some of the societal implications....

☞ "The top 25 hedge fund managers collectively earned $25.3 billion in 2009, and just to make it into this elite group required an estimated payout of $350 million." – Simon Lack, *The Hedge Fund Mirage: The Illusion of Big Money and Why It's Too Good to Be True* (2012)

---

24 Most hedge funds will implement a *High Water Mark Provision*. This is an investor-friendly term, as it does not allow the manager to collect incentive fees during periods of positive performance below peak values. For example, assume an investor makes a $1MM subscription to a hedge fund, and the fund immediately falls 50 percent, only to be followed by a 100 percent increase. In this illustration, without a high water mark, the investor would have to pay an incentive fee on the 100 percent increase, even though he has derived no economic gain ($500k to $1MM). The high water mark would disallow any collection of incentive fees until the investor's position in the fund eclipsed the peak value of $1MM.

What exactly do these hedge funds do anyway? Here are a few of the more popular strategies:

Distressed Debt – Purchasing the bonds of troubled companies, often at steep discounts. Ideally, they are good companies with bad balance sheets and the company can be repaired through operational improvements or some financial engineering.

Long/Short – Buying stock in companies that they like, just like the everyday investor. They also have short positions where they sell borrowed stocks. The objective here is to try to profit from overpriced companies set for a correction.

Global Macro – An unconstrained style that typically bets on the direction of government bonds, currencies, equities and/or interest rates. They'll go both long and short, using futures and derivatives, in this cowboy-esque approach.

"All somebody has to do now is say, 'I'm a hedge fund,' and he gets a whole lot more money." – Jim Rogers, as quoted in *Inside the House of Money* by Steven Drobny (2006)

Hedge funds are more expensive than conventional stock or bond offerings, and that has appeal, given our natural inclination to believe that 'expensive' equals 'better.' Certainly, some are worth the extra cost. Yet, not all hedge funds are created equal. The ones you covet should have some sort of edge; you want your compass pointing to them. Sadly, it is a bit of a clubby space and getting in with the good ones takes more than a nice smile. In many ways, they adhere to the maxim that, "it's not what you know, but who you know." To put it another way: alternatives are just as much an asset class as they are an access class.

Investors also need to be deferential to the natural life cycle of managers, which should weigh heavily on the hedge fund search and selection process. In fact, the average shelf life of a hedge fund is roughly four years. The cause of this attrition in the space might be somewhat surprising, as roughly half of all hedge fund failures result from operational or business issues (e.g. defections of key personnel or failure of a prime broker), as opposed to adverse market movements. It's a big tally, as between 2000 and 2009, about 5,000 hedge funds went out of business. In 2004 alone, approximately 1,000 funds shut their doors[25]. These numbers make it clear that hedge funds need to be assessed with a careful eye towards business risk....

⚐ "There are some outstanding hedge funds, but they are considerably outnumbered by the multitudes of lousy ones." – Robert Arnott (April 2013)

Hedge funds are just like any other business enterprise, in that the majority starts off from humble beginnings. Steve Jobs and Steve Wozniak famously started Apple from Jobs's parents' garage. They made the first batch of the company's computers themselves and immersed themselves in the business. Hedge fund start-ups often possess that same entrepreneurial zest. However, they tend to be staring at computers, as opposed to making them. These newbies have a lot of start-up risk and the failure rate is certainly important to consider. However, the energy they devote to shortening their success runway is invaluable. In fact, research shows that, over the past twenty years, these hungry emerging managers have performed twice as well as their emerged brethren that perhaps have let their vigor wane

> Given the elevated fees and illiquid nature, the thoughtful investor needs to 'rationalize the structure.' Don't pay '2 and 20' if you can get similar exposures in a publicly traded, liquid solution. Also, there are now many high quality hedge funds in a mutual fund structure, with the advantage of no incentive fee and daily liquidity.

---

25 Sebastian Mallaby, *More Money Than God* (New York: Penguin, 2010) and Barton Biggs, *Hedgehogging* (Hoboken, NJ: Wiley, 2008)

just a bit.[26] That's not a bad return premium, if you can find the ones that make it out of the garage.

On the other end of the spectrum are the mature, brand name hedge funds. These are the ones with principals who buy professional sports team or Gatsby-esque palaces in the Hamptons or Vail. They've made more money than they could spend in three lifetimes, though they're certainly trying. These brand name funds do have a lot going for them. For starters, they can afford to cut big checks to attract top talent. They also have minimized business risk by developing world-class operations and infrastructure. Yet, are they still as hungry as they were when their names didn't adorn the financial press? That's the operative question, and it's a tricky one. Many are fueled by a need to maintain their legacy, which is a pretty powerful motivator. Yet, it can also be a recipe for mediocrity, as they might look to deliver a Goldilocks type of return: not too low to irritate their investors, and not risky enough to deliver stratospheric performance. That may be fine to many, but trying to get into the mindset of the hedge fund lever pullers is certainly a must to determine what future performance will look like....

- ඏ "every investor in hedge funds should consider where the fund's managers are in their personal motivation cycle." – Barton Biggs, *Hedgehogging* (2008)

As you may infer by now, alternative investments provide no guarantee for outsized results....

- ඏ "If all the money that's ever been invested in hedge funds had been put in treasury bills instead, the results would have been twice as good." – Simon Lack, *The Hedge Fund Mirage: The Illusion of Big Money and Why It's Too Good to Be True* (2012)

- ඏ "Hedge funds are marketed as an 'asset class' that provides generous returns during all stock market environments and thus

---

26 Alex Dunnin, "Emerging Managers Add Twice the Alpha," *Financial Standard,* June 5, 2012.

serves as excellent diversification for an all-equity portfolio . . . . we found that hedge funds have returns lower than commonly supposed." – Burton G. Malkiel and Atanu Saha, "Hedge Funds: Risk and Return," *Financial Analysts Journal* (November/December 2005)

Alfred W. Jones has been credited with starting the first modern hedge fund in 1949. This structure shorted stocks, used leverage, and solely charged an incentive fee. The hedge fund industry has since come a long way, and still continues to grow. It's important to note that the hedge fund is just a legal structure. Translated: anyone can start a hedge fund. With limited barriers to entry, we have seen just that. Remember all that jazz about the S-Curve and the whole notion of how plush margins attract new entrants? Well, the hedge fund space is no exception. Hedge funds now manage nearly $3 trillion in unlevered assets, which compares to $40 billion in 1990. This has a downside, because, as the space proliferates, returns may become more pedestrian....

☞ "Hedge funds in aggregate are going to look more and more like the broader market as their asset base continues to grow." – Carl Friedrich, CIO at Piermont Wealth Management Inc., "Property Crushes Hedge Funds in Alternative Markets," *Bloomberg* (July 10th, 2013)

Yet, illiquid investments do have their merits. They can offer diversification and return opportunities if you hold them over a multi-year period....

☞ "Viewed in the time frame appropriate for a long-term investor, well-chosen positions in illiquid assets perform better than otherwise comparable liquid assets." – David F. Swensen, 2010 Yale University Endowment Report

☞ "Alternative assets, by their very nature, tend to be less efficiently priced than traditional marketable securities, providing an opportunity to exploit market inefficiencies through active management." – David F. Swensen, 2010 Yale University Endowment Report

☞ "If you can put a bunch of money into these idiosyncratic investments, then you get a lot of diversification benefit because the returns are very uncorrelated [to the broader market] . . . . So even though you are putting a riskier asset in your portfolio, because it's not correlated with everything else that you own, the portfolio volatility actually comes down." – Hamilton "Tony" James, president of Blackstone Group, LP, as quoted by Devin Banerjee, "Property Crushes Hedge Funds in Alternative Markets," *Bloomberg* (July 10th, 2013)

While hedge funds are not invincible, certain more risk-minded funds can help serve to limit directionality in your portfolio. For instance, in 2008, the mother of all stress tests, the HFRX Global Hedge Fund Index, ended down by more than 23 percent. While this is not positive in terms of absolute performance, and is not something that would warrant popping the champagne, the average hedge fund did still perform considerably better than the equity markets, as the S&P 500 fell 37 percent. Further, there were some standouts. Some hedge funds battened down the hatches before the credit crisis arrived and lost very little, and some even miraculously made money. With asset prices melting down everywhere, these were the *hedged* funds. Thus, funds that are proven and adept risk managers (e.g. low net and gross exposures) can be a great

Gauging hedge fund performance is a challenge. Hedge fund benchmarks are tainted by a number of biases, including survivorship bias, selection bias, and backfill bias. According to Mesirow Financial's 2011 whitepaper, "Understanding Hedge Fund Indices, Biases, and Methodologies," industry-wide hedge fund index returns are said to have an artificial upward bias of 3-4 percent.

tactical addition to a portfolio when asset valuations are rich or when an economic expansion is getting long in the tooth.[27]

Short-selling, betting on a stock to fall, is one unconventional tactic that a hedge fund has at its disposal, which can help to limit their directionality of returns. When 'shorts' are combined with 'longs' in a portfolio the overall market exposure can be reduced. The mechanics of short selling are to borrow a security with an accompanying obligation to deliver back the borrowed position at a future date. The premise is that the security will depreciate and the short seller will deliver back shares at a lesser value and profit from the difference.

Shorting is a valuable risk management instrument, but it is arguably a more risky endeavor when compared to going long, or buying a stock and profiting from it going up. For starters, shorting is betting against the general long-term direction of the market. Also, an investor's financial downside if he goes long on a security is limited to the capital invested (assuming it is an unlevered transaction), as a security cannot fall below $0. However, the theoretical downside for a short position is unlimited, since there are no boundaries to a security's appreciation. So it should come as no surprise that the HFRI Equity Hedge Short Biased Index, a collection of hedge funds that live and breathe to short stocks, has a ten year annualized return of -5.2 percent through January 31st, 2014. There are some good career short sellers out there, such as Jim Chanos (read more about him in the biography section), but it takes a lot of skill to make repeated profits....

- ☞ "Don't waste time short-selling. Show me the short-sellers' yachts." – Ron Baron, founder of Baron Capital Group

- ☞ "Currently, the hedge fund industry is generally disillusioned with its ability to earn alpha on the short side."[28] – Barton Biggs, *Hedgehogging* (2008)

---

27 Net exposure is a measure of how correlated the hedge fund is to its respective market. Gross exposure is used synonymously with fund leverage. If both figures are under 100 percent, the fund is on the more conservative end of the hedge fund spectrum.

28 Alpha is a term used to describe excess return achieved over a designated benchmark. Positive alpha is indicative of managerial skill.

OVERTIME....

The LTCM Vendetta

On August 17th, 1998, the Russian government defaulted, forcing a crisis upon a highly levered hedge fund called Long Term Capital Management (LTCM).[29] The fund was large and greatly intertwined with Wall Street. Its symbiotic relationship with the financial system, and by extension the broader economy, was an unhealthy one. So much so that William McDonough, president of the Federal Reserve Bank of New York at the time, said that, "an abrupt and disorderly close-out of Long-Term Capital's positions would have posed unacceptable risks to the American economy."[30] Thus, in the eyes of the Fed power brokers, letting LTCM fail just wasn't in the cards. Out of deemed necessity, the Federal Reserve intervened and orchestrated a bailout of the fund to avoid the hypothetical systemic financial damage. The bailout was for $3.6 billion, with contributions from 14 financial institutions.

> Look not at what the manager owns, but also who owns the fund. Be very leery of a concentrated investor base, as you will be beholden to a small number of investors, or even a single one, that accounts for the majority of assets. If such investor(s) decide to redeem, the selling pressures could harm your interest in the fund.

Guess who wasn't one of the 14? Conspicuously absent from the bailout consortium was Bear Stearns, and ten years later the firm effectively failed. The 85-year old investment firm got seduced by the false profits to be made with subprime mortgages, and when trouble surfaced they found no helping hands with bailout dollars. It was a remarkable fall from grace as Bear

---

29 Just prior to its failure, LTCM was levered close to 100:1. In other words, for every $1 it possessed it simultaneously owed $100.

30 Comments before the House of Representatives Committee on Banking and Financial Services (October 1st, 2008).

Stearns traded at close to $170 in January 2007, and just 14 months later was sold to JP Morgan for $10 per share (originally acquired for $2 per share). In fact, its stock imploded from $87 to under $5 over the course of a mere twelve trading days in March 2008. Surely, it was a humbling turn of events for the once venerable firm and its tough-talking CEO Jimmy Cayne, one that conspiracy theorists will tell you was a vendetta a decade in the making.

Decoding Private Equity

Private equity and hedge funds have some similarities. They are offered in illiquid structures, are magnets for top talent, and are 'access' classes. In fact, the difference between the 'haves' and 'have not's' in the private equity universe is stark. For instance, the return differential between managers in the 25th and 75th percentile in United States Venture Capital is roughly 20 percent per annum, according to the 2012 Yale Endowment Annual Report. Compare that to a dispersion of less than one per-

There is an inverse relationship between private equity and hedge funds. You want to more heavily allocate to private equity during economic troughs and hedge funds (the adroit risk manager variety) during the late stages of an economic rally. The best private equity vintage years are when the economy is exiting a recession and when they can acquire assets at depressed pricing. *Hedged* funds, on the other hand, will not fully participate in the upswing in asset values, but they will help to protect a portfolio when they start to correct.

cent for active managers in fixed income. Thus, private equity is a space that can generate attractive results, but that is predicated on being with the *right* manager. Unfortunately, for most investors looking to dabble in the private equity space, the good managers don't want your money, but the bad ones do. It's a catch-22 in that regard. When the good managers want to raise capital, they have people banging down their door. To get a slot in the fund you either have to have a pre-existing relationship or have big bucks (millions, not thousands) to bring to the table. Further, 'average' just doesn't cut it with private equity. Unless you are with the top performing managers you would be better off with just a plain vanilla equity index product. Private equity is a space that, once again, typifies the mantra of, "it's not what you know, but who you know."

It is also no mystery that private equity investors need to have very lengthy time horizons. These illiquid investments can tie your money up for more than decade, much longer than the typical hedge fund. Patience is a prerequisite, as returns are not instantly delivered. Private equity returns typically follow the path of a J-curve. Returns can often be negative in the beginning years, as investments are carried at cost and manager fees are assessed. It often takes a few years for private equity managers to cultivate their acquisitions, after which performance, ide-ally, turns positive. Further, private equity funds will typically only offer quarterly performance estimates. This can mask the true volatility of these investments. For instance, if venture capital returns (one of the riskier segments of private equity) were measured real time, as opposed to quarterly, then their volatility could be close to twice that of the S&P 500.[31][32] This volatility is not necessarily a bad thing, but it is certainly not for everyone.

Private equity transactions can leave an imprint on other asset classes, which is important for investors to consider. A typical Leverage Buyout (LBO) transaction can illuminate this concept. Consummation of a LBO, where a private equity firm uses a great deal of debt as a currency for a purchase, brings mixed fortunes for the target's equity and bondholders. It's a favorable development for equity holders, as the company is usually acquired at a premium. However, bondholders suffer from the laws of supply and demand as more debt is added to the pur-chased company's balance sheet. As a related aside, given the increased

---

31 Venture capital is a segment of private equity that deploys capital to high potential companies in the early stages of their life cycle. Facebook and Twitter are two examples of recipients of venture capital.

32 "Understanding Hedge Fund Indices, Biases and Methodologies," *Mesirow Financial*, 2011.

debt service, companies that generate high levels of cash make ideal LBO targets.

With $3 trillion under management, the private equity industry has obvious staying power. Further, through their acquisitions, they have a lot of individuals on their payroll. KKR, Blackstone, and Apollo are three private equity heavyweights. Collectively, they employ over two million people through their portfolio companies, illustrating that the private equity industry is a key cog in the economy, and this won't be changing overnight.[33]

---

33 Devin Banerjee, "Property Crushes Hedge Funds in Alternative Markets," *Bloomberg*, July 10, 2013.

COMMODITIES

Commodities are marketable goods used in commerce all around us. Common examples include oil, corn and natural gas. Another defining trait is that they are difficult to differentiate and can be easily substituted for each other. For instance, most people couldn't tell the difference in taste between sweet and field corn, including myself. Yet, commodities certainly aren't boring, as the narrative on the investment front has become a lot more interesting. The securitization of the commodities market has paved the way for increased traction as an investable solution. Consider that it is estimated that commodity index investments rose from $13 billion at the end of 2003 to $317 billion in July 2008, right before the arrival of the credit crisis.[34] In fact, investment trading for most commodities far exceeds the corresponding commercial activity. In other words, we can eat corn or gas our car, but our first priority now would be to gauge their investment merits instead.

Commodities aren't for the faint of heart. Their volatility has been more than 20 percent higher than the S&P 500 for the five years preceding February 2014. However, more erratic returns haven't deterred investor interest. The case for commodities over the past few years has been in large measure a derivative of the emerging market growth story. As the heavily populated emerging markets become wealthier, their consumption patterns should increase in tandem. Commodities, which are basic staples in general commerce, will be needed to accommodate this burgeoning demand....

---

34 Harrison Hong and Motohiro Yogo, "Commodity Market Interest and Asset Return Predictability," March 25, 2010.

☞ "In the long run commodity prices are governed by one law – the economic law of supply and demand." – Edwin LeFevre, *Reminiscences of a Stock Operator* (1923)

Commodity pricing will also be supported by population growth. The more people there are on Earth (currently over seven billion), the greater the need for oil, cotton, corn, etc.…

☞ "the power of population is indefinitely greater than the power in the earth to produce subsistence for man." – Robert Malthus, *An Essay on the Principle of Population* (1798)

Commodities also offer diversification benefits. Commodities and equities have a Dickensian relationship. The best of times for equities often coincides with the worst of times for commodities. In fact, commodities were up in the challenged economic decades of the 1930's and 1970's, while equities languished. There is a certain psychological underpinning to this financial behavior, as in times of great anxiety and cynicism, investors covet things they can see and feel, like a barrel of oil or bushel of corn.…

☞ "Commodities tend to zig when the equity markets zag." – Jim Rogers, co-founder of the Quantum Fund

Commodities are an insurance policy of sorts, as they are a good defense against the vagaries of currencies. In particular, they can help hedge the adverse impact resulting from the decline of the United States dollar, as there is an inverse relationship between commodities and currencies. Here's how that works. The first thing you need to know is that most commodities are priced in good old US dollars. So, if the dollar declines, commodities prove more enticing to foreign buyers who can get more bang for their buck with their stronger currency. Also, all else equal, if the greenback falls, the value of commodities should rise, because it now takes more dollars to buy them. Make sense? If you don't trust me on this, reflect back to the 1970's when the US dollar plummeted and gas prices went to the moon. All told, owning commodities can soften the blow when the dollar falls.

Commodity investing has it merits, but it's far from simple. The complexity starts with the fact that it is most often done through futures - contractual obligations to buy a certain asset at a predetermined price and date. This presents different considerations than conventional bond or stock investing. Rule of thumb: if you don't know what contango or backwardation mean (yes, those are actual investing terms, not obscure botanical diseases), then tread lightly with futures[35]....

> "The problem with commodities is that you are betting on what someone else would pay for them in six months. The commodity itself isn't going to do anything for you . . . it is an entirely different game to buy a lump of something and hope that somebody else pays you more for that lump two years from now than it is to buy something that you expect to produce income for you over time." – Warren Buffett, interview with Wade Slome, "Here's What Warren Buffett Says About Gold and Commodities," *Wall St. Cheat Sheet* (March 8th, 2011)

Despite the aforementioned benefits, there are those with a well-entrenched, unflattering view of commodity investing....

> "The only consistently profitable extractive industry is dentistry." – attributed to Warren Buffett

> "An investment by definition is either current income or a stream of future income. When you buy a commodity you have to be

---

35 If the futures curve slopes upward (spot price is less than the futures price), it is in a state of contango. There is a negative roll yield when the market is in this state, as when your futures contract expires your only alternative is a more expensive contract if you would like to roll the proceeds back into the futures market for the same commodity. Backwardation has a positive roll yield, as the spot price is more expensive than the futures price.

assuming that you are going to be able to sell it at a higher price to someone else because it has no income. That is not investing – it is speculating." – Barton Biggs, *Diary of a Hedgehog* (2012)

Commodities can also serve as a currency for corruption. It may sound counter-intuitive that windfall wealth from natural resource finds can send an economy in reverse, but it happens. The riches may go to only the very top members of government. The wealth is then used to solidify their power, and not for more productive purposes, like education. Moreover, the economy may become undiversified, as capital is re-routed to bring the natural resource online.

According to Chuck Jeannes, the costs of production for gold hovers between $1,000 and $1,100 per ounce ("Goldcorp CEO says cost of Gold Production Rising," *Emerging Money*, March 28th, 2013).

A corollary to this is *Dutch Disease*, where a country wounds itself economically after a discovery of natural resources, or following an abrupt influx of foreign currency or foreign aid. The name was coined after the negative fallout from a natural gas field find by the Netherlands in 1959. The country's economy became increasingly one-dimensional after the gas find due to the neglect of other sectors that could have conceivably proved better yielding in terms of technological progress. The resource

There is quite a compelling secular investment case for agricultural commodities. The amount of arable land is declining, farming yields are falling and the world's population is growing and needs to eat. However, weather and its corresponding impact on harvests can overpower prices during the short-term.

exports subsequently caused the country's currency to inflate, and eventually made pricing uncompetitive on the global stage. The Dutch's windfall energy find proved to be more of a curse than a blessing, as they were left with a bloated currency and an undiversified economy. We

159

have seen this movie before when a country's short-term interests come at the expense of longer-term economic viability....

ஒ "When a nation is over-reliant on one or two commodities like oil or precious minerals, corrupt government ministers and their dodgy associates hoard profits and taxes instead of properly allocating them to schools and hospitals." – Bono, lead singer for U2 (2012)

The costs of production – the expenses incurred to bring a resource to a consumer – are a critical determinant of commodity pricing. This includes more than just the upfront expense of building an oil rig or gold mine. Ongoing labor costs, taxes, insurance premiums, and more fall under this figure. The costs of production are not a constant for commodity producers. They will vary depending on a number of factors, including where they operate and how efficiently the business is managed....

ஒ "The exchangeable value of all commodities, rises as the difficulties of their production increase." – David Ricardo, *The Principles of Political Economy and Taxation* (1821)

According to the U.S. Energy Information Administration, the price of crude oil accounts for 71 percent of the retail price of gasoline (national average). The rest is attributed to taxes, refining profits, and distribution and marketing costs.

ஒ "The true cost of consuming a good is the labor and other scarce resources we have to employ to obtain it." – Dani Rodrik, *The Globalization Paradox: Democracy and the Future of the World Economy* (2012)

ஒ "The real price of everything, what everything really costs to the man who wants to acquire it, is the toil and trouble of acquiring it." – Adam Smith, *An Inquiry into the Nature and Causes of the Wealth of Nations* (1776)

Commodities ultimately adhere to the laws of supply and demand, and imbalances are not cured overnight. Consumer preferences rarely change abruptly, and transformative new supply doesn't arrive easily. In fact, commodity bull markets are generally very long in the tooth and average at least a decade. The reason is that it takes a long time to build commodity-related infrastructure, such as oil rigs and pipelines. The upshot of all of this is that higher commodity pricing serves as a magnet for capital, innovation, and infrastructure investment, which ultimately leads to new supply. Enterprising individuals see high prices as an opportunity and look to profit from an otherwise unpleasant situation....

> The United States has long played a pivotal role in the oil market, both as a consumer and producer, ever since Edwin Drake drilled the first commercial well in 1859 near Titusville, Pennsylvania. The supply side of the ledger is certainly getting more interesting. Keep in mind that the United States has a significant impact on oil demand, as it uses one-fourth of the world's supply while representing less than five percent of the world's population.

⌘ "The best cure for high prices is high prices" – attributed to Henry Clews, 19th-20th century financier

A good case study to showcase how the laws of supply and demand impact commodities is that of natural gas. Technological advancements have created an explosion of new supply that has outpaced the level of demand. This has resulted in natural gas pricing that fell from over $13/British Thermal Unit (btu) in 2008 to just over $4/btu in 2014. There are a multitude of obvious beneficiaries, including consumers with lower heating costs and manufacturers with reduced expenses. Further, energy companies have recently taken aim at shale oil reserves in the hopes of replicating their extractions success achieved with shale gas, and the benefits should reverberate throughout the globe. According to the International Monetary Fund, a 10 percent rise in oil prices pares an estimated 0.2-0.3 percent from global GDP growth. Of course, there are skeptics about this possible energy revolution….

> ☞ "Nobody disputes that cheap natural gas would be a good thing for the economy. The question is, is this a sustainable new development that can be counted on for decades to come, or simply a 'bubble' brought on by a land grab and drilling frenzy?" – Jeff Goodell, "Rolling Stone Responds to Chesapeake Energy on 'The Fracking Bubble'," *Rolling Stone* (March 6th, 2012)

The reshaping of our energy future has environmental considerations as well. They have a positive economic impact, but are less environmentally friendly than other energy sources, like wind or tidal power….

> ☞ "Investing in oil is investing in the past and it's investing in climate change." – Daniel Kessler, spokesman for environmentalist group 350.org

OVERTIME....

Sorry Hubbert

In 1956, M. King Hubbert predicted that the United States would face a permanent structural decline in domestic oil production between 1965 and 1971. Hubbert's Peak had validity for decades, but it would eventually be upended by technological advancement. Hydraulic fracturing (also known as 'fracking,' a process that has actually been around since 1947) and horizontal drilling have proven transformative to the US energy complex. The fracking process involves the injection of water and other chemicals to release oil and gas trapped in shale rocks. These advancements in oil and gas extraction have led to a supply renaissance. Consider that in 1996, the U.S. produced just 0.3 trillion cubic feet of shale gas. By 2011, however, that figure had leapt to 7.8 trillion, allowing America to transform itself from an importer to a pending exporter of gas. The shale oil story got a bit of a later start, but the end result is that the United States should overtake Saudi Arabia to become the world's biggest oil producer before 2020, and will become energy independent along the way, according to a recent forecast by the International Energy Agency. Sorry, Hubbert, but your models were slightly off; the power of human ingenuity and innovation should never be underestimated.

This new oil and gas narrative has spillover implications across the globe. Natural gas is not uniformly priced internationally. In the United States, it is generally priced at $3-$4/btu range. However, in

Economists refer to the water involved in growing and manufacturing of products as *Virtual Demand.* The United States is the biggest net exporter of virtual water. It exports close to a third of all the water it withdraws from the natural environment. Much of this is in grains, either directly or via meat, according to *When the Rivers Run Dry* by Fred Pearce (2006).

Japan the price is \$19.8/btu, and even in resource-rich Brazil the cost is \$16.8/btu.[36] It's conceivable, though, that the global pricing of gas should start to converge as the United States starts to export gas and other countries start to use fracking and horizontal drilling to tap their own reserves. The shale gas revolution started in the United States, but the benefits may soon be felt worldwide.

Then there is the impact to OPEC, or the Organization of the Petroleum Exporting Countries. OPEC is an oil cartel with twelve members, including Saudi Arabia and Venezuela, but not the United States. OPEC has historically produced roughly 40 percent of the world's crude oil supply, which is a valuable political currency. Unfortunately, many of the OPEC member countries are relatively one-dimensional in regards to their exports, due to their heavy reliance on oil and gas revenues. So, OPEC seems destined to lose some political sway and see increased fragility with their respective economies. Amy Meyers Jeffe put it in these words: "As political uncertainty spreads across the Mideast, rising U.S. shale-oil production may become a more critical touchstone to market stability. In fact, the U.S. shale-oil boom might roll back the clock to the 1960s, when a U.S. oil surplus (via the Texas Railroad Commission) put Washington, not Riyadh, as the world's swing producer."[37]

The Water-Diamond Paradox

Water resides at the base of Maslow's Hierarchy of Needs. It's an indispensable resource for everyday life, right up there with the air we breathe. Yet, the price doesn't seem to show it, as water is decidedly cheap. Notably, tap water is priced at pennies on the gallon, well less than a comparable volume of gasoline or soda.

> The structural challenges facing water also represent an opportunity for businessmen and investors. As they say in the American West, "water flows uphill towards money."

---

36 "Natural Gas Landed Prices Around World," *Real Clear Energy*, March 18, 2013.
37 "The Experts: How the U.S. Oil Boom Will Change the Markets and Geopolitics," *The Wall Street Journal*, March 27, 2013.

Also consider that a unit of water will cost considerably less than that of a diamond, even though water represents a basic necessity and diamonds are largely an unnecessary luxury. You would think that something that serves no biological need would be priced less than something we cannot live without. This paradox of value is a concept first discussed by Adam Smith in his 1776 *An Inquiry into the Nature and Causes of the Wealth of Nations*. This pricing conundrum persists because diamonds are rare and more difficult to acquire than water. The scarcity, rather than utility, of diamonds determines its value. Hence, as long as soda, gasoline, or diamonds are perceived to be less accessible than water, they will command a pricing premium.

Water is scarcer then you may realize. Yes, water surrounds us. However, 97.5 percent of the water on earth is salt water that is not fit for consumption in its current form. Of the remainder, only a miniscule fraction is accessible, potable water. Further, the demand for water is projected to dwarf supply over the coming decades. You'd be surprised about how much water is used in the production of all things around us, from food to cellphones. Consider that it takes 880 gallons of water to make one gallon of coffee, while one pound of beef requires 1,799 gallons of water, according to National Geographic. As the world becomes more industrialized and endeavors to live more like the Western world, the demands for water will accelerate. Yet, for now, water is an enigma of value that fails to conform to the basic tenets of supply and demand.

Without adequate price signals for water (i.e. making it more expensive) we may be destined for a *Tragedy of the Commons*, a concept that refers to the collective actions of individuals that lead to the depletion of a shared resource. Individuals act independently and in their own self-interest, although they may understand the debilitating long-term effect of doing so. These people would essentially say, "I know water is cheap and its future bleak, but I am going to count on everyone else to solve the problem." Hopefully, we cure the structural issues facing water before it's too late. As Benjamin Franklin said, "When the well's dry, we know the worth of water."[38]

---

38 *Poor Richard's Almanack* (1746).

Investing in Plumbing

Advancements in oil and gas extraction have created an energy supply boom. The process has been so abrupt that it has actually outpaced
our ability to utilize it. In fact, in some instances, excess supply is being
burned off because it is more economical than storing it. Bringing
this new supply online to the end consumer is no small feat, as there
is a need for an estimated $100 billion in funding over the next three
years for the development of energy-related infrastructure. Enter *Master
Limited Partnerships* or MLPs, which are businesses that own and build
pipelines and storage facilities that facilitate the transport of oil and
gas throughout the domestic economy. MLPs are not exactly glitzy businesses. However, they fill the vital role of what is in essence owning and
operating the necessary plumbing for the energy complex.

Not too long ago, MLPs were an obscure and untouched corner of
the investing world. In 2000, the MLP universe was comprised of 18
companies with a meager collective market value of around $14 billion.
Since then, MLPs have burst onto the investing scene. Now there are 106
public companies with an aggregate market capitalization in excess of
$400 billion. They have blossomed as an asset class, but are still on the
small side. Consider that Exxon Mobil alone had a $420 billion market
value at the start of 2014. Yet, their relative size has not diminished their
investment interest, which may still have a lot of runway if this energy
story is still heating up.

Investors have gravitated to MLPs due to their advantageous mix
of public market liquidity and partnership taxation (no corporate tax).
Further, many MLPs (i.e. 'midstream' MLPs) tend to have their fortunes
tied to commodity volumes (not pricing), which is rather inelastic and
pretty predictable. This helps limit the volatility of MLPs, which is about
two-thirds of that of the S&P 500. Finally, they also have to distribute 90
percent of their retained earnings, which gives them allure to the yield-
oriented investor (the Alerian MLP Index has a yield in the vicinity of
six percent as of March 2014).

MLPs do carry their fair share of risks. Notably, the MLP is a creation of 1980's tax reform, so this gives MLPs some political risk, as the structure can be simply legislated away. This threat shouldn't be dismissed, as Canada rather abruptly ended the favorable tax treatment of the Canada Royalty Trust in 2011, a comparable structure to MLPs. Further, not all MLPs are created equal, and the space is not immune to bankruptcies and earning impairments. Therefore, a diversified solution is the more prudent way to gain exposure to the space (ex. buy a MLP index solution). While MLPs are not risk-impervious, they do continue to play a role in an energy narrative that seems to have a few more chapters left.

ART & COLLECTIBLES

A rt and collectibles can fulfill a dual role, unlike most investments. They have aesthetic appeal and can also be the source of financial gain. The downside is that they are emotional assets. This can lead to troublesome results if logic is pushed aside in these rather opaque markets that have high trading costs. Art and collectibles may have visual appeal, but that doesn't necessarily mean they'll also have investment appeal.

Art, meet globalization. Globalization, meet art. The top three artists in 2011 in terms of auction revenues (volume and price) were Andy Warhol, Qi Bai Shi, and Zhang Daqian. The Chinese have a nationalistic approach to art purchases, which explains the demand for these top-selling artists that many in the Western world wouldn't recognize. It also shows that the steamroller that is globalization has reached the art market.

The reality is that art and collectibles should adhere to the same rules of supply and demand that govern conventional asset classes. This means that pricing will not be immune to the impact of varying fortunes of the economy. When the economy thrives, disposable income increases, leading to higher aggregate demand for luxury items. For instance, during the economic resurgence from 2009 through 2012, the pricing for the collectible car market reportedly rose by roughly 33 percent. In fact, the state of the art market can be quite telling….

☞ "The arts are an even better barometer of what is happening in our world than the stock market or the debates in congress." – Henrik Willem Van Loon, historian, journalist, and author

☞ "The arts are simply the signature of civilizations." – Beverly Sills, American opera star

The value of art is a function of a number of factors, including size, medium, artist, subject matter, condition, and rarity. This much may seem obvious – not all art is created equal. What is probably not so obvious is its risk management potential....

☞ "It outperforms in times of economic turmoil and trouble. It has outperformed during all of the wars of the 20th century. It's outperformed during the last 27 recessions." – Cappy Price, from a discussion with Uri Berliner, "The Art of Investing: The Rewards Aren't Always Financial," *NPR* (June 19th, 2013)

Of course, there is a cynical side to everything. Remember the Greater Fool Theory....

☞ "we might as well call the art market what it is, a pyramid scheme. Art is only valuable if there are two more people coming after you who want to buy it for more than you paid, inflation or no." – Marion Maneker, "How Overheated Is the Art Market? Maybe Not So Much," *The Big Picture* (December 18th, 2013)

As Elbert Hubbard, American writer and artist, once said: "art is not a thing – it is a way."[39] Hubbard passed away in 1915, but his words are quite prophetic. Art and collectibles can be a path to riches, but, like most assets acquired at a premium, they can also pave the way to financial hardship.

---

39 Elbert Hubbard, *Journeys to the Homes of Great Teachers* (1908; reprint, New York: Wm. H. Wise & Co., 1916).

FINANCIAL INNOVATION

The investing landscape is dynamic and ever-changing. New solutions are manufactured at a seemingly blistering pace. We now have CMOs, CMBS, CDOs, (Wall Street has never met an acronym it didn't like) and a host of other financial instruments that didn't exist a generation ago. There is also the proliferation of private equity and hedge funds, which has added some exoticism to the investing arena. The motive is usually to provide ways to channel liquidity more effectively to capital starved areas or provide more advanced tools to manage risk. Financial innovation was intended to bring about positive change....

- "But recent regulatory reform, coupled with innovative technologies, has stimulated the development of financial products, such as asset-backed securities, collateral loan obligations, and credit default swaps that facilitate the dispersion of risk.... These increasingly complex financial instruments have contributed to the development of a far more flexible, efficient, and hence resilient financial system than the one that existed just a quarter-century ago." – Alan Greenspan, before the National Italian American Foundation, Washington, D.C. (October 12th, 2005)

- "all good things which exist are the fruits of originality." – John Stuart Mill, *On Liberty* (1859)

Some of this innovation has lived up to its billing, some has not. This has led to divergent opinions on the financial innovation story. Take financial derivatives, which include equity options such as puts and calls. On one hand, as Warren Buffett said in his 2002 Letter to Shareholders, "In my view, derivatives are financial weapons of mass destruction, carrying dangers that, while now latent, are potentially lethal." At the same time, Warren Buffett is a user of them. For instance, he sold some protective puts that reportedly expire several years from now, which is a way to express a bullish stance on the market. Opinions are mixed, but financial innovation will likely continue to redefine the investing landscape for some time....

⟐ "In exchange for capital, corporations can offer investors any set of rights that can be described by words, subject to any conceivable set of qualifications, and in consideration of any conceivable set of offsetting obligations." – D.P. Hariton, "Distinguishing Between Equity and Debt in the New Financial Environment" (1994)

These complex innovations play right to human nature. There is an instinctive lure that draws us to the new and mysterious, especially when there is the potential of swift, outsized financial gain. For instance, despite Warren Buffett's cautionary comments, derivatives trading approached $700 billion in 2008, as reflected by the notional value of outstanding over-the-counter contracts. That represents an approximate seven-fold increase when compared to 1998 levels[40]....

⟐ "You always admire what you really don't understand."- Eleanor Roosevelt, *Meet the Press* (September 16th, 1956). This quote is often attributed to Blaise Pascal as well.

So it should come as no surprise that the economics of complexity are quite compelling....

⟐ "Simplicity is a great virtue but it requires hard work to achieve it and education to appreciate it. And to make matters worse:

---

[40] "OTC derivatives market activity in the first half of 2008," *Bank for International Settlements*, November 2008.

complexity sells better." – Edsger W. Dijkstra, Dutch computer scientist, "On the nature of Computing Science" (1984)

However, there are many that argue that complex innovation has not left the world better off. Understand that obscurity does not guarantee performance....

- "It is better to remember the obvious than to grasp the esoteric." – Charlie Munger

- "Beware of geeks bearing formulas." – Warren Buffett, as quoted in Sebastian Mallaby's *More Money than God* (2010)

- "I sincerely believe that banking institutions are more dangerous to our liberties than standing armies." – attributed to Thomas Jefferson, paraphrase of a statement made in a letter to John Taylor (1816)

- "The financial markets that we have constructed are now so complex, and the speed of transactions so fast, that apparently isolated actions and even minor events can have catastrophic consequences . . . . Virtually all mishaps over the past decades had their roots in the complex structure of the financial markets themselves." – Richard Bookstaber, *A Demon of Our Own Design: Markets, Hedge Funds, and the Perils of Financial Innovation* (2008)

- "financial markets cannot predict economic downturns accurately, but they can cause them." – George Soros, *The New Paradigm for Financial Markets: The Credit Crisis of 2008 and What It Means* (2008)

- "Autonomy and Freedom of choice are critical to our well being, and choice is critical to freedom and autonomy. Nonetheless, though modern Americans have more choice than any group of people ever has before, and thus, presumably, more freedom and autonomy, we don't seem to be benefiting from it psychologically." – Barry Schwartz, *The Paradox of Choice: Why More is Less* (2004)

☞ "Investment success cannot be captured in a mathematical equation or a computer program." – Seth Klarman, *Margin of Safety: Risk-Averse Value Investing Strategies for the Thoughtful Investor* (1991)

☞ "The rocket scientists [at financial institutions] managed to create a missile that landed on themselves." – Anthony Sanders, professor of real estate finance at George Mason University (November 2007)

☞ "The CDO [collateralized debt obligation] was, in effect, a credit laundering service for the residents of Lower Middle Class America. [But for Wall Street it] turned lead into gold." – Michael Lewis, *The Big Short: Inside the Doomsday Machine* (2011)

☞ "I wish someone would give me one shred of neutral evidence that financial innovation has led to economic growth — one shred of evidence." – Paul Volcker, Former Federal Reserve Chairman (2009)

☞ "Lack of transparency, underestimation of risk, and cluelessness about how new financial products might behave when subject to significant stresses are recurrent problems in many crises, past, and present." – Nouriel Roubini and Stephen Mihm, *Crisis Economics: A Crash Course in the Future of Finance* (2011)

☞ "The only simplicity for which I would give a straw is that which is on the other side of the complex — not that which never has divined it." – Oliver Wendell Holmes Jr., *Holmes-Pollock Letters:*

The Correspondence of Mr. Justice Holmes and Sir Frederick Pollock, 1874-1932 (1961)

ๆ "Everything should be made as simple as possible, but not simpler." – attributed to Albert Einstein

"The most important financial innovation that I have seen the past 20 years is the automatic teller machine." – Paul Volcker, Former Federal Reserve Chairman (2009)

Keep in mind that the value inherent in the innovation of today may not be appreciated for years to come....

ๆ "There is no reason anyone would want a computer in their home." – Ken Olsen, Founder of Digital Equipment Corp. (1977)

ๆ "Television won't be able to hold on to any market it captures after the first six months. People will soon get tired of staring at a plywood box every night." – Darryl Zanuck, executive at 20th Century Fox (1946)

As with many things, there are two types of innovation: simple and complex. The critics would say that complex innovation has led to instruments of modern day financial alchemy that have done little to improve the broader well-being of society. Some of the criticism regarding this alphabet soup of new investment options (ex. CDS, CMO) is justified, given their contributions to the global credit crisis. Complexity has led to fragility, as these instruments were owned by many who did not fully understand the potential risks. However, some complex innovations do have merit, otherwise they would be extinct. Thus, it doesn't make sense to typecast all complex innovation as evil. On the other hand, simple innovation does not tend to elicit such a vitriolic response. In fact, simple innovation may deliver positive results with huge impacts....

- "And, indeed, simplification is one mark of real genius." – Dan Ariely, *Predictably Irrational* (2009)

Index funds arguably fall into the category of simple innovation. They are low-cost, passive investments that provide a rather predictable return pattern that mirrors a designated benchmark, such as the S&P 500 or Dow Jones Industrial Average. They are rather straightforward, perhaps boring, and deliver a perfectly mediocre result. The downside is that they include all parts of a benchmark, even the undesirable constituents. However, while they are nothing fancy and not without criticism, they can be quite effective....

- "Any intelligent fool can make things bigger, more complex, and more violent. It takes a touch of genius – and a lot of courage – to move in the opposite direction." – E.F. Schumacher, "Small is Beautiful" (1973)

- "When you look at the results on an after-fee, after-tax basis over reasonably long periods of time, there's almost no chance that you end up beating the index fund." – David F. Swensen, *NPR* interview (April 2008)

- "Fiduciaries should strongly consider index funds as an alternative to actively managed funds. Index funds incur about 80 percent less in transaction costs than actively managed funds." – Michael C. Keenan, finance and insurance industry veteran, "The Elephant in the Living Room," *Financial Advisor* (May 1st, 2008)

- "Passive investing is a difficult concept for many to accept, perhaps because of its fundamental paradox: when we aim at the average we perform better than the average." – David Stein, Parametric Portfolio Associates (2003)

☞ "If you invested in a very low cost index fund – where you don't put the money in at one time, but average in over 10 years – you'll do better than 90 percent of people who start investing at the same time." – Warren Buffet, Berkshire Hathaway Annual Meeting (2004)

Passive investing helps one avoid having to constantly agonize over the markets and economy. A laissez-faire approach that utilizes index funds will keep it simple....

> Efficiency is the degree to which all relevant information is incorporated into a security's price. It is a function of a few things, such as liquidity and analyst coverage. For instance, large cap US equities are generally considered more efficient than emerging market equities, at least by US investors. However, just because a market is efficient does not mean that the current price is correct. Investors are not infallible.

☞ "A provision of endless apparatus, a bustle of infinite enquiry and research, or even the mere mechanical labour of copying, may be employed, to evade and shuffle off real labour, – the real labour of thinking." – Sir Joshua Reynolds, English painter (1784)

Believers of the *Efficient Market Hypothesis (EMH)* will gravitate towards passive index products. This theory states that it is impossible to beat the market over an extended period, as prices always reflect all relevant information. There is no informational edge to be had, and one may as well wave the white flag and buy the entire market instead....

☞ "past, present and even discounted future events are reflected in market price" – Louis Bachelier, *The Theory of Speculation* (1900)

☞ "A random walk is one in which future steps or directions cannot be predicted on the basis of past actions. When the term is applied to the stock market, it means that short-run changes in stock prices cannot be predicted." – Burton G. Malkiel, *A Random Walk Down Wall Street* (1973)

Passive investing has it merits, but there are those who arrive at a different conclusion about the efficient market hypothesis....

⌕ "Unfortunately, this argument for the efficient market hypothesis does not tell us that the stock market cannot go through periods of significant mispricing lasting years or even decades." – Robert Shiller, *Irrational Exuberance* (2005)

⌕ "In relatively calm markets – where there are relatively few systemic shocks to the economy – the EMH is a pretty good approximation to reality. When market conditions change and you experience large macro shocks, then simple heuristics like 60/40 no longer work as well because financial markets have changed in their dynamics." – Andrew Lo, "The Volatility of Volatility," *CFA Institute Magazine* (Sept/Oct 2013)

⌕ "While markets are not totally crazy, they contain quite substantial noise, so substantial that it dominates the movements in the aggregate market." – Robert Shiller, as quoted in *Crisis Economics* by Nouriel Roubini and Stephen Mihm (2011)

We benefit from simple innovations in many walks of life. For instance, in 1847, Ignaz Semmelweis became the first medical professional to require doctors and staff of his clinic to frequently wash their hands. Fast forward to today, and, according to the United States Centers of Disease Control and Prevention (CDC), "Hand washing is the single most important means of preventing the spread of infection."

Lastly, passive investing has its limitations....

- "It is impossible to produce superior performance unless you do something different from the majority." – Sir John Templeton, founder of Templeton Growth Fund, Inc.

OVERTIME....

A New Breed of Index

Not all indices and related funds are created equal. Traditional indices, like the S&P 500, are market capitalization (current stock price multiplied by company shares outstanding) weighted, which means the best performers will naturally be larger constituents. *Fundamental Indexation* (also called smart beta strategies) aims to break the relationship between price and index weighting. This methodology molds indices based off certain factors, such as the P/E multiple and Price/Sales, instead of capitalization. Naysayers of fundamental indexation will tell you they are not indices! The construction methodology is no different than how active managers operate. Furthermore, fundamental indexation has an inherent value bias, as it systemically shies away from the top performers. Fundamental indexation may or may not be a new breed of 'index,' but it does provide another tool for an investor looking for simple and inexpensive exposure to the equity space.

Perhaps the best case against fundamental indexation is the belief that a new breed of index is simply unnecessary. Frankly, passive management has a pretty impressive performance track record when stacked up next to their active manager counterparts. For instance, in the five-year period ending June 2012, only 24 percent of active managers beat their passive equivalent in intermediate-term municipal bond asset class, and only 22 percent and 32 percent beat their active peers in large cap domestic equities and large cap foreign equities, respectively.[41] There are just a lot of smart people mining these opportunity sets, which limits active managers in their pursuit of repeatable, outsized returns compared to an index. Passive solutions don't have to carry this burden of finding these increasingly rare mispriced securities. They *are* the index, which

---

41 Rick Ferri, "Indexes Beat Active Funds Again in S&P Study," *Forbes*, October 11, 2012.

is, appropriately, their source of strong performance. Fundamental indexation could be a 'better mousetrap' for gaining index exposure, but it does have some stiff competition from the capitalization-weighted incumbent.

INFLATION

Milk prices rising, health care costs marching higher, real estate prices skyrocketing – that would be inflation influencing your daily narrative. Inflation, the increase in the general price for goods and services, is ubiquitous. You see evidence of it on Main Street, Wall Street, Walmart, Bloomingdales, and just about any corner of the world around us. There are some quick definitions of it, such as the common "too much money chasing too few goods." Or, for the business school student or investment practitioner, it can be seen as the erosion of purchasing power, and synonymous with currency depreciation. No matter how you skin it, inflation is a consideration for consumers and investors, the rich and poor, young and old, everyone.

You can look at inflation in a few different ways, but at least for investors, the primary consideration is where inflation is headed. In order to understand the future, you must know the drivers of inflation. There is the *Demand-Induced* variety. You'll see this type when an economy starts to overheat and total spending exceeds production. Another defining characteristic of demand-induced inflation is a scarcity of labor and the consequent acceleration of wages. When people get paid more, they spend more, and that lays the foundation for higher prices. However, this isn't in the cards for the

Innovation is often born out of inflation. Enterprising individuals realize that there is a profit to be made by providing relief to the high costs associated with inflation. For instance, it's no surprise that the advancements in natural gas and oil extraction followed the spectacular rise in their prices.

foreseeable future, as globalization has supersized the potential labor pool. There is also *Cost-Push* inflation, which results from an unexpected shock to the supply chain (i.e. supply shocks). The 1970's oil embargo in U.S. and the resulting rise in prices is a commonly cited example of cost-push inflation. This type of inflation is rather uncommon, and rarely does it have a massive impact, though it certainly has happened. Again, globalization, along with technology advancements, has made curing supply imbalances a lot easier. Inflation should be tame in the future, but should not be marginalized, as it is woven into the fabric of general commerce....

- ☞ "A nickel ain't worth a dime anymore." – attributed to Yogi Berra, MLB hall of famer

- ☞ "I don't mind going back to daylight saving time. With inflation, the hour will be the only thing I've saved all year." – Victor Borge, 20th century Danish comedian and musician

- ☞ "Inflation is as violent as a mugger, as frightening as an armed robber, and as deadly as a hit man." – Ronald Reagan (1978)

- ☞ "For just over my price range, I can get something way under my quality expectation level. Thanks, inflation!" – Jarod Kintz, *This Book Has No Title* (2012)

- ☞ "Inflation is when you pay fifteen dollars for the ten-dollar haircut you used to get for five dollars when you had hair." – attributed to Sam Ewing, American humorist and television producer

- ☞ "There are two main drivers of asset class returns – inflation and growth." – Ray Dalio

Inflation is often referred to as an invisible tax, which is a rather convenient policy tool. As Milton Friedman famously said, "Inflation is the one form of taxation that can be imposed without legislation." That's what makes inflation so insidious and perhaps now more so than ever. Yes, the textbook drivers of inflation don't seem to be much of a danger. However, given the sad state of fiscal finances for developed economies, the threat of inflation is ever-present, and investors should always be on the lookout.

Getting your hands on inflation now and its future path is important. Further, when you fail to consider inflation, your investment results are somewhat artificial. Fortunately, the math to get there is pretty straightforward, as you can approximate the 'real' return for an investment by simply subtracting the rate of inflation.[42] For instance, a five-percent return is really around three-percent in an environment with a very realistic two-percent rate of inflation. In other words, a five percent return commands roughly 40 percent less purchasing power if inflation has risen at a two percent clip. Thus, even in small doses, inflation matters.

Deflation, the opposite of inflation, has a rather curious impact on real returns. Consider the real returns of bonds from Japan and the United States from early 2013. Japan had a CPI rate of -0.5 percent and a +0.75 percent rate on its 10 Year Sovereign bond, which equates to a real return of +1.25 percent. The United States has a rate of +1.9 percent on its 10 Year Treasury bond and a CPI of +1.5 percent. On the surface, the United States bond seems like the better option given the higher rate. However, the real return on a United States Treasury bond is 70 percent *less* than that of a comparable maturity Japanese sovereign bond. Therefore, the 'nominal' (pre-inflation) rate of return may be a misleading way of viewing investment results.

> Deflation may be bad for equities, but can be good for fixed income. As prices fall, the value of the coupon has increasing purchasing power.

---

42 This calculation for determining the real inflation rate is a bit crude and inexact, but gets you real close, real quickly to the right answer. The more precise, but slightly more arduous approach, calculation is as follows: ((1+Return)/(1+Inflation Rate)) – 1.

Unfortunately, we all have mindset that tends toward the 'nominal,' rather than the 'real.' *Money Illusion* is an economic concept that refers to a predisposition for individuals to think of money in nominal terms. For instance, studies show that individuals feel better about a pay increase of 2 percent when inflation runs at 4 percent as compared to a 2 percent pay cut when inflation is zero (the inflation adjusted results are exactly the same in both instances). It behooves investors to think in real terms and always be mindful of the threat of inflation....

- "If it looks like a tax, acts like a tax and takes away your resources like a tax, then it's a tax." – Thomas Sowell, "Taxing the Poor," *National Review* (December 11th, 2012)

- "I do not think it is an exaggeration to say history is largely a history of inflation, usually inflations engineered by governments for the gain of governments" – Friedrich August von Hayek, *Denationalisation of Money: The Argument Refined* (1978)

- "By a continuing process of inflation, governments can confiscate, secretly and unobserved, an important part of the wealth of their citizens." – John Maynard Keynes, *The Economic Consequences of the Peace* (1919)

Inflation is a global phenomenon. Of late, the emerging markets have imported inflation as a result of money printing by the governments of developed markets. At the same time, developed markets have imported disinflation, that is, a decline in the rate of inflation, from the emerging markets, due to the lower cost of labor. Inflation is not uniform across counties, and its impact varies depending on one's income class. Unfortunately, the 'little guy' tends to lose out when inflation surfaces....

- "The rise of prices that follows an expansion of [paper money does] not affect all descriptions of labor and commodities, at the same time, in an equal degree . . . . The working man finds all the articles he uses in his family rising in price, while the money rate of his own wages remains unchanged." William Gouge, treasury adviser for Andrew Jackson, *A Short History of Money and Banking* (1833)

☞ "Inflation is a hidden tax that disproportionately affects those least able to pay it: the middle class and the poor." – Michael G. Pento, *The Coming Bond Market Collapse: How to Survive the Demise of the U.S. Debt Market* (2013)

The quantity of inflation is also not constant. It varies depending on where you live and fluctuates over time....

☞ "The price of everything rises and falls from time to time and place to place; and with every such change the purchasing power of money changes so far as that thing goes." – Alfred Marshall, *Principles of Economics* (1890)

As was touched on in the monetary policy chapter, there are concerns that the aggressive policies by Central Banks will ignite inflation. The money injected into the economy is kindling for rampant inflation, but the lighter (velocity) is currently broken. Velocity, the rate at which liquidity flows through the economy, in the United States has slowed to a glacial pace and is now at a 65 year low. Both liquidity and velocity are necessary ingredients for inflation....

☞ "Inflation is always and everywhere a monetary phenomenon" – Milton Friedman, "The Counter-Revolution in Monetary Theory" (1970)

The impact of these Central Bank policies will not be limited to Americans. Capital is very portable these days and often finds its way to emerging markets. In fact, Friedman was right...sort of. Central Bank money printing can lead to inflation, even in other countries. For instance, the International Monetary Fund estimates that, through January 2014, $470 billion of the liquidity created by the Federal Reserve's asset purchases was invested in Emerging Markets. This is arguably more troubling in emerging markets given the nature of individuals' expenditures. Families in these countries can spend half to three-quarters of their income on food. Americans used to spend over 40 percent of their budget on food nearly a century ago (1917 – 1919), but that number has since fallen to under 20 percent, according to a report from the Bureau of Labor Statistics.[43] So, while we may grumble over milk or bread prices, in India or China, a sharp spike in food prices could be a matter of life or death.

Inflation has its dangers, but it is not categorically bad. Notably, it can have a better outcome than deflation, as you will read in a moment. However, don't assume rising prices are necessarily the result of organic economic growth....

> Inflation is a bit of a zero-sum game. Inflation is toxic to lenders, but bliss for borrowers (borrowers pay back in cheaper dollars). Thus, a good hedge against inflation is having a fixed-rate mortgage, assuming a reasonable interest rate.

☞ "Mere inflation – that is, the mere issuance of more money, with the consequence of higher wages and prices – may look like the creation of more demand. But in terms of the actual production and exchange of real things it is not." – Henry Hazlitt, *Economics in One Lesson: The Shortest and Surest Way to Understand Basic Economics* (1946)

Deflation (decline in general level of prices in an economy) is perhaps even more sinister than inflation. It stymies consumer spending, which results in a chiseling of corporate earnings, investment, and innovation. Japan offers a telling tale of the impact of deflation, which

---

43 David S. Johnson et al., "A century of family budgets in the United States," *Monthly Labor Review* (May 2001).

followed one of the greatest asset bubble collapses in history. To say asset prices at its peak were inflated and disconnected from economic reality was an understatement. Consider that the Tokyo Imperial Palace Grounds, the signature appraisal at the time, was said to be worth more than all of the real estate in California, even though it covered only 1.32 square miles. When the bubble burst, the wreckage was not confined to real estate. The Nikkei 225 (Japan's version of the S&P 500) peaked in December 1989 at close to 39,000, with a stratospheric Price/Earnings valuation multiple of 80x At its peak, the Nikkei astonishingly represented close to half of the aggregate global stock market value. When the index bottomed in 2009 it had lost more than 80 percent of its peak value....

☞ "Deflation is in almost all cases a side effect of a collapse in aggregate demand – a drop in spending so severe that producers must cut prices on an ongoing basis in order to find buyers." – Ben Bernanke, before National Economists Club (December 21st, 2012)

Source: Yahoo! Finance

❧ "As Japan has demonstrated, deflation is a very insidious plague because low or declining nominal GDP emasculates consumer spending (don't buy now because it will cost less later) and corporate profits." – Barton Biggs, *Diary of a Hedgehog* (2012)

Naturally, there are exceptions to the notion that deflation occurs only during dire economic times….

❧ "People associate deflation with the awful Great Depression, but most don't know that the consumer price index (CPI) steadily fell (albeit much more gently) from late 1925 through 1929, in the midst of the Roaring Twenties – hardly a time associated with economic stagnation." – Michael G. Pento, *The Coming Bond Market Collapse: How to Survive the Demise of the U.S. Debt Market* (2013)

Illustrated below is the precipitous decline in value of the German mark compared to the United States dollar:

January 1913: 4.2 marks per dollar

January 1919: 8.9

June 1922: 350

January 1923: 18,000

November 1923: 4.2 trillion

Source: Gene Smiley, *Rethinking the Great Depression* (Chicago: Ivan R. Dee, 2002).

Disinflation, or a decline in rate of inflation, represents another challenge for investors. When there are whiffs of deflation in the air, equities can, and likely will, come under pressure….

❧ "When inflation falls below 2 percent, it is no longer good for equities; it is bad and price-to-earnings ratios fall." – Barton Biggs, *Diary of a Hedgehog* (2012)

Inflation can also ravage investment results for all asset classes….

☞ "It is no longer a secret that stocks, like bonds, do poorly in an inflationary environment . . . . The main reason, I believe, is that stocks, in economic substance, are really very similar to bonds." – Warren Buffett (1977)

☞ "Inflation is the crabgrass in your savings." – Robert Orben, American humorist

Or perhaps it doesn't ravage *all* asset classes, at least in the case of equities....

☞ "On this point we can be categorical. There is no close time connection between inflationary (or deflationary) conditions and the movement of common-stock earnings and prices." – Benjamin Graham, *The Intelligent Investor* (1949)

The most dangerous variety of inflation is hyperinflation. Hyperinflation is a period with very high monthly rates of inflation exceeding 50 percent, according to Philip Cagan.[44] Further, the inflation rate in this case is typically difficult to control and is often a byproduct of war. The United States is not immune to hyperinflation, as it has suffered through bouts of it during the Revolution and the Civil War. Yet, hyperinflation is most often associated with Germany's Weimar Republic in the early 1920's, or modern day Zimbabwe (inflation peaked at an estimated 79.6 billion percent in November 2008). As a related aside, the German hyperinflation episode, in conjunction with the resulting recession, was said to have led to the rise of Hitler.[45] Unsurprisingly, the Germans highly covet monetary stability and get anxious over even the smallest hint of hyperinflation....

---

44 "The Monetary Dynamics of Hyperinflation," in *Studies in the Quantity Theory of Money*, ed. Milton Friedman (Chicago: University of Chicago Press, 1956).
45 "Zimbabwe after hyperinflation," *The Economist*, April 27th 2013.

- ☞ "When runaway inflation and bank failures struck in Germany in the 1920s, the middle class was destroyed, which led directly to the rise of the Nazis." – Nick Clooney, American journalist and television host (and yes, father of George Clooney)

- ☞ "Hyperinflation can take virtually your entire life's savings, without the government having to bother raising the official tax rate at all." – Thomas Sowell, "Taxing the Poor," *National Review* (December 11th, 2012)

BEHAVIORAL FINANCE

B uy low – sell high is an investment mantra that is rarely contested, yet is very difficult to put into practice. The reason? We are often our own worst enemies. We are hardwired to do more harm than good, as we have an innate tendency to invest on emotions, not science or reasoning. Our behavioral biases, if left unchecked, will too often result in self-inflicted investment wounds.

Investor psychology can materially shape investment results in a few ways. First, they can add a punctuation mark to a market movement. Fear (market collapses) and greed (market bubbles) are self-feeding and can send asset class prices well beyond the boundaries of reason. Our emotions are rarely hidden from the world around us. When we see people despondent or euphoric, we can't help but be influenced by them. Further, the economic landscape impacts our psyche. For instance,

The *Plucking Model* was a concept popularized by Milton Friedman in 1964. It suggests that the economy is like a plucked string, as the farther you pull it, the more forcefully it snaps back. The take away is that you should try not to sell low, as economic troughs are typically followed by periods of resurgence, which can be a boon for the disciplined investor.

we are most gullible and complacent when we are most happy, and the broader economy does serve as stimuli. So, when the economy is in high gear and life is good, we have a tendency to become more of a risk taker. It should be the other way around. You want to be very pricedisciplined, and the odds are that asset class valuations will be rich when the economy is sending the all-clear signal. Further, inexpensive assets, curiously enough, can be terrifying. Investing is the opposite of consumer shopping. When there is a sale, people tend to run away. You should know, as well, that we are all pre-disposed to behavioral biases, and even the brightest minds can fall victim to a lack of self-awareness....

⚓ "Success in investing doesn't correlate with I.Q. once you're above a level of 25. Once you have ordinary intelligence, what you need is the temperament to control the urges that get other people into trouble in investing." – Warren Buffett (1999)

⚓ "All people are biased, no matter what. All that you can hope for is that you do your best to be aware of your biases. You can't pretend you don't have them." – Peter Hatemi, Associate Professor of Political Science, Microbiology and Biochemistry at Penn State University

⚓ "The market is fond of making mountains out of molehills and exaggerating ordinary vicissitudes into major setbacks." – Benjamin Graham, *The Intelligent Investor* (1949)

⚓ "Man's enemies are not demons, but human beings like himself." – Lao Tzu, *Tao Te Ching* (6th century BC)

⚓ "People in both fields operate with beliefs and biases. To the extent you can eliminate both and replace them with data, you gain a clear advantage." – John Henry, American businessman and owner of the Boston Red Sox, as quoted in Michael Lewis, *Moneyball: The Art of Winning an Unfair Game* (2004)

⚓ "Most, probably, of our decisions to do something positive, the full consequences of which will be drawn out over many days to come, can only be taken as the result of animal spirits – a spontaneous urge to action rather than inaction, and not as the outcome of a weighted average of quantitative benefits multiplied by quantitative probabilities." – John Maynard Keynes, *The General Theory of Employment, Interest and Money* (1936)

- ☞ "No matter how good fundamentals may be, humans exercising their greed and propensity to err have the ability to screw things up." – Howard Marks, *The Most Important Thing: Uncommon Sense for the Thoughtful Investor* (2011)

- ☞ "When we remember we are all mad, the mysteries disappear and life stands explained." – Mark Twain (1898)

- ☞ "We are not only irrational, but pre-dictably irrational – that our irratio-nality happens the same way, again and again." – Dan Ariely, *Predictably Irrational* (2009)

As early 20th century publishing magnate William Randolph Hearst once supposedly said, "The public likes entertainment better than it likes information."

- ☞ "What a piece of work is a man!" – William Shakespeare, *The Tragedy of Hamlet, Prince of Denmark* (c. 1599-1602)

We have our behavioral vulnerabilities, but so does everyone else. There are opportunities when we notice there are price dislocations in the market due to widespread emotional investing. Some of the obvious examples are avoiding technology stocks in the late 1990's, or owning equities in early 2009 when the general consensus was that the economy was beyond repair....

- ☞ "The most important single factor in shaping security markets is public psychology." – Gerald Loeb, founder of E.F. Hutton & Co., *The Battle for Investment Survival* (1935)

How do we get to these extremes? For one, we are pre-disposed to negativity and the media plays to this....

☞ "If it bleeds, it leads." – Journalism adage

We are also quite nearsighted. Studies show that humans are predisposed to believe that the long-term outcome can be predicted by short-term events. So, when markets fall, we think they will fall further. Yet, when markets fall, what generally happens is that valuations improve and we are left with a better entry point. Similarly, when markets rise, our natural response is to get a piece of the action, even though valuations might be less compelling. As you might suspect, the best advertisement for the stock market is a frothy rally....

Sir Isaac Newton once said that he "could calculate the motion of erratic bodies, but not the madness of a multitude." This certainly makes sense, as Newton lost the equivalent of several million of today's dollars courtesy of some ill-advised speculation in the South Sea Company.

☞ "A large body of research in psychology and economics shows that human beings tend to form their expectations by relying on past experiences – especially *recent* ones." – Robert Arnott & Denis Chaves, "Mind the (Expectations) Gap" (July 3rd, 2013)

☞ "Rising prices are a narcotic that affects the reasoning power up and down the line." – Warren Buffett, testimony to Congress (June 2nd, 2010)

☞ "When you feel like bragging, it's probably time to sell." – John Neff, *John Neff on Investing* (2001)

We all have free will, but you wouldn't often know it. We are innate imitators, not initiators. Investors often need to fend off peer pressure but it's not comfortable to have a trade or opinion that is contrary to consensus. Sometimes we need to break free from the herd in order to avoid financial loss. As we will learn more when we discuss bubbles, following the crowd is a seductive, convenient, potentially dangerous habit….

- ☞ "Different causes determine the appearance of these characteristics peculiar to crowds, and not possessed by isolated individuals. The first is that the individual forming part of a crowd acquires, solely from numerical considerations, a sentiment of invincible power which allows him to yield to instincts which, had he been alone, he would perforce have kept under restraint." – Gustave Le Bon, *The Crowd: A Study of the Popular Mind* (1895)

- ☞ "When things are going well and prices are high, investors rush to buy, forgetting all prudence. Then, when there's chaos all around and assets are on the bargain counter, they lose all willingness to bear risk and rush to sell. And it will be ever so." – Howard Marks, *The Most Important Thing: Uncommon Sense for the Thoughtful Investor* (2011)

- ☞ "In crowds it is stupidity and not mother-wit that is accumulated." – Gustave Le Bon, *The Crowd: A Study of the Popular Mind* (1896)

- ☞ "Where all think alike, no one thinks very much." – Walter Lippmann, Pulitzer Prize winning journalist, with Albert Einstein getting credit for the quote on occasion

- ☞ "[The] central principle of investment is to go contrary to general opinion, on the ground that, if everyone is agreed about its merits, the investment is inevitably too dear and therefore unattractive." – John Maynard Keynes

- ☞ "The masses have never thirsted after truth. They turn aside from evidence that is not to their taste, preferring to deify error, if error seduces them. Whoever can supply them with illusions is easily their master; whoever attempts to destroy their illusions is always their victim." – Gustave Le Bon, *The Crowd: A Study of the Popular Mind* (1896)

Doing what's smart can be very different from doing what's popular. If investors can muster the courage to go against the crowd it can actually prove quite lucrative, particularly during market panics. The pain experienced with a financial loss is twice as potent as the euphoria from a gain. Thus, we are disproportionately emotional when the markets head south. This panicked and dour state can make the unwitting investor sell something at perhaps the worst time possible. It also can lead to paying an excessive premium for assets when there is a cheery consensus. We can blame the amygdala, which is the part of the brain that plays a primary role in our corresponding fear of loss. Irrespective of the biology, assets can be heavily discounted when panics ensue and this can lead to great riches for the disciplined buyer. In other words, sometimes bad news is good news for the disciplined investor, as assets can go on sale....

- ☞ "Buy when there's blood in the streets, even if the blood is your own." – Baron Nathan Rothschild, British banker and member of the Rothschild banking family

- ☞ "If you can keep your head when all about you
  Are losing theirs and blaming it on you,
  If you can trust yourself when all men doubt you,
  . . . .
  Yours is the Earth and everything that's in it" – Rudyard Kipling, "If–" (1895)

- ☞ "There is no security on this earth; there is only opportunity." – Douglas MacArthur, commander of U.S. forces in the Pacific theater of the Second World War

- "In capital markets, price is set by the most panicked seller at the end of a trading day. Value, which is determined by cash flows and assets, is not." – attributed to Seth Klarman

- "You can have cheap equity prices or good news, but you can't have both at the same time." – Joe Rosenberg, from an interview with Andrew Bary, "The Best Opportunities in a Half-Century," *Barron's* (December 3rd, 2011)

- "Nothing gives one person so much advantage over another as to remain always cool and unruffled under all circumstances." – attributed to Thomas Jefferson

- "The time of maximum pessimism is the best time to buy, and the time of maximum optimism is the best time to sell." – Sir John Templeton

- "Generally speaking, the more an investment thesis is at odds with the generally prevailing view, the greater the financial rewards one can reap if it turns out to be correct." – George Soros, *The New Paradigm for Financial Markets: The Credit Crisis of 2008 and What It Means* (2008)

- "Investors should remember that excitement and expenses are their enemies. And if they insist on trying to time their participation in equities, they should try to be fearful when others are greedy and greedy only when others are fearful." – Warren Buffett, 2004 Letter to Shareholders

- "Fortunately or unfortunately, experience teaches that the likelihood of a market decline is inversely proportional to the size of your cash position and the lowness of your net long, and the likelihood of the decline being reversed is in direct proportion to the amount of selling you do during the decline." – Barton Biggs, *Diary of a Hedgehog* (2012)

ఞ "To buy when others are despondently selling and to sell when others are euphorically buying takes the greatest courage, but provides the greatest profit." – Sir John Templeton

ఞ "Whenever you find yourself on the side of the majority, it is time to reform (or pause and reflect)." – Mark Twain (1904)

ఞ "It takes patience, discipline, and courage to follow the 'contrarian' route to investment success: to buy when others are despondently selling, to sell when others are avidly buying. However, based on a half century of experience, I can attest to the rewards at the end of the journey." – Sir John Templeton

ఞ "In investing, what is comfortable is rarely profitable." - Robert Arnott

ఞ "The public buys the most at the top and the least at the bottom." – Bob Farrell, Wall Street veteran

There will always be a reason to be bearish and there will always be a reason to be bullish, but there is never a reason to lose your sense of discipline. The best defense against emotional investing is being dispassionate and conducting thorough and exhaustive research (what we learned about in Chapter 1)....

> We are more motivated when it comes to loss aversion, compared to pursuit of a comparable gain. For instance, homeowners feel more duty-bound to add insulation to their residence when they're told how much money they could lose relative to being told how much they can save.

- "You are neither right nor wrong because the crowd disagrees with you. You are right because your data and reasoning are right." – Benjamin Graham

- "Everything beautiful and noble is the result of reason and calculation." – Charles Baudelaire, "In Praise of Cosmetics" (1863)

- "Successful investors tend to be unemotional, allowing the greed and fear of others to play into their hands. By having confidence in their own analysis and judgment, they respond to market forces not with blind emotion but with calculated reason. Successful investors, for example, demonstrate caution in frothy markets and steadfast conviction in panicky ones. Indeed, the very way an investor views the market and it's price fluctuations is a key factor in his or her ultimate investment success or failure." – Seth Klarman, *Margin of Safety: Risk-Averse Value Investing Strategies for the Thoughtful Investor* (1991)

- "Trust, but verify." –attributed to Ronald Reagan, though originally a Russian proverb

- "Human biases tend to force people to focus exclusively on the good side of trades, which can be very dangerous . . . we are somehow preprogrammed to look for confirmation and not disconfirmation." – Jim Leitner, Falcon Management, as quoted in *Inside the House of Money* by Steven Drobny (2006)

- "When you develop your opinions on the basis of weak evidence, you will have difficulty interpreting subsequent information that contradicts these opinions, even if this new information is obviously more accurate." – Nassim Taleb, *The Black Swan: The Impact of the Highly Improbable* (2007)

☞ "Don't let the noise of others' opinions drown out your own inner voice." – Steve Jobs, Stanford commencement speech (2005)

☞ "The seeker after truth must, once in the course of his life, doubt everything, as far as possible." – René Descartes, *Principles of Philosophy* (1644)

☞ "Courage is the resistance to fear, mastery of fear – not absence of fear." – Mark Twain, *Pudd'nhead Wilson* (1894)

☞ "There is always a good deal of doubt with regard to the correct time for applying the simple principle of 'buy low and sell high.'" – Benjamin Graham & David Dodd, *Security Analysis* (1934)

☞ "Pessimistic visions about almost anything always strike the public as more erudite than optimistic ones." – Joseph Schumpeter

There is some correlation between demographics and behavior. For instance, males, particularly the alpha dogs, have a tendency to be overconfident and that could make them more susceptible to imprudent decision-making during times of market turbulence.[46] It also leads to excessive trading, which tends to do more harm than good. Yet, generally speaking, young, old, rich, poor, and even the successful business types all alike have bad wiring. You need to be a little detached, unemotional, and disciplined when investing in order to avoid the irrational behavior that comes with the territory....

☞ "Bulls make money, bears make money, pigs get slaughtered." – Wall Street maxim

☞ "Obviously the stock market is quite irrational in thus varying its valuation of a company proportionately with the temporary

---

46 Jar Ritter, "Behavioral Finance," *Pacific-Basin Finance Journal* 11, no. 4 (September 2003).

changes in its reported profits . . . it would seem that its errors should afford profitable opportunities to the more logically minded to buy common stocks at the low prices occasioned by temporarily reduced earnings and to sell them at inflated levels created by abnormal prosperity." – Benjamin Graham and David Dodd, *Security Analysis* (1934)

- "The stock market is filled with individuals who know the price of everything, but the value of nothing." – Phillip Fisher

- "You are entitled to your opinion. But you are not entitled to your own facts." – commonly attributed Daniel Patrick Moynihan, former New York State senator

- "Opinions are the cheapest commodities on earth." – Napoleon Hill, *Think and Grow Rich* (1937)

- "Rhetoric is cheap, evidence comes more dearly." – John Fund, American political journalist

- "Conventional wisdom is an oxymoron." – Anonymous

As a cautionary tale, know that just weeks before the stock market crashed in October 1929, Irving Fisher, a prominent Yale economist, assured the nation that, "Stock prices have reached what looks like a permanently high plateau." Many accepted this on face value, and it certainly did not serve them well.

Engrain this notion in your head – rationalizing the unsustainable is a dangerous proposition. This is another takeaway from the aforementioned Fischer anecdote. The economic speedster from the 'roaring twenties' ran out of gas, as will all future periods of robust growth. There are laws of financial gravity that cannot be denied. What goes up often must ultimately come down. It's all just a matter of time. Another example: many tried to convince themselves that technology stocks with no earnings and outrageous valuations would continue their uninterrupted ascension in the late 1990's, which was a costly mistake. Their spectacular rise and fall is best illustrated through the movement of the NASDAQ index; note that this tech-heavy index has yet to return to its March 2000 peak....

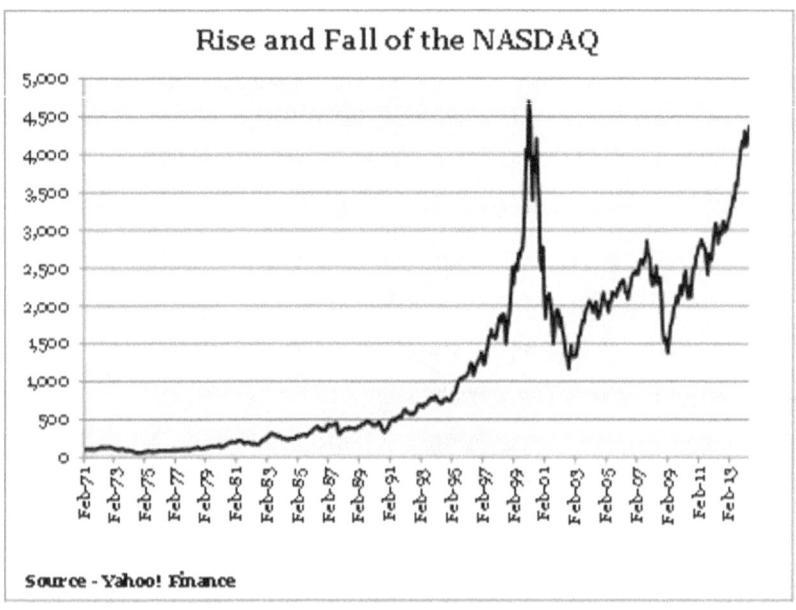

Rise and Fall of the NASDAQ

Source - Yahoo! Finance

⊕ "The four most dangerous words in investing: 'it's different this time.'" – Sir John Templeton

It is a much more comfortable position to be in the majority, not the minority. This is true in most walks of life, with the investment business being no exception. Asset managers that go out on a limb with a particular position are on the clock. If they aren't proven correct in a short amount of time, their business, reputation, and professional careers will be put in jeopardy. Thus, siding with the majority is the path of least resistance....

⊕ "Worldly wisdom teaches that it is better for reputation to fail conventionally than to succeed unconventionally." – John

Maynard Keynes, *The General Theory of Employment, Interest and Money* (1936)

⌾ "Many portfolio managers in large investment companies face a tough choice if they don't follow the herd: they have to choose between a prudent strategy of avoiding big risks or following the herd and accepting those risks. Separating from the herd may sacrifice a year or two of the great returns earned by their competitors. The joy at seeing that they may eventually be right is more than offset by the risk of losing their jobs because of below-average earnings during the interim. Their incentives lead them to act in their own interest, not in the interest of their investors." – Allan H. Meltzer, American economist and professor at Carnegie Mellon University (August 2007)

⌾ "It has been more profitable for us to bind together in the wrong direction than to be alone in the right one." – Nassim Taleb, *The Black Swan: The Impact of the Highly Improbable* (2007)

⌾ "In any great organization it is far, far safer to be wrong with the majority than to be right alone." – John Kenneth Galbraith

⌾ "By far the biggest problem for professionals in investing is dealing with career and business risk: protecting your own job as an agent. The second curse of professional investing is over-management caused by the need to be seen to be busy, to be earning your keep. The individual is far better-positioned to wait patiently for the right pitch while paying no regard to what others are doing, which is almost impossible for professionals." – Jeremy Grantham (2012)

We are not infallible, nor are the many lessons espoused in this book. In light of that, a premium should be placed on humility and pragmatism. Don't overestimate your abilities, know your limitations, and steer clear of ventures that are outside your skill set. Similarly, learn from the mistakes and hubris of others. Excessive pride is been an overarching theme in the demise of many once-fabled institutions, such as Long Term Capital Management and Lehman Brothers....

- ✆ "Blessed is he who expects nothing, for he shall never be disappointed." – Alexander Pope, 18th century English poet

- ✆ "You will be much more in control if you realize how much you are not in control." – Antonio Damasio, professor of neuroscience

- ✆ When asked which single book he would take with him to a desert island, William F. Buckley, Jr. was said to respond "a book on shipbuilding."

- ✆ "It ain't what you don't know that gets you into trouble. It's what you know for sure that just ain't so." – attributed to Mark Twain

- ✆ "I'm only rich because I know when I'm wrong." – George Soros

- ✆ "There are two kinds of people who lose money: those who know nothing and those who know everything." – Henry Kaufman, economist

- ✆ "One of the greatest pieces of economic wisdom is to know what you do not know." – John Kenneth Galbraith

- ✆ "Investors should invest in what they know. The biggest mistake is to invest on what they don't know." – Mohamed El-Erian, former CEO and co-chief investment officer of PIMCO

- ✆ "He who knows not and knows that he knows not is a wise man." – Anonymous

- "It's frightening to think that you might not know something, but more frightening to think that, by and large, the world is run by people who have faith that they know exactly what's going on." – Amos Tversky, cognitive psychologist

- "Unlike dice, markets are subject not merely to risk, an arithmetic concept, but also to the broader uncertainty that shadows the future generally." – Roger Lowenstein, *When Genius Failed* (2000)

Of course, there is a counter-argument. Maybe being a little cocky and self-assured will work out….

- "Modesty is a vastly overrated virtue." – John Kenneth Galbraith

OVERTIME...

Emotions Barometer

Specific catalysts for market disruptions are nearly impossible to predict. It's hard to figure precisely when a dictator will want to advance his military agenda, or when a really rotten earnings announcement will make investors question the market at large. Yet, we do know the odds of a market downturn are higher after bouts of complacency. Fortunately, there is some science to tracking investor emotions, courtesy of Professor Robert Whaley and the Chicago Board Options Exchange. Launched in 1993, the VIX tracks short-term implied volatility in the S&P 500. The VIX's official name is the Chicago Board Options Exchange Market Volatility Index. That's quite the mouthful. Hence, it is often referred to simply as the 'fear gauge.' The index has a long-term average of approximately 20, and a contrarian might construe a value below this level indicative of widespread complacency, or even greed, and treat it as a sell signal. Conversely, elevated values tend to occur during times of market panic, as happened during the credit crisis. Don't treat the VIX as an automatic trigger, as it can stay at subdued or elevated levels for extended periods (months or even years). Further, it should not be your only tool when formulating an investment thesis. However, it does offer a way to quantify investor sentiment, which can be valuable in the battle of behavioral finance, and the VIX can warn investors when market volatility may be about to rear its ugly head.

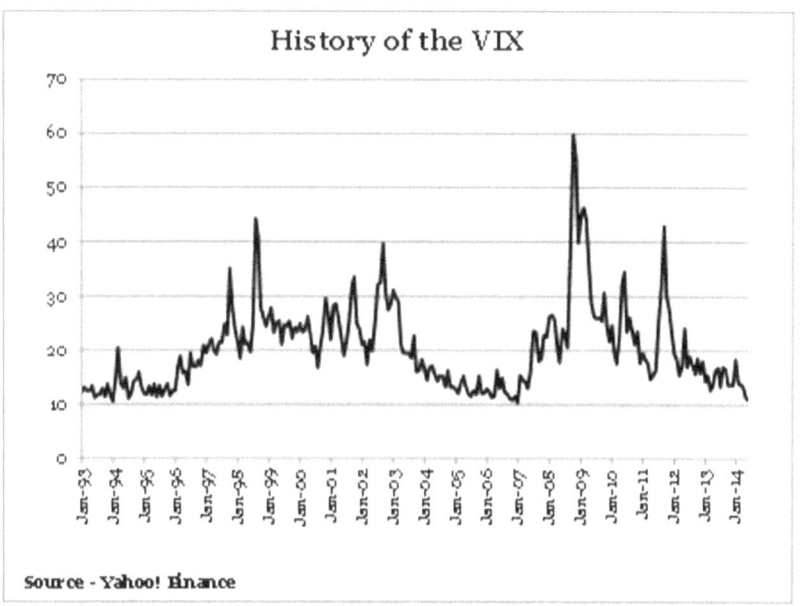

History of the VIX

Source - Yahoo! Finance

A Menu of Biases

We are subject to a number of biases that can impact our investment decision-making. Thus, having a detailed list can bring some self-awareness and hopefully prove valuable on the investing front:

⚉ Overconfidence bias or the *Lake Wobegon Effect*: We have a natural tendency to believe we have superior abilities in many facets of life. About 80 percent of people, group after group, rate themselves "above average" as friends, conversationalists, drivers, or dancers, and in having a good sense of humor, good judgment, and being trustworthy.[47]

 ⚉ *Investment implication: overconfidence can lead to insufficient due diligence, which goes against the core principle of rigor. More*

---

47 Charles Ellis, "Murder on the Orient Express: The Mystery of Underperformance," *Financial Analysts Journal* 68, no. 4 (July/August 2012).

specifically, we underestimate risk and only consider a few possible scenarios of what could go wrong.

⊕ We also tend to overvalue what we own, which is called the *Endowment Effect.*

    ⊕ *Investment implication: seen most regularly and vividly in the real estate market when we value our primary residence for more than what the market will bear. It's not necessarily a bad thing to hold out for premium pricing, but opportunity costs can mount.*

⊕ The *Availability Bias* occurs when rational individuals act irrationally due to recent and traumatic events.

    ⊕ *Investment implication: We are predisposed to focus on the here and now. For instance, many investors sold equities in the aftermath of the 2008 global credit crisis, despite generational low valuations. What is viewed as permanent in the innately cyclical markets and economy is always temporary.*

⊕ As Isaac Asimov said, "All things being equal, you root for your own sex, your own culture, your own locality." Unsurprisingly, we tend to have a *Home Bias* when it comes to investing, which is a disproportionate allocation to companies close to your residence. For example, an academic study from the late 1980s showed that although Sweden possessed a capitalization that only represented about one percent of the world's market value of equities, Swedish investors put their money almost exclusively into domestic investments.[48] The *Home Bias* can breed a level of complacency and produce structural concentrations, inviting risk along the way.

---

48 "Home Bias," *Investopedia*, accessed August 3rd, 2014, http://www.investopedia. com/terms/h/homebias.asp.

☞ *Investment implication: we tend to be systemically underinvested to foreign assets. This can unnecessarily leave return and diversification opportunities off the table.*

Americans are not immune to the *Home Bias,* particularly when it comes to fixed income. As of December 31, 2010, American investors allocated 72 percent of their equity holdings to stocks domiciled in the United States, while the U.S. represented 43 percent of global stock market capitalization. For bond investors, the study found a 60 percent gap between Americans' allocation to domestic bonds and the United States' share of the global fixed income market.

☞ Another one is the *Status Quo* bias, or a preference for the current state of affairs.

Source: Chris Phillips, "For many investors, there's no place like home," *Vanguard* (September 6th, 2012)

☞ *Investment implication: this can create investor inertia. Notably, studies have shown many instances of no asset allocation changes over the lifetime of retirement plan participants. This is a bit alarming, as asset allocation should become progressively more conservative as your time horizon shrinks.*

☞ *Hindsight Bias* creates a false sense that the world is more predictable than it really is. When the past seems less random in the rearview mirror, it may lead to an under-appreciation of what risk the future might bring.

☞ *Investment implication: Bernie Madoff's fraud, the housing market collapse, Enron, and the list goes on and on. Sometimes the unthinkable happens and this can lead to financial ruin.*

- *Myopic Loss Aversion* is a phenomenon where investors tend to weigh short-term losses more heavily than potential gains, even when they are expected to stay invested for the long term.[49]

    - *Investment implication: don't feel ashamed to cut your losses. To do otherwise is to let emotions get in the way of logic. Further, for some, realized losses can create a tax benefit.*

- People become more confident and self-assured *after* they make a bet than immediately *before*, according to a study done by Canadian psychologists[50].

    - *Investment implication: due diligence does not and should stop once you buy something and have real skin in the game.*

- The *Social Proof* principle states that we look to what others do or say in order to determine what we think is correct. To repeat a point from an earlier section: we are innate imitators, not initiators.

    - *Investment implication: this helps explains the new turnover paradigm – when besieged with news items and opinion pieces, we are predisposed to act.*

- The *Confirmatory Bias* is the tendency to ignore information that is contrary to your opinion.

    - *Investment implication: there is real downside when we fail to consider material factors that influence pricing.*

---

49   Shlomo Benartzi and Richard Thaler, "Myopic Loss Aversion and the Equity Premium Puzzle," *National Bureau of Economic Research, Asset Pricing Program* (May 1993).
50   Business World, *What You Can Do In Bubbles,* January 31, 2014

Bubbles, Manias, and the Inevitable Crash

Bubbles (of the investment variety) are the intersection of fantasy and finance. They occur when prices rise for no apparent reason, or when there's a sharp increase in the value of an investment fueled by grandiose visions of quick, outsized returns. Bubbles are not a new phenomenon, as they have a history going back centuries. The Dutch Tulip Bulb craze, which took place from 1634 to 1637, is generally considered the first speculative bubble in modern history. At their peak, tulip bulbs were valued as much as ten times the annual income of a skilled craftsman and a single bulb could change hands close to ten times a day.[51] Initially, bubbles are often somewhat grounded in economic reality, but then greed takes over and sends prices to an unsustainable level. At this point, bubbles typically collapse under the own weight, leaving financial hardship in their wake....

⚲ "the term bubble should indicate a price that no reasonable future outcome can justify. I believe that tech stocks in early 2000 fit this description. I don't think there were assumptions – short of them owning the GDP of the Earth – that justified their valuations." – Cliff Asness, co-founder of AQR Capital, "My Top 10 Peeves," *CFA Institute* (2014)

---

51   Michael G. Pento, *The Coming Bond Market Collapse: How to Survive the Demise of the U.S. Debt Market* (Hoboken, NJ: Wiley, 2013).

Not all bubbles are created equal. For instance, the late 1990's 'tech' bubble, even though it created financial suffering for many, deployed capital that led to enduring, impactful innovations in tele-communications and other technology. On the other hand, the 17th century tulip bulb bubble only left in its wake a number of individu-als with overpriced flowers. Bubbles come in different forms, but the overarching thread is that they are effectively pyramid schemes, with early investors deriving profits from those late to the game. They also exhibit exponential and viral growth among the euphoric masses until their ultimate demise caused by unsustainable and excessive valuations….

- "It is not crowds, but mobs, greed, and excessive liquidity that create bubbles." – Barton Biggs, *Diary of a Hedgehog* (2012)

- "I define a speculative bubble as a situation in which the news of price increases spurs investor enthusiasm, which spreads by psychological contagion from person to person, in the process amplifying stories that might justify the price increases and bringing in larger and larger class of investors, who, despite doubts about the real value of investment, are drawn to it partly through envy of others' successes and partly through a gambler's excitement." – Robert Shiller, *Irrational Exuberance* (2005)

- "all three elements of a classic asset bubble that we have dis-cussed: massive oversupply, an unsustainably high price level, and ownership of the asset class in question." – Michael G. Pento, *The Coming Bond Market Collapse: How to Survive the Demise of the U.S. Debt Market* (2013)

- "but the real disasters in life begin when you get what you want." – Irving Kristol, *Pornography, Obscenity, and the Case for Censorship* (1971)

- "History cautions that people experiencing long periods of relative stability are prone to excess." – Alan Greenspan, testimony to Senate Banking, Housing and Urban Affairs Committee (February 16th, 2005)

- "The first lesson of economics is scarcity: there is never enough of anything to fully satisfy all those who want it. The first lesson of politics is to disregard the first lesson of economics." – Thomas Sowell, *Is Reality Optional? and Other Essays* (1993)

> The way to think about meteoric rises in the asset classes is that it tends to cannibalize future performance. This train of thought is of the same vein as trying to avoid being a linear thinker and extrapolating out recent market actions.

- "To be a great wealth manager, you need to err on the side of prudence and forego the big returns that sometimes come from speculating on bubbles." – Paul Strebel, chair of the Board of Directors at IMD, the Lausanne-based business school

- "Men, it has been well said, think in herds. It will be seen that they go mad in herds, while they only recover their senses slowly, and one by one." – Charles Mackay, *Extraordinary Popular Delusions and the Madness of Crowds* (1841)

- "Insanity in individuals is something rare – but in groups, parties, nations, and epochs it is the rule." – Friedrich Nietzsche, *Beyond Good and Evil* (1886)

- "What the wise man does in the beginning, the fool does in the end." – old proverb

- "I do not believe in the collective wisdom of individual ignorance." – Thomas Carlyle, 19th British historian and essayist

☞ "I've searched all the parks in all the cities — and found no statues of Committees." – G.K. Chesterton

☞ "The big money in booms is always made first by the public – on paper. And it remains on paper." – Edwin LeFevre, *Reminiscences of a Stock Operator* (1923)

The unraveling of a bubble can be abrupt and violent. While bubbles are typically years in the making, once the fault lines appear, the burst can be swift and last a mere matter of weeks or months. Case in point is the -22 percent return for the S&P 500 in the 4th quarter of 2008, during the eye of the storm of the credit crisis. The S&P 500 delivered positive returns in the preceding five calendar years (2003 – 2007) and lulled many investors into a false sense of comfort. Thus, investors need to always be on the lookout for symptoms of bubbles and have a quick trigger finger. Otherwise, the bursting of a bubble can hit you like a ton of bricks….

☞ "Whatever the reason (and it is unimportant), the absolute certainty, as earlier observed, is that the world ends not with a whimper but with a bang."[52] – John Kenneth Galbraith, *A Short History of Financial Euphoria* (1990)

How do you know when you are in a bubble? If you look around, you can usually see some clues. The following provides some

Interestingly, the 2000's was a worse decade for domestic stocks than the 1930's, the Great Depression decade. In the 2000's, the annualized total return for the S&P 500 was -1.2 percent, compared to -0.8 percent during the 1930's, even though from 1929 through 1939 real GDP contracted 32 percent from peak to trough. Putting in perspective, during the recent 'Great Recession' (2008-2009), GDP fell only four percent.

---

52 "This is the way the world ends / This is the way the world ends / This is the way the world ends / Not with a bang but a whimper." – T. S. Eliot, "The Hollow Men," (1925)

context of the mood right before the market crash that preceded the Great Depression….

☞ "Taxi drivers told you what to buy. The shoeshine boy could give you a summary of the day's financial news as he worked with rag and polish. An old beggar who regularly patrolled the street in front of my office now gave me tips and, I suppose, spent the money I and others gave him in the market. My cook had a brokerage account and followed the ticker closely. Her paper profits were quickly blown away in the gale of 1929." – Bernard Baruch, personal memoirs

☞ "When the time comes that a shoeshine boy knows as much as I do about what is going on in the stock market . . . it's time for me to get out." – Joseph Kennedy, father of JFK and RFK

The fallout from bubbles is surely unpleasant. Sadly, the carnage is not quarantined to investment results either: there is a societal impact. When the bubble bursts there is a tendency for crime and even suicide rates to increase. Further, the financial decimation from the bursting of bubbles is often disproportionately felt by the Main Street investor. They are too often blindsided and rudderless when the bubble bursts. They typically don't have the bankroll to pay for good investment counsel. This means that they are the last ones to hear about the ballooning asset prices and consequently participate in only a modest fraction of the upside. This can prove crippling to the finances of those who live paycheck to paycheck. It's a sad state of affairs, with the little guy generally getting the worst of it.

One upshot of bubbles bursting is the purging of bad characters. When bubbles pop, fraudsters tend to be exposed. A lot of fraudulent schemes are predicated on rising markets. Thus, when markets come crashing down, the veil is lifted on some of the unscrupulous characters in the industry. For instance, it should come as no surprise that the notorious Bernie Madoff had his mammoth Ponzi scheme exposed in the wake of the global credit crisis. Further, litigation is another salient characteristic of market collapses, not just to bring justice to the bad actors, but to also try through the force of the law to recover some of what the markets and the unwitting asset managers have taken away. The gloves come off when people feel swindled. It's a truism that we live in a litigious society, but this is taken to new heights when mixed with the emotional side of finance.

We also might be staring down the barrel of another financial crisis. Let's just hope we can address the high debt levels issued by many governments before an actual crisis....

> ☞ "Only a crisis – actual or perceived – produces real change."
> – Milton Freidman, *Capitalism and Freedom* (1962)

Participating in bubbles is dangerous, but very tempting given the allure of easy profit. There is the risk of permanent capital loss if investors don't proceed with caution when a bubble begins to form. This may be avoidable if you have price discipline and a lot of patience. Value investors may be best situated for sidestepping bubbles as they, by their very nature, refuse to pay an inordinate premium for an asset. Yet, it may be emotionally trying, as the bursting of a bubble may occur well after the point of reason. In fact, many thought Warren Buffett had lost his touch as he steered clear of the technology names that ran up to unimaginable heights in the late 1990's. The market came crashing down starting in March 2000, vindicating his prudence. Yet, the social pressures can be weighty. Greed and herd behavior can call your thinking into question. That's what makes well-refined self-awareness and a well-tuned investment process so invaluable. Further, do know that surgical precision on an exit is highly improbable. Thus, don't be too afraid to take some chips off the table and cash out early....

> ☞ "I made my money by selling too soon." – attributed to Bernard Baruch

Not everyone loses when the bubble bursts – John Paulson (more on him in the biography section at the end of the book) can attest to that notion. In fact, the Paulson Credit Opportunities fund delivered an astounding return of 589 percent in 2007. There will be casualties, but it also cleanses some of the excess from the markets and can foster helpful change....

- ☞ "Nothing is born nor destroyed, but things that exist are combined then separated again." – Anaxagoras, ancient Greek philosopher

- ☞ "Nothing is lost, nothing is created, everything is transformed." – Antoine Lavoisier, paraphrased from *Traité Élémentaire de Chimie* (1789)

THE SOVEREIGN DEBT BUBBLE

"The era of big government is over."
– Bill Clinton, State of the Union address (January 23rd, 1996)

There is a lot of rhetoric about a bond bubble being caused by excessive debt issuance, quantitative easing (asset purchases by the Central Bank), and general fiscal irresponsibility by many developed countries, including the United States. The thought is that the laws of supply and demand will ultimately deliver a punishing blow to holders of sovereign debt.…

- "It is incumbent on every generation to pay its own debts as it goes. A principle which if acted on would save one-half the wars of the world." – Thomas Jefferson, a letter to Antoine Louis Claude Destutt de Tracy (December 26th, 1820)

- "It must, indeed, be one of these two events; either the nation must destroy public credit, or public credit will destroy the nation." – David Hume, philosopher, Essay IX: Of Public Credit (1752)

- "Boom-bust processes, or bubbles, are more commonly associated with leveraging of debt rather than equity leveraging." – George Soros, *The New Paradigm for Financial Markets: The Credit Crisis of 2008 and What It Means* (2008)

- "The Treasury secretary told us that we are going to solve the problem of too much debt and too much consumption with more debt and more consumption; that is like telling Tiger Woods you get another girlfriend and that will solve your problems or five more girlfriends to solve your problems." – Jim Rogers, CNBC interview (December 10th, 2009)

☞ "All crises have involved debt that, in one fashion or another, has become dangerously out of scale in relation to the underlying means of payment." – John Kenneth Galbraith, *A Short History of Financial Euphoria* (1990)

☞ "The worst loans are made in the best of times. The best loans are made in the worst of times" – Anonymous

☞ "When people go into the market and purchase with money which they hope to receive hereafter . . . . At periods of this kind a great extension of credit takes place. Not only do all whom the contagion reaches employ their credit much more freely than usual; but they really have more credit, because they seem to be making unusual gains; but they really have more credit, because they seem to be making unusual gains, and because a generally reckless and adventurous feeling prevails, which disposes people to give as well as take credit more largely than at other times, and give it to persons not entitled to it." – John Stuart Mill, *Principles of Political Economy* (1848)

The innate problem is that it is our elected officials are incentivized to spend, not cut. Austerity is typically not the path to re-election. Sadly, we need some fiscal sanity, and that will be in short supply until the basic legislative foundation has been re-worked....

> A typical bubble is fueled by greed, which makes this current bond bubble a curious case, as the upside is limited given generational low yields.

☞ "There is no new paradigm; through-out history, nations have never printed their way to prosperity. This time is no exception." – Michael G. Pento, *The Coming Bond Market Collapse: How to Survive the Demise of the U.S. Debt Market* (2013)

◈ "A billion here, a billion there, and pretty soon you're talking real money." – attributed to Everett Dirksen, former Senate Republican leader

◈ "In this present crisis, government is not the solution to our problem. Government is the problem." – Ronald Reagan, Inaugural Address (January 20th, 1981)

◈ "You and I, as individuals, can, by borrowing, live beyond our means, but for only a limited period of time. Why, then, should we think collectively, as a nation, we are not bound by the same limitation?" – Ronald Reagan, Inaugural Address (January 20th, 1981)

Some view the curing of the debt burden as a moral imperative. We don't want to saddle our future generations with a smothering debt that they were not responsible for....

The return on investment for debt issued in the United States has been on the decline over the past few decades. In other words, GDP growth has not kept pace with the increase in our debt burden. It would be interesting if we could treat the government like a publicly traded stock. My hunch is that it would be a terrific shorting candidate. Quite frankly, if the U.S. was subject to GAAP (generally accepted accounting principles) accounting, it would be deemed bankrupt.

◈ "the principle of spending money to be paid by posterity, under the name of funding, is but swindling futurity on a large scale." – attributed to Thomas Jefferson, paraphrase of a statement made in a letter to John Taylor (1816)

There is a long history of stretching the purse strings in the United States. The Louisiana Purchase in 1803 was financed with an $11.25 million loan, at a time when the federal budget was around $4 million. Further, there is precedent for bond market upheaval in the United States....

♔ "The United States itself had a checkered history of honoring debts, with many of the states having defaulted throughout the nineteenth century." – Dani Rodrik, *The Globalization Paradox: Democracy and the Future of the World Economy* (2012)

Yet, as the moment, with still generational low rates, the dreaded 'bond vigilantes' have yet to arrive to enforce fiscal discipline. In other words, with bond prices still high, the United States has gotten away with their largesse. That could change abruptly if you don't do what the bond vigilantes want. For instance, Greece, a famously leveraged economy, failed to take any actions to address their debt stock, such as enacting pension reform. It sounds made-up, but workers in any field, regardless of how arduous their profession was, could retire at age 55 (50 for women) and start to collect a pension. It was too good to be true, and the bond vigilantes finally ushered in the corrective process.

Greece failed to proactively put a governor on their debt issuance. The result was a spike in the rate on their 10-year debt from under six percent to over 35 percent from the start of 2010 to the end of 2011. The moral of the story is that bond vigilantes can quickly send rates soaring....

♔ "I used to think if there was a reincarnation, I wanted to come back as the President or the Pope or a .400 baseball hitter. But now I want to come back as the bond market. You can intimidate everyone." – James Carville, Bill Clinton campaign strategist (1993)

Part of the reason the United States government has been able to continue their ways is because they are not alone in their largesse. Many developed economies in Europe and Japan have been gorging on debt as well....

⚘ "If Europe today accounts for just over 7 per cent of the world's population, produces around 25 percent of global GDP and has to finance 50 per cent of global social spending, then it's obvious that it will have to work very hard to maintain its prosperity and way of life." – Angela Merkel, German Chancellor (December 2012)

On the other hand, there are those who defend the use of debt even if it is a staggering sum....

⚘ "Our national debt after all is an internal debt owed not only by the Nation but to the Nation. If our children have to pay interest on it they will pay that interest to themselves. A reasonable internal debt will not impoverish our children or put the Nation into bankruptcy." – Franklin Delano Roosevelt, speech (May 22nd, 1939)

Further, the United States, like Japan (but unlike members of the European Union), has its own currency, which creates the ability to inflate its way out of its fiscal troubles. This can keep the bond vigilantes at bay for some time....

⚘ "Both the S&P and its competitor Moody's downgraded Japan in 2002, at a time when the Japanese economy's situation resembled that of the United States in 2011, and nothing at all happened." – Paul Krugman, *End This Depression Now!* (2012)

OVERTIME....

The Cold Hard Facts

T his may read more like a horror story, but here are some of the alarming truths about the sovereign debt bubble. Keep in mind that there was already a wakeup call on August 5th, 2011 when the United States lost its pristine AAA credit rating with Standard & Poor's, who re-graded the U.S. to AA+:

- In 2011, Social Security, Medicaid and Medicare accounted for 44 percent of the government's $3.7 trillion in expenditures, up from 34 percent in 1990, according to statistics compiled by the government's Bureau of Economic Analysis. There were 40 million people in the U.S. 65 and over, according to the 2010 U.S. Census, the year before the first baby boomers hit retirement age. By 2020, that number will rise to 55 million.

> You can't hide if the debt vigilantes arrive and the U.S. Treasury market sells off. The price of credit is derived, in large measure, from the Treasury yield curve. Bondholders: you should pay attention. While the impact will vary, the credit markets at large will not be immune if Treasury yields spiked.

- According to the Congressional Budget Office, year-over-year government expenditures, adjusted for inflation, have fallen only four times since 1980: 1987, 1993, 2007, and 2010.

- In 2010, the U.S. Social Security fund went cash flow negative for the first time since the early 1980's. The costs of the benefits now exceed the tax collections paid in to the fund. This does not mean that the fund is insolvent, but there is an increased chance that many in the future will receive less than what they paid in.

⊛ According to the U.S. Department of the Treasury, since 1960 Congress has had to "permanently raise, temporarily extend, or revise the definition of the debt limit" 78 times through March 2013.[53] This occurred 49 times under Republican presidents and 29 times under Democratic presidents. Think of the debt ceiling as the limit on United States' credit card.

⊛ By 2030, there will be about two workers per retiree, down from 3.4 workers in 2000, according to the Social Security Administration. If a three-year-old today is taxed at the same rate as today's working population, he will get less than half of the benefits that our current seniors are getting.

⊛ "740 [billion dollars], 750 billion, that's our defense budget. And the defense budget of the other 15 top countries on earth, including Russia and China, combined is 540 [billion]." – Senator Alan Simpson (September 17th, 2012)

⊛ The Federal Reserve's balance sheet has expanded from close to $800 billion in 2008 to approximately $3.84 trillion as of October 31st, 2013. Prior to 2008, their balance sheet was almost entirely U.S. Treasury debt. Now Treasuries comprise only 55 percent of the portfolio. The residual is mainly mortgage-backed securities (34 percent) with federal agency debt securities (1.5 percent) and foreign currency denominated assets (0.6 percent) being the next largest positions, according to the November 2013 Federal Reserve Balance Sheet Quarterly Report. Thus, the Fed has in large part swapped the credit risk of the U.S. government with that of the average homeowner. The latter gets taxed, the

---

53 "Debt limit," *U.S. Department of the Treasury*, last modified March 20, 2014.

former can levy taxes. Arguably, the complexion of the Fed's balance sheet is now a riskier one.

⊙ The ever growing national debt is everyone's problem. It's a contingent liability that if proportionately realized could prove financially crippling to many. This debt obligation comes out to nearly $53,000 if every person living in the U.S., including children and unemployed had to pay a share, according to a 2012 Harvard report.[54]

⊙ On its present course, Medicare and Social Security will consume the entire United States federal budget by around 2040. We are victims of our own success in ways, at least as it relates to advancements in the medical field. The longer we live, the more financial stress we place on the entitlement system.

---

54 Kellie Ryan, "Students produce FY 2012 Annual report of the U.S.A. on debt, revenues and spending," *Harvard University Institute of Politics*, October 16, 2013.

TAXES

―――――――――❧❧❧―――――――――

"Don't tax you. Don't tax me. Tax the fellow behind the tree."
– attributed to Senator Russell B. Long

Taxes are a bitter pill, but an inescapable reality. Taxes have been a common gripe long before the 1913 ratification of the 16th Amendment, often considered the origin of the United States income tax. As unpopular as they may be, they represent a necessary evil as they serve as a funding source for education, infrastructure, and national defense initiatives. They also influence corporate decision making, serve as obvious hunting grounds for topics in the popular media, and impact returns for the taxable investor. In fact, taxable investors in stocks might lose as much as 3.5 percentage points per year to taxes.[55] Taxes may not change the quality of an investment, but they can change the quantity of the result....

- ❧ "The tax on capital gains directly affects investment decisions, the mobility and flow of risk capital . . . the ease or difficulty experienced by new ventures in obtaining capital, and thereby the strength and potential for growth in the economy." – John F. Kennedy (1963)

- ❧ "That the power to tax involves the power to destroy." – Chief Justice John Marshall, *McCulloch v. Maryland* (1819)

―――――――――――

55 David Poterba, "Tax Policy and Corporate Saving," *Brookings Papers on Economic Activity* (1987).

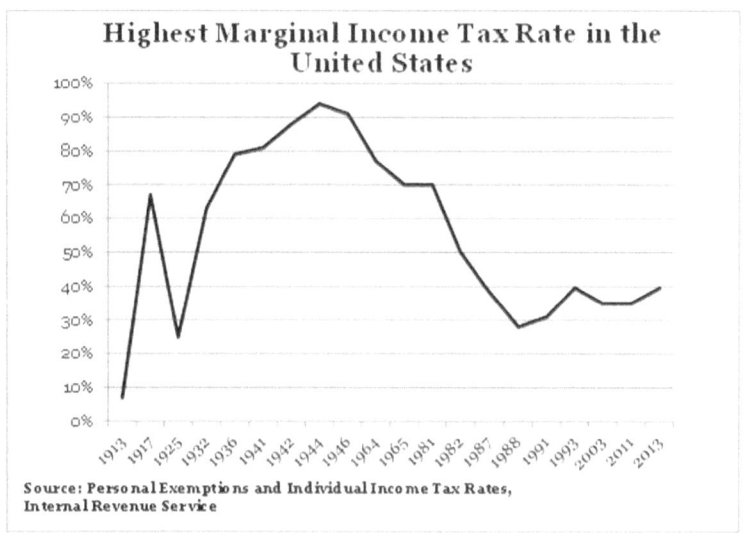

Source: Personal Exemptions and Individual Income Tax Rates, Internal Revenue Service

☞ "whatever you tax, you get less of and if you're taxing the economy, regrettably that's what inevitably happens" – Alan Greenspan, testimony in front of President Bush's Advisory Panel on Federal Tax Reform (March 3ʳᵈ, 2005)

☞ "It's not what you make, it's what you keep." – Anonymous

The goal for all investors should be to think in terms of after-tax results, and minimize the resulting tax liability where possible....

At 60.2 percent (2012 rate), Denmark has the dubious distinction of having the highest top personal income tax rate among the 34 countries in the OECD.

☞ "Any one may so arrange his affairs that his taxes shall be as low as possible: he is not bound to choose that pattern which will best pay the Treasury: there is not even a patriotic duty to increase one's taxes." – *Helvering vs. Gregory* (1935)

☞ "The avoidance of taxes is the only pursuit that still carries any reward." – John Maynard Keynes

❧ "For all long-term investors, there is only one objective – maximum total real return after taxes." – Sir John Templeton

Maximizing after-tax results is easier said than done, as the tax code is decidedly complex. Americans spend countless hours and an estimated $100 billion on tax preparation....

❧ "The hardest thing in the world to understand is the income tax." – attributed to Albert Einstein

Yet, tax complexity or taxes in general should not be a non-starter for a sound investment. If you have a great business idea or investment, you should still pursue it even if your after-tax bounty at the end of the day is less than what you feel is fair....

❧ "Those that can do a good trade don't wrangle over taxes." – Old Chinese proverb

> Think taxes are punitive now? In the 1950's, the top marginal tax rate for individuals in the United States was 91 percent.

Taxes are a natural and inevitable part of our political discourse. Conservatives will argue that taxes hinder economic growth. They cite low tax regimes outside the United States, like Hong Kong, that have commensurately higher economic growth. The pro-tax camp will argue they are a necessary social policy mechanism. In other words: somebody has to fund our schools, military, etc....

❧ "All taxes are a drag on economic growth. It's only a question of degree." – attributed to Alan Greenspan

❧ "Elections should be held on April 16th – the day after we pay our income taxes. That is one of the few things that might discourage politicians from being big spenders." – Thomas Sowell

- "The only difference between a tax man and a taxidermist is that the taxidermist leaves the skin." – attributed to Mark Twain

- "You don't even pay taxes – they take taxes . . . . That's not a payment – that's a jack." – Chris Rock, *Bigger and Blacker* (1999)

- "There is no art which one government sooner learns of another, than that of draining money from the pockets of people." – Adam Smith, *An Inquiry into the Nature and Causes of the Wealth of Nations* (1776)

- "There are two distinct classes of men . . . those who pay taxes and those who receive and live upon taxes." –Thomas Paine, 18th century author and political activist

- "A citizen can hardly distinguish between a tax and a fine, except that the fine is generally much lighter." – G. K. Chesterton

- "Lower rates of taxation will stimulate economic activity and so raise the levels of personal and corporate income as to yield – not a reduced – flow of revenues to the federal government." – John F. Kennedy, speech to Congress (January 1963)

Consider that in 1913, when the income tax was born, the US Tax Code was only 400 pages in length, while today it numbers close to a mind-boggling 74,000 pages, and continues to expand. Tax simplification is a noble endeavor, but it often fails to gain any legislative traction, as it would be such a herculean undertaking. The Tax Code is intimidating to even look at, and is far from a friendly read. It's inherent complexity and daunting length fuel part of the popular rage with taxes in general. Yet, the multitude of deductions and credits embedded in the Tax Code are a latent opportunity for the thoughtful investor or businessman. It can be an asset, but that doesn't stop the masses from viewing it as a liability....

❧ "I would like to electrocute everyone who uses the word 'fair' in connection with income tax policies." – William F. Buckley, Jr.

❧ "[American tax laws] are constantly changing as our elected representatives seek new ways to ensure that whatever tax advice we receive is incorrect." – Dave Barry, Pulitzer Prize winning author and columnist

❧ "The art of taxation consists in so plucking the goose as to obtain the largest amount of feathers with smallest amount of hissing." – Jean-Baptiste Colbert, finance minister for Louis XIV of France in the 17th century

Taxes are a decidedly divisive subject. Nobody likes paying them and it seems as if fairness is so elusive. There is broad consensus that tax cuts can stimulate an economy. Yet, in these days of fiscal instability there's often debate about how to address the reduction in tax revenue....

❧ "Look, I'm very much in favor of tax cuts, but not with borrowed money. And the problem that we've gotten into in recent years is spending programs with borrowed money, tax cuts with borrowed money, and at the end of the day that proves disastrous. And my view is I don't think we can play subtle policy here." – Alan Greenspan, Meet the Press (August 1st, 2010)

❧ "The first truth is that the current tax rates cannot support the promises made to middle-class Americans." – Cliff Asness, *We Are the 98 Percent*, The American (January 7th, 2013)

At the root of the debate is our progressive tax scheme: if you make more, you pay more. This 'Robin Hood' system assesses a higher stated tax rate on higher earners. Consider that in 2009, the top one percent of New York City taxpayers (the 34,598 households making above $493,439 annually) paid 43.2 percent of city income taxes (they made

33.9 percent of income), according to the city's Independent Budget Office. This translated into an average tax bill of $75,477 for these families. Granted, the effective (actual) tax rate for these top one-percenters was less than the stated tax rate, but they do quite a bit of the heavy lifting when it comes to filling the government coffers. The argument is that high taxes are a redistribution mechanism that penalizes success and discourages investment. It also keeps accountants and financial planners gainfully employed, as they offer counsel to those looking to reduce their tax expenditures. Hence, it may not even be the most effective mousetrap for governmental revenues, as high tax rates also incentivize actions to reduce your taxable base. So it may be politics, not math, that are the controlling force behind the design of our tax code....

☞ "In fact, such a flat tax rate, even with no change whatsoever in other features of the law, would yield a higher revenue because a larger amount of taxable income would be reported." – Milton Friedman, *Capitalism and Freedom* (1962)

In order to garner public support for increased taxes on the wealthy, Warren Buffett has famously stated that his tax rate is lower than that of his secretary.[56] Of course, the truth, they say, is always somewhere in the middle. He is afforded such a generous

The *Laffer Curve*, at its core, suggests an inverse relationship between government revenues and tax rates. Essentially, the idea behind it is that elevated tax rates prove counterproductive, as individuals reconstruct their finances to minimize their tax burden. Likewise, a decline in tax rates will increase government revenues, as individuals will have a greater incentive to work and invest, since they keep more of what they earn. The Laffer Curve was named after Arthur Laffer, a member of Ronald Reagan's Economic Policy Advisory Board.

---

56 In 2007, Buffett's tax rate was 17.7 percent, according to N. Gregory Mankiw, "Fair Taxes? Depends What You Mean by 'Fair'," *New York Times*, July 15, 2007.

tax rate because he taketh what the Internal Revenue Service (IRS) Code giveth. His income is made up of largely dividends and capital gains that, ever since the Bush tax cuts (more on this later) have a preferred tax rate compared to regular wages. In 2014, qualified dividends and long-term capital gains had a top federal tax rate of 20 percent. At the same time, salary and compensation for the top earners are taxed at 39.6 percent. You can't blame the Oracle for not subjecting himself to a higher tax rate. You also can't blame him for using his pulpit to present a way to usher in more fiscal discipline to plug the gaping hole in the federal government's finances. However, nowhere in the IRS Code is there a prohibition to give more to the Treasury Department than your computed tax liability. Something for Warren to consider if he feels so obliged.

The corporate tax is another topic that has impact to investors. For instance, higher corporate tax rates can be passed through to consumers in the form of higher prices, or can result in lower dividends or employee wages. The United States has the highest statutory corporate federal income tax rate of developed countries at 35 percent, not to mention any applicable state or local taxes. The effective rate is lower for many corporations that take advantage of the countless corporate tax exemptions. Large, well-staffed U.S. corporations paid an average effective federal tax rate of 12.6 percent in 2010, according to the Government Accountability Office. Not only does the level of taxes matter, but also the fact that not all forms of capital for a company are treated uniformly. In particular, interest deductibility can make debt instruments look more appealing in the eyes of corporate decision makers....

> Assuming no taxes, bankruptcy costs, and perfect information, the value of a firm should not be impacted by its capital structure (i.e. the amount of leverage it assumes). This theory, which was put forth by Franco Modigliani and Merton Miller, is referred to as the *Capital Structure Irrelevance Principle* and helped Modigliani win the 1985 Nobel Prize in Economics.

☞ "The resulting increase in the cost of capital needed to finance new investment will lead to lower capital formation, thereby future output and productivity. An additional distortion resulting from the present law corporate income tax rules is the incentive to finance new investments from debt rather than equity on account of the deductibility of interest payments on debt but no comparable deductions for dividends paid on equity." – Excerpt from Joint Committee on Taxation, *Present Law and Background Relating to Selected Business Tax Issues* (September 16th, 2006)

OVERTIME....

Taxes and Dividends...Not so Fast[57]

U p until about a decade ago, the layered taxation on dividends was perceived as a disincentive for corporations to issue dividends. The earnings which gave rise to dividends were already subject to corporate taxes, and once dividends were paid out to top earners they would be hit with another round of income taxes. Corporate executives, who make decisions on dividend policy, could effectively alleviate their personal tax burden by retaining earnings. The classic example of the time was Microsoft. As long as Bill Gates, who owned a ton of the company's stock, was at the helm the company, they would never issue a dividend.

All this changed with the 2003 Bush Tax Cut legislation, which established a preferred tax rate on dividends. It is thought to have changed the way corporations thought about dividend issuance. In the two years following the cuts, 145 companies initiated dividends, as they were no longer taxed by the recipient at ordinary income rates. However, the evidence is a bit porous on the influence of taxation. Consider that REIT dividend issuance also surged during this period, even though their dividends were not qualified. Also, share repurchases increased at a faster rate than dividends.[58] Importantly, in 2003, corporate earnings were on the rise, as the economy had moved past the 2001 recession. Consequently, corporations were in a better position to issue dividends. Dividends did increase after the legislation, but during a period when earnings accelerated at even faster pace. Therefore, dividend payout ratios did not increase. Further, earnings (EBITDA) and dividend

---

57 Select data used in this vignette sourced from the following: "Buybacks Expected to Increase," *New York Times*, November 28, 2012, and Jesse Edgerton, "Four Facts about Dividend Payouts and the 2003 Tax Cut," *International Tax and Public Finance*, (July 2012).

58 Repurchases were slightly lower than dividends in 2002 but nearly two times higher in 2007.

payouts had close to a perfect positive correlation from 1995 to 2007. Taxes influence corporate decision-making, but are hardly the controlling factor.

Good Turnover

Not all forms of turnover are created equal, and *Tax Loss Harvesting* can be very beneficial to the taxable investor. Think of tax loss harvesting as good turnover; if done well, it can turn lemons (bad investments) into lemonade (better after-tax results). Tax loss harvesting entails selling a security trading at an unrealized loss while simultaneously buying a similar, but substantially different, security during the wash sale period (30 days after the sale). If you happen to violate the wash sale rule, the tax benefit is deferred, which means you cannot immediately use the realized loss to lessen your tax bill. After the wash sale expires, the capital loss is secured, and then the individual re-enters the security that they had initially sold. Unfortunately, there is no official IRS guide telling you what "substantially different" entails, as the potential combination of investments is incalculable. However, if executed effectively, studies show that tax loss harvesting can add up to one percent in performance per annum to results for the taxable investor. In sum, tax loss harvesting can generate a tax benefit with limited slippage to pre-tax performance.

Tax loss harvesting is easier said than done, with gold offering a great case study to support this notion. Gold had a challenging 2013, which likely converted many positions from unrealized gain to loss. There are two popular, very liquid exchange traded funds (tickers IAU and GLD) that give exposure to the price of gold bullion. If a taxable investor was intent on maintaining his gold exposure, the first place to look would be the other aforementioned gold solution. They both have differences in terms of fees, liquidity, and the gold exchange (New York Mercantile vs. London) they are designed to track. Perhaps these differences rise to the level of substantial differentiation, but there is a risk that the IRS would disagree. If you didn't want to roll the dice, you could hold obviously dissimilar investments, like gold miner stocks or even silver bullion. However, these are historically more volatile investments than gold. So, an investor is faced with a choice between the potential disallowance of the tax loss or more unpredictability related to their pre-tax results. This goes to show you that tax-loss harvesting is no free lunch.

GLOBALIZATION

Globalization, the magnetic force that has been integrating the world around us, has had immense implications for investors, citizens, and consumers. Ideas, labor, capital, and technology now move much more seamlessly around the planet, along with a quicker pace of adoption. There are the more vivid, overt examples of globalization's presence, such as people in remote outposts of the globe with smart phones and the corresponding plethora of information at their fingertips. There are also more subtle examples. You now have people eating sushi in South America, or people wearing backwards baseball caps in Southeast Asia. These latter examples may be of lesser consequence for the investor, but the totality of globalization's impact has been profound, as it has resulted in millions of individuals lifted out of poverty and an improved way of life for countless more.

Globalization has also taken corporations to new financial heights, due to their increased ability to access consumers from all corners of the globe. In particular, there is a focus on the developing world, home to over 80 percent of the world's population. Consider that in 2010, of the 226 million new Internet users, an estimated 162 million were from developing markets.[59] It should come as no surprise that roughly 30 percent of the earnings of the big U.S. and European multinationals now come from the developing economies….

ᴄᴐ   "No one has succeeded in turning back the evolution of the world or the force of globalization since Adam and Eve." – James

---

59   International Telecommunications Union, "ITU Estimates Two Billion People Online by End 2010," *International Telecommunications Union*, October 19, 2010.

Wolfensohn, economist and former president of The World Bank (August 1ˢᵗ, 2001)

- "It has been said that arguing against globalization is like arguing against the laws of gravity." – Kofi Annan, former Secretary-General of the United Nations (August 2000)

- "Globalization is best thought of as the growing interconnectedness in the world. It is the result of a series of historical processes (economic, political, and cultural) through which the world has become compressed and which have led to awareness that the world has become a single place." – Ronald Robertson

- "A man's feet should be planted in his country, but his eyes should survey the world." – George Santayana, *Life of Reason* (1905)

There should be some soft-pedaling on the merits of globalization, as there will be winners and losers....

- "globalization of trade, knowledge, innovation, industrialization and entrepreneurial culture is increasing at a rapid rate and the net result is more distribution of wealth and power. A new world order is imminent. The countries that succeed will be those with better socioeconomic policies, more cash, natural resources and creativity. The US can embrace this change and compete or we can resist it and lose." – Med Jones, "Global Economic Outlook 2011," *CEO Quarterly Magazine*, (January 3ʳᵈ, 2011)

- "Where globalization means, as it so often does, that the rich and powerful now have new means to further enrich and empower themselves at the cost of the poorer and weaker, we have a responsibility to protest in the name of universal freedom." – Nelson Mandela, Speech on receiving the Freedom Award from the National Civil Rights Museum (November 2000)

Globalization is also a narrative about convergence as the emerging world closes the standard of living gap with the developed economies. This trend will not occur in an uninterrupted fashion, but it does have legitimacy, with South Korea as a prime exhibit. Goldman Sachs and the World Bank have estimated that by 2020 close to 50 percent of the world's growth will come from emerging economies, and by 2030, about 60 percent (not adjusted for purchasing power parity)....

☞ "Never before have so many people – or so large a proportion of the world's population – enjoyed such large rises in their standard of living." – Martin Wolf, *Why Globalization Works* (2004)

Globalization is not just about more integrated commerce and communications: it has also led to the exportation of political and economic ideologies. Many say that the rise of the emerging world is attributed to the adoption of capitalist principles....

"By almost any economically relevant metric, distances have shrunk considerably in recent decades. As a consequence, economically speaking, Wausau [Wisconsin] and Wuhan [China] are today closer and more interdependent than ever before." – Ben Bernanke, Jackson Hole Speech (August 25th, 2006)

☞ "It's worth pondering the reasons for this Asian reversal, and its implications. One obvious, if too often forgotten, lesson is that the wealth of a nation is not a birthright. Prosperity has to be earned year after year, through sound economic policies that unleash the natural talents of a nation's people." – "Japan as Number Three: Beijing's rise, Tokyo's fall and the Wealth of Nations," *The Wall Street Journal* (August 17th, 2010)

☞ "Globalization is the worldwide extension of capitalism." – Dani Rodrik, *The Globalization Paradox: Democracy and the Future of the World Economy* (2012)

The economic ascension of emerging markets has arguably come at the expense of industrialized nations, like the United States, which could soon render the following quotation irrelevant....

⌖ "When the United States sneezes, the rest of the world catches a cold." – Wall Street adage

The emerging markets' transformation to more significant economic cogs may just be a return to normalcy. The emerging markets may have been economic under-achievers a decade or so ago, but that wasn't always the case. In fact, India and China shared a position as the center of economic gravity for the better part of the last two millennia. Our memory banks instantly regurgitate that the United States and the United Kingdom have been the dominant forces on the global stage ever since the Industrial Revolution took hold. That's true, but prior to that the global economy was more Asia-centric. Now the pendulum may be shifting back to what once was. *Mean Reversion* is Wall Street technical speak for what goes up, most come down and vice versa. This wave of globalization may just be mean reversion on steroids.

This globalization wave is a profound one, with far-reaching effects. Increased global trade, and its corresponding benefits, has been a plot line in this recent wave of globalization. This development may just deliver the biggest bounty. Interestingly, the big winner might be domestic multi-national corporations and their respective investors, as they can now more easily tap into the emerging market consumer segment. This has proven a great way to both diversify and enhance their top-lines (i.e. revenues). Why? The emerging market consumer is typically eager to showcase their newfound wealth and spend, spend, spend. According to a 2012 McKinsey study, annual consumption from the developing economies will grow by more than 300 percent by 2020, to about $30 trillion; double that of the United States. There are many more potential customers outside the U.S. than within its borders, and these potential customers are ready to buy....

⊕ "No nation was ever ruined by trade, even seemingly the most disadvantageous." – Benjamin Franklin & George Whatley, *Principles of Trade* (1774)

⊕ "Free trade is indeed just like technological progress." – attributed to Henry Martyn, 17th-18th century Anglican missionary

⊕ "Globalization and free trade do spur economic growth, and they lead to lower prices on many goods." – Robert Reich, former Sectary of Labor (September 27th, 2005)

⊕ "Under a system of perfectly free commerce, each country naturally devotes its capital and labour to such employments as are most beneficial to each. This pursuit of individual advantage is admirably connected with the universal good of the whole. By stimulating industry, by rewarding ingenuity, and by using most efficaciously the peculiar powers bestowed by nature, it distributes labour most effectively and most economically: while, by increasing the general mass of productions, it diffuses general benefit, and binds together, by one common tie of interest and intercourse, the universal society of nations throughout the civilized world." – David Ricardo, *The Principles of Political Economy and Taxation* (1821)

⊕ "peace, commerce, and honest friendship with all nations, entangling alliances with none." – Thomas Jefferson, first inaugural address (March 4th, 1801)

⊕ "Wouldn't it be a similar waste to employ workers in England if the textiles they produced can be obtained from India by putting fewer people to work?" – Dani Rodrik, *The Globalization Paradox: Democracy and the Future of the World Economy* (2012)

More open trade can help optimize the global economy, according to David Ricardo's *Law of Comparative Advantage*....

☞ "Under a system of perfectly free commerce, each country naturally devotes its capital and labour to such employments as are most beneficial to each. This pursuit of individual advantage is admirably connected with the universal good of the whole. By stimulating industry, by rewarding ingenuity, and by using most efficaciously the peculiar powers bestowed by nature, it distributes labour most effectively and most economically: while, by increasing the general mass of productions, it diffuses general benefit, and binds together, by one common tie of interest and intercourse, the universal society of nations throughout the civilized world."

This isn't entirely rosy. Increased global trade (via trade agreements) does have negative repercussions....

☞ "Trade agreements have other detrimental implications. They discriminate against lower-cost imports from countries that are not part of the treaty." – Michael G. Pento, *The Coming Bond Market Collapse: How to Survive the Demise of the U.S. Debt Market* (2013)

Further, isolationism, or de-globalization, does have some merit, as this dogma helps to keep the fate of a country largely in its own hands. Globalization can lead to the importation of political and economic missteps or sins of other countries....

☞ "The great rule of conduct for us in regard to foreign nations is extending our commercial relations, to have with them as little political connection as possible....Why, by interweaving our destiny with that of any part of Europe, entangle our peace and prosperity in the toils of European ambition, rivalship, interest, humor, or caprice?" – George Washington, Farewell Address (1796)

Globalization does have a shadowy side, particularly as financial capital and corresponding risk has become much more portable and can end up in the wrong hands....

⌨ "The inevitable conclusion is that financial globalization has failed us. Countries that have opened themselves up to international capital markets have faced greater risks, without compensating benefits in the form of higher economic growth." – Dani Rodrik, *The Globalization Paradox: Democracy and the Future of the World Economy* (2012)

⌨ "If financial capital is free to move about, it becomes difficult for any state to tax it or to regulate it because it can move somewhere else." – George Soros, *The New Paradigm for Financial Markets: The Credit Crisis of 2008 and What It Means* (2008)

Similarly, increased labor force mobility, in an effort to improve corporate profit margins, has negative repercussions….

⌨ "but merchants have no country. The mere spot they stand on does not constitute so strong an attachment as that from which they draw their gains." – Thomas Jefferson, letter to Horatio G. Spafford (March 17th, 1814)

⌨ "Reliable data on the outsourcing of American jobs is sorely missing from the debate on globalization." – Congressman Dan Lipinski, *Lipinski Presses for Release of Information on Outsourcing of U.S. Jobs* (April 5th, 2006)

⌨ "some groups will *necessarily* suffer long-term losses in income from free trade. In a wealthy country, such as in the United States, these are likely to be unskilled workers such as high school dropouts. This renders the whole notion of "gains from free trade" suspect, since it is not at all clear how we can decide whether a country *as a whole* is better off when some people gain and some people lose." – Dani Rodrik, *The Globalization Paradox: Democracy and the Future of the World Economy* (2012)

Outsourcing, despite its reputation, has its benefits. For starters, the shifting of labor overseas often results in higher corporate profit margins, which benefits corporate shareholders. Consumers enjoy otherwise lower costs, particularly of manufactured goods. This does come at the expense of lost domestic jobs or shrunken wages. Thus, corporate profit growth does not mean commensurate wage growth. In fact, there can be an inverse relationship between the two in this day of portable labor....

⌨ "Outsourcing and globalization of manufacturing allows companies to reduce costs, benefits consumers with lower cost goods and services, causes economic expansion that reduces unemployment, and increases productivity and job creation. According to the McKinsey Global Institute, for every $1 outsourced, the economic gain to the U.S. as a whole is $1.12 to $1.14." – Larry Elder, "Lou Dobbs to outsourcing: Drop dead," *WND.com* Commentary (March 10th, 2005)

Many countries have not fully participated in this recent wave of globalization. This in some measure is due to the formidability of multinational businesses. Since globalization has broken down many geographic barriers to entry, some foreign businesses have captured the profits that once accrued to domestic companies. Globalization has removed the geographic moat once enjoyed by many businesses....

⌨ "At the onset of the Industrial Revolution, the gap between the richest and poorest regions of the world was of the order of 2:1. Today, the same ratio stands at 20:1. The gap between the richest and poorest country has risen to about 80:1." – Dani Rodrik, *The Globalization Paradox: Democracy and the Future of the World Economy* (2012)

⌨ "Rapid economic globalization is bringing about greater market access and new partners for development, but also putting the weaker economies in a more vulnerable and disadvantageous position, and in an uneven competition." – Phan Van, former Prime Minister of Vietnam

The other blemish, if you can call it that, with globalization is the political instability it can invite. Whether it's the Arab Spring in Egypt or riots in Thailand, oppressive political regimes will not be tolerated for any extended period. There has also been a corresponding rise in revolutions, as well as, unfortunately acts of terrorism, as this wave of globalization has gained steam. Terrorism and revolutions are words that are often mentioned in the same breath. They shouldn't. Unlike terrorism, which is downright unacceptable, there are multiple ways to view revolutions....

☞ "All successful revolutions are the kicking in of a rotten door." – John Kenneth Galbraith, *The Age of Uncertainty* (1977)

☞ "A revolution is an idea which has found its bayonets." – Napoleon Bonaparte

☞ "Revolution requires extensive and widespread destruction, a fecund and renovating destruction, since in this way and only this way are new worlds born." – Mikhail Bakunin, *Statism and Anarchy* (1873)

☞ "Economically considered, war and revolution are always bad business." – Ludwig Von Mises, *Nation, State, and Economy* (1919)

OVERTIME....

The Next Investing Frontier

Investors are always on the lookout for the next big thing. Everyone wants a piece of the next Apple, Google, and the same goes for countries. *Frontier Markets,* which include the likes of Saudi Arabia and Nigeria, are the next generation of Chinas and Indias or so some think. They are a collection of countries that *could* rise to emerging economy status. In that vein, they are kind of like Facebook. There are hundreds of millions of potential customers, but no obvious path to monetization. Yet, while they do not have the market depth or economic might to warrant emerging market status, they now have a blueprint to follow, courtesy of countries such as South Korea. They are an eclectic mix, but many of these countries are rich in natural resources and have a youthful and motivated population, both of which are generally considered ingredients for robust economic growth.

Frontier markets are unified by their potential, but also their unpredictability. Their economic growth rates are volatile and capital market behavior even more so. This is due to questionable rule of law and business dealings, among other factors. This is why the conversation surrounding frontier markets needs to be balanced. As Ben Levishon put it, "frontier markets today are essentially what emerging markets were more than a decade ago – in both positive and negative respects. There's the outsized growth, sure, but that comes with higher-than-average risks. Most frontier-market stocks trade infrequently, are expensive to enter and exit, and come with idiosyncratic factors that can cause markets to plunge or freeze up completely. It's not a bet for the faint of heart – or an easy market to play."[60]

---

60 Ben Levishon, "Braving the Frontier Markets," *Barron's*, February 9, 2013.

Globalization in Reverse

Globalization comes in waves. The first period of globalization started in 1880 and lasted close to 25 years. The most recent wave started around the end of Cold War. The Berlin Wall physically came down, as did many barriers of commerce around the world. Global trade has kicked into high gear as a result. According to data from the Department of Commerce, the United States exported $26 billion and imported $22 billion in goods and services in 1960. In the *month* of June 2011, exports were more than $170 billion and imports exceeded $223 billion, which even far surpasses the 1960 annual results when adjusted for inflation.[61] Overall, global trade has doubled in the last decade, with the GWP (Gross World Product) now over $70 trillion, according to the World Bank.

Corporations have reaped the benefits of globalization as well. For instance, S&P 500 companies are becoming increasingly reliant on revenues from overseas. This gives them an opportunity to both diversify and enhance their revenues. Foreign sales accounted for 34 percent of aggregate revenue for the S&P 500 in 2012, which has almost doubled over the past ten years. Thus, calling the S&P 500 a U.S. index may now be a bit of a misnomer.

In an October 1939 radio broadcast, Winston Churchill described Russia as a "riddle, wrapped in a mystery inside an enigma." Perhaps, but Russia's one-dimensional economy isn't much of an unknown. It lives and dies by the pricing and demand for oil and gas, which account for close to three-quarters of the country's exports.

Given all of the benefits, it is certainly peculiar that globalization has started to abate. There has been evidence of a rise of localism (i.e. "Buy American"), or reverse globalization, as global trade in the past three years has grown at a rate less than that of global economic growth, which last occurred in the 1940's. This may be transitory, as there are

---

61 If adjusted to match 2011 dollars, the 1960 results would be, respectively, 198 billion and 167 billion.

many significant trade pacts in the queue. Notably, the Obama administration is on the verge of a cross-Pacific trade agreement with many Asian countries called the Trans-Pacific Partnership (TPP). It is also pursuing a trade agreement with Europe called the Transatlantic Trade and Investment Partnership (TTIP). These two trade pacts could boost global economic output by $600 billion, equivalent to almost the entire GDP of Switzerland. These agreements may never get to the finish line, but don't let this course correction make you think differently of the positives that have occurred during the recent globalization wave.

False Monikers

The emerging markets are decidedly eclectic. Yet, they have more than their fair share of acronyms and nicknames for certain subsets that falsely make them appear a little more homogenous. Perhaps the most popular is *BRIC*. Jim O'Neil coined this acronym in a 2001 report entitled *Building Better Global Economic BRIC's*. It's short for Brazil, Russia, India, and China, which represent four of the largest emerging countries. They certainly are meaningful economic actors, as in 2010 the BRIC's imported more goods than the United States for the first time ever, according to the International Monetary Fund. Yet, their size, and the acronym itself, might be the only unifying thread, as these four countries have different languages, cultures, and economic drivers.

The nicknames don't stop with the BRIC's. There is The Andean *Pumas* consisting of Colombia, Peru, and Chile, which represent an emerging economic force in Latin America. There are also the *MIPS* (Malaysia, Indonesia, Philippines, and South Africa) and the *MIST* (Mexico, Indonesia, Korea, and Turkey). Lastly, there is the *Fragile Five*, which includes Turkey, Brazil, Indonesia, South Africa, and India. These countries have been awarded this dubious moniker due to their shaky fiscal situations and reliance on foreign capital. There surely will be more nicknames to come, but that doesn't mean that any of the constituents of the emerging market are any less unique in terms of their cultures, resources, or investment opportunities.

CHINA

"Should a people allow its customs to become too firmly rooted, it can no longer change, and becomes like China, incapable of improvement."
– Gustave Le Bon, The Crowd:
A Study of the Popular Mind (1898)

L e Bon's comments may have been true in 1898, and ultimately held true for the subsequent eighty years. However, they have been rendered an anachronism as a result of the Reform Era, a strategic plan to modernize and enhance China's economic standing. This ended their philosophy of economic isolationism, and after decades of economic stasis, China has awoken....

☞ "Let China sleep, for when she awakes she will shake the world." – attributed to Napoleon Bonaparte

"The experience of the last thirty years has taught us: we cannot adopt a closed door policy to develop our economy." – Deng Xiaoping, former Chinese leader

Now, the discussion about globalization goes hand-in-hand with that of the rise of China as an economic force. China has become the face of the emerging markets and their accompanying economic significance. In fact, China may have already 'emerged.' China now stands as the second largest economy on the planet, recently displacing Japan. Its ascension has been swift, with its per-capita GDP climbing from just $517 in 1993 to $6,076 in 2012. China's transformation has not been a ripple, but a wave, and it is changing the center of economic gravity for the globe. With national growth rates that are triple most developed economies for the last decade, and a population of nearly 1.4 billion people, its metamorphosis is profound....

☞ "Just think about it: Today, China is the world's fourth largest economy (second largest in terms of purchasing power), and yet just half a century ago it had abolished private ownership of assets and had the most anti-business policies in the world." – Burton G. Malkiel and Patricia Taylor, *From Wall Street to the Great Wall: How Investors Can Profit from China's Booming Economy* (2008)

China's economic rise has reverberated throughout the globe....

☞ "China's growth this way is different from anything we've seen before, because its economic linkages are much greater than we've seen with previous rising powers." – Odd Arne Westad, *Reading China's future through its past*, China Daily (December 20th, 2013)

☞ "China is the equivalent of a company with revolutionary technology: it has been highly disruptive, destroying competitors while lifting up nations that supply and feed off its growth momentum." – Ruchir Sharma, *Breakout Nations: In Pursuit of the Next Economic Miracles* (2012)

China and the United States have a rather unholy alliance. They buy our debt so we can continue our political largesse. We import their cheap manufactured goods, which keeps their populous gainfully employed. Neither can change their behavior abruptly, as the result would be a matter of mutually assured economic destruction.

This type of exponential growth does have costs. For instance, in order to accommodate its expansive population that is becoming increasingly wealthy, China is making strategic investments of natural resources internationally and exploiting their own domestically. There are negative externalities here, as pollution (more on this soon) and increasing prices for basic staples due to an enlarged appetite from the Chinese may be a new norm. Economic growth at a blistering pace for more than a billion people sounds good, but has a dark side to it.

China's growth has its consequences, and the journey will certainly be choppy as they adjust their sails. This growth story will be interrupted and surely have its naysayers along the way. While it won't be a straight line, its economic ascension is likely to continue….

> ☞ "China alone will probably have the largest economy, surpassing that of the United States a few years before 2030." – U.S. National Intelligence Council (December 10th, 2012)

In the mid-19th century, Horace Greeley, or John B. L. Soule, depending on whom you ask, in support of American expansion, wrote, "Go West, young man, Go West." But, considering China's recent emergence and rapid growth, perhaps it would work better now as "Go east, young man, go east."

It sounds counter-intuitive, but foreign investors may have not fully participated commensurately in this modern day Industrial Revolution. The MSCI China Free Index compounded at an annualized total return (dividends plus appreciation) of 5.0 percent over the past seven years (typical duration of a full business cycle) ending in March 2014. That's not too shabby, but it trails behind any of the country's annual growth rates during this same stretch, including 2008 when the global economy nearly melted down. The index also trailed the S&P 500 by 1.3 percent or roughly 13 percent on a cumulative basis. Further, it only surpassed the Barclays Treasury Index by a meager 0.3 percent, but did so with more than five times the volatility.[62] This gyrating market has certainly not delivered the best return per unit of risk, which points to some flaws,

---

62 Data from Callan Associates' PEP Database.

curious given the context of a macroeconomic boom. It indicates that many Chinese companies have room for improvement, as bottom-line earnings have not kept pace with their top-line potential. In large part, the culprit is underwhelming corporate governance structures. There is an Enron-esque discount typically embedded into Chinese stocks prices that will persist until these companies more closely resemble the, seemingly, more efficient and transparent Western world enterprises.

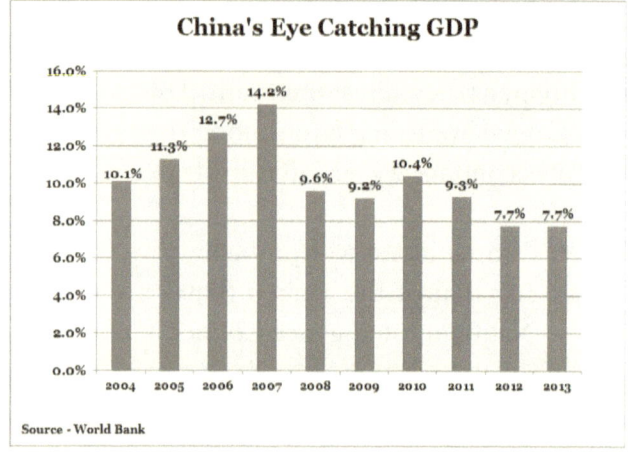

Its underachieving stock market shows that China does have its blemishes. For starters, the cost of conducting business can be more than just financial: just ask foreign businessmen who have been detained by the Chinese government. When operating in China, one needs to keep in mind that it is still, despite its free-market tendencies, a communist country...

   ☞ "Leniency to those who confess, severity to those who resist." – old Communist Party saying

China is just like any company; it has liabilities and assets. On the liability side, its loan growth has been accelerating at an alarming pace of over 100 percent per annum at times in recent years. It is doubtful that these loans were subject to unblemished underwriting, and cumulative debt levels are now reaching worrisome heights. A report by the National Audit Office issued at the end of 2013 said that borrowing by local governments had reached 17.9 trillion Yuan ($2.96 trillion) as of that June, an increase of more than sixty percent from the end of 2010. We have seen this movie before. Debt growing at a faster clip than the general economy can send a country into a malaise when the bill is due.

Things may be heating up in the Chinese corporate sector as well. In early March 2014, corporate China experienced its first bond default ($14.7 million missed interest payment) from a tiny solar panel firm called Shanghai Chaori Solar Energy. The math behind this event is a bit of a rounding error, given that China is a roughly $9 trillion economy. However, what is most interesting is that the government did not intervene. China has endeavored to be a more market-oriented economy, and to do so it means that the government must cut back on its meddling and let corporate failure occur. However, one event does not make a trend, and China does not appear to be a true free-market economy just yet.

China's opaqueness is another liability. It has its fair share of crony capitalism and back door deals that help maintain the status quo for the well-established. Not to mention some of the funny math you see for the country at large. China has yet to build a brand that escapes accusations of being a black box, with official economic statistics subject to manipulation. In fact, even Premier Li Keqiang admitted in 2007 that Chinese GDP data was suspect and said it was "for reference only." Fortunately, there are some clever ways to look through this veil of secrecy and get a better handle on the country's economic trajectory. For instance, electricity or power consumption data can be quite telling and also difficult to manipulate. This public information is readily available for the studious investor.[63]

China will also have to confront the law of large numbers, which stipulates that as company or economy grows it becomes increasingly more difficult to maintain the same level of past growth. For example, 10 percent growth is more difficult to achieve with a $100 billion market capitalization company, as compared to one at $100 million. China is no exception to the rule....

> ☞ "China's economy has grown rapidly over the past decade to make it the second-largest in the world. But at some point in the

---

63 To see this data, go to http://www.stats.gov.cn/english/.

economic development trajectory, the size of an economy starts to impede its growth, and it appears that China may be finding it difficult to grow its larger economic base at a higher sustained level." – Sean Lynch, Wells Fargo Wealth Management (July 18th, 2013)

China also took rather drastic measures to curtail its population growth. Its infamous 'one child policy' enacted in 1979 has distorted the demographic complexion of the country and this profound exercise in central planning has led to some unintended consequences....

☞ "The aging of the population will put pressure on the working class to increase its productivity, in order to support all those new retirees, and the shrinking labor pool will put pressure on businesses to raise wages." – Ruchir Sharma, *Breakout Nations: In Pursuit of the Next Economic Miracles* (2012)

Yet, on the other side of the ledger, China possesses a number of assets. For starters, it has a considerable population of over 1.3 billion, which is becomingly increasingly educated. That's a lot of economic lottery tickets. As we have seen, even one person can prove transformative to an economy. Just think of the impact of Thomas Edison, Henry Ford, or Bill Gates. China is increasing its odds of having one or a few of these luminaries in their populous helping to re-write their economic narrative for the better. Moreover, China's citizens are increasingly motivated courtesy of social media and increased access to television. They now see the way the Western world lives, and are envious. That's one potent asset to have: millions and millions of people who are hitting the books and eager to improve their way of life.

China's has also accumulated a significant trade surplus due to its successes as an export-centric economy. Their currency reserves now have a value close to two trillion dollars, in large measure due to their manufacturing prowess. It's hard to bet against a country with this kind of lever to pull. However, China will have to address their overzealous real estate and infrastructure investments. This was popularized in a 2013 *60 Minutes* segment that showed the extent of China's vacant commercial and residential complexes. It wasn't just a few empty homes here and there. Not just ghost towns, but ghost *cities* have been created. These excesses need to be said in the same breathe as their massive currency surplus. Their real estate binge could be incendiary, but their currency reserves could help put out the flames.

The verdict on China is still out and may not be issued any time soon, but you'll have plenty of economic theatre to enjoy along the way. China's economic model blends authoritarian and capitalist tenets. It's certainly a unique concoction, not to mention the mammoth proportions of this market: China's economy alone accounts for 15.4 percent of global GDP.[64] Thus, China's economic results will weigh mightily on the global economy. That's what makes this economic experiment interesting, exciting, and even a bit frightening....

☞ "We have seen the future, and it is China." – paraphrase of Lincoln Steffens, turn of the 20th century American journalist

---

64 "World Economic Outlook," *International Monetary Fund,* April 2014.

OVERTIME....

China: Math 101

The math associated with a country that is home to over a billion people is just unbelievable. Here is a laundry list of facts and statistics that illustrates the staggering influence of China and its citizens:

⊛ In 2010, China purchased roughly 6.3 million *more* vehicles than the United States.[65] This is a remarkable turn of events for a country in which the bicycle was a cultural icon and aspirational product as recently as the 1980's.

⊛ The Chinese consumer does love to shop. Historically, Chinese consumers shop almost five times more often than their US counterparts, though this number has been decreasing, recently.[66] In addition, in 2012, former Chinese Commerce Minister Chen Deming predicted that China could become the world's largest consumer market by 2015.[67]

⊛ By 2025, China will have more than 221 cities with populations of more than one million people each.[68] There are currently only nine cities in the United States with a million or more people.

⊛ Despite its shortage of arable land, agriculture is still a vital industry in China. According to a February 2013 report from the USDA Foreign Agricultural Service, China's total agricultural

---

65   ISI Group, November 2010.

66   Yuval Atsmon, et al., "China's new pragmatic consumers," *McKinsey & Company*, October 2010.

67   Kenneth Rapoza, "China Official Says Country to Top U.S. Market by 2015," *Forbes*, May 25, 2012.

68   Jonathan Woetzal, et al., "Preparing for China's Urban Billion," *McKinsey & Company*, February 2009.

trade increased by more than nine percent in 2012 to top $205.6 billion. China is a leader in worldwide farm output, primarily producing pork, rice, wheat, potatoes, peanuts, tea, barley, cotton, oilseed, and fish.

☞ In 1987, there were 140 billionaires on the planet. The United States led the way with 41 on the list, followed by Japan and Germany with 24 and 13, respectively.[69] By 2013, the global billionaire tally had grown to 1,426. The United States still leads with 442, but China and Russia now take second and third with 130 and 110, respectively.[70]

☞ China recently eclipsed the United States as the world's top trading partner (imports and exports), as total trade in 2013 reached $4.2 trillion.

☞ China is expected to use roughly twice as much energy (gigawatts) as the United States by 2040, according to the Energy Information Administration.

The Dirty Little Secret

China's economic fortunes have been on the rise over the past few decades due to its manufacturing prowess. However, this is a high volume, low margin business. In a 2005 study of the production of the 30 gigabyte Apple iPod, a product made in China by the company Foxconn, estimated that, "it cost about $144 to make each iPod unit. Of this amount, only about $4, or 2.8 percent of the total cost, was attributable to the Chinese workers who assembled it."[71] Wages correlate with this

69 Sean Kilachand, "Forbes History: The Original 1987 List of International Billionaires," *Forbes*, March 21, 2012.

70 Luisa Kroll, "Inside the 2013: Billionaires List: Facts and Figures," *Forbes*, March 4, 2013.

71 Wayne M. Morrison, "China-U.S. Trade Issues," *Congressional Research Service*, July 17, 2013.

slim piece of the revenues. As such, although China is a really a great 'assembler' nation, a great deal of their population does not share in these fantastic manufacturing fortunes.

This does have a somewhat positive upshot, as it keeps a lid on global consumer prices. The Chinese have been getting raises over the past few years, however, though with limited inflationary impact. Between 2005 and 2010, China's average yearly minimum salary increase was 12.5 percent. At the same time, the price of goods exported to the USA rose less than five percent, even with an appreciating Chinese currency (the renminbi).[72] Yes, the Chinese are getting paid a little more, but their cost of labor advantage has been diminishing. Consider that in 2002, the average manufacturing wage in China was 240 percent lower that of Mexico. As of 2010 that gap was only 14 percent.[73] Unsurprisingly, many businesses, particularly automakers, have been building plants in Mexico. As mentioned, this is part of the shadowy side of globalization as labor can be ported over to lower wage regimes. That's the dirty little secret about China. The average citizen doesn't make much, but when they do start to get higher wages, this may result in businesses heading elsewhere. That's good for the world's consumers in regards to the price of manufactured goods, but not so good for a country that needs to keep hundreds of millions gainfully employed. It is also said that rich countries make rich things. While China has emerged onto the global stage, it seems like its transformation to an economic power remains incomplete.

China vs. The Environment

Smog, pollution, and animal endangerment have all been byproducts of China's unbridled quest for economic significance. As we know, the impact of China's actions always seems magnified. In fact, pollution

---

72 "Rising Costs: the End of China as a Production Base?" *China Integrated*, March 2012.

73 Andres Oppenheimer, "China's wage hikes could benefit Latin America," *Miami Herald*, March 3, 2012.

and dust generated in China has been found settling as far away as California, and sixteen of the world's twenty most polluted cities are in China. These environmental issues have created economic and health issues, and will continue to do so if left unaddressed. Unsurprisingly, Premier Li Keqiang declared a "war on pollution" in March 2014.

Behind every challenge there is an opportunity, with China being no exception to this notion. For instance, in Japan, recycling is a $360 billion industry. In the U.S. it's a $100 billion industry. In China, however, recycling revenues are only $5.4 billion a year, according to Li Qiaofeng, the executive director of China National Resources Development Holdings. There is some obvious low hanging fruit for the enterprising individual, but there is a lot of work to be done to help put China on a more sustainable path as it relates to the environment. As you will read about in the next section, there is a green movement afoot, and there are agents of change committed to solving issues not just for China, but the entire planet.

IMPACT INVESTING

Once a cottage industry, *Impact Investing* is now a significant force in the business. There is no fine-tuned, formulaic definition of impact investing, but think of it as the melding of philanthropy and financial returns. The hunting ground used by impact investors is vast, but generally includes clean technology and socially responsible investing, as well as adjacent investment areas. The conventional thinking is that these are corners of the investment arena that would deliver underwhelming financial returns. Impact investors look to dispel that notion. They have an overarching dual mandate: improving the social and environmental conditions of our planet along with generating positive financial returns. Thus, the world wins, and so do investors. It also has a risk management benefit, as investors can steer clear of companies with latent environmental or reputational liabilities. Impact investing is a blossoming space, with eye-catching estimates that it could grow to $1 trillion worldwide by 2020 according to a 2012 forecast by JP Morgan....

- "I believe wholeheartedly that a new form of capitalism is emerging. More stakeholders (customers, employees, shareholders, and the larger community) want their business to . . . have a purpose bigger than their product." – Mats Lederhausen, Investor and former McDonald's executive, as quoted in Daniel Pink's *Drive* (2009)

- "Pursuit of profit with a purpose." – Antony Bugg-Levine and Jed Emerson, *Impact Investing* (2011)

⊕ "Not all profit is equal. Profits involving a social purpose represent a higher form of capitalism, one that creates a positive cycle of company and community prosperity." – Michael Porter and Mark Kramer, *The Big Idea: Creating Shared Value* (January/February 2011)

⊕ "Resources are limited; creativity is unlimited." – motto for POSCO, a South Korean steelmaker.

⊕ "The environment is the only stakeholder that is silent." – John Mackey, Rajendra S. Sisodia, and Bill George, *Conscious Capitalism* (2013)

Impact investing is becoming increasingly fashionable, particularly among the younger demographic who want to have a more positive impact on the world. Performance at all costs just doesn't seem right. Of course, there is a counter-argument. Those naysayers believe that impact investing is just a distortion of the markets, as capital is routed away from more productive areas. Further, when the government tries to get involved in this game and spend taxpayer dollars on 'green' investments, it has had a few notable whiffs (we'll get to Solyndra in a second)....

⊕ "There is one and only one social responsibility of business – to use its resources and engage in activities designed to increase its profits." – Milton Friedman, *Capitalism and Freedom* (1962)

⊕ "When governments try to invest in emerging industries, they often swing and

Microfinance is the lending of small amounts of money to less affluent individuals who often lack any collateral to pledge. In 2010, microfinance financed served more than 100 million clients with more than $50 billion in loans across the globe, according to Antony Bugg-Levine and Jed Emerson in *Impact Investing* (2011).

miss." - W. James Antle III, *Devouring Freedom: Can Big Government Ever be Stopped?* (2013)

⊛ "But no major academic study has been able to demonstrate a link between providing microfinance and long-term economic development." – Antony Bugg-Levine and Jed Emerson, *Impact Investing* (2011)

I'm all for an economic regime that is less punishing to the atmosphere and surrounding ecosystem. Yet, there is a lot to consider. For starters, the capital outlay for green energy facilities is significant, and the financials may be predicated by government subsidies. Further, there is an intermittency factor. The sun doesn't shine all day and wind is not a constant. Thus, solar panels and wind farms face idle time that can be costly. This makes them risky, expensive propositions with viability based on factors outside one's control.

Impact investing is an emotional subject, to say the least. I don't think there are many rooting for more smog and animal extinctions. That's not the crux of the matter. Green initiatives are just complicated and expensive decisions, and need to be well thought out. That's why I am supportive of a healthy debate. That said, there often tends to be two parallel scientific narratives for any given facet of the impact investing conversation and both may have some validity. This helps fuel the emotional response, not to mention the confusion. When there is science to support your argument, you can become emboldened and perhaps even tune out the competing views. This creates a very shaky foundation for a constructive dialogue to solve some of daunting problems that ourselves and future generations face. It's a bit disheartening, but when it comes to impact investing and the green discourse, a surplus of science has delivered a corresponding surplus of emotion.

Consider the work of Bjørn Lomborg – a staunch environmentalist turned skeptic. Lomborg, a former Greenpeace supporter, brazenly challenged some of the conventional green initiatives, including the Kyoto Protocol, and his outspoken and controversial stance was at first deemed heretical and consequently he was nearly exiled from the scientific community. The fiery response he once faced has since dulled, but his work is still not without its own skeptics. He remains a slightly misunderstood character, as his rhetoric about green efforts does not mean he wants to stiff-arm the creativity and innovation necessary to solve the vexing problems facing our planet. Rather, he's a bright guy (he has a PhD in political science) who gets that the status quo is not satisfactory. Lomborg just feels that some of the debate's discourse is misguided and alarmist. This combination, he contends, has led to a very material misallocation of capital….

☞ "Listen, global warming is a real problem, but it's not the end of the world. A 30-centimetre sea level rise is just not going to bring the world to a standstill, just like it didn't over the last 150 years." – Bjørn Lomborg, author of *The Skeptical Environmentalist.*

☞ "European Union will spend $250 billion a year to cut 20 percent of carbon emissions by 2020. This will only reduce the temperature by .1 percent of a degree by 2100." – Bjørn Lomborg

I am not a scientist, but I do recognize that there is a parallel narrative that disputes his comments. Yet, for the sake of argument, let's just take his comments at face value and assume they are correct. They're clearly engaging, but they are also risky. Even if he *was* right, does that mean he will continue to be right? For instance, some predictions have sea levels rising as high as 6.6 feet (200 centimeters) by 2100. We also know that the damage to the ecosystem can be self-feeding and thus exponential in nature. That's what makes me wonder if they do more harm than good. Yes, the right science desperately needs to be added to the conversation, but complacency has always been a gripe of mine, as an investor, an environmental steward, and a parent.

You could surely write a treatise on our environment and the various ways to rectify what ails it. There is such an expansive encyclopedia of research out there to mull through. It can also be quite dizzying if you were to toggle back and forth on the various viewpoints. Get your Imodium ready as here is a small sampling of excerpts that may prove to be a head-scratcher as they go against the grain of conventional wisdom. And, yes, there is science that challenges these as well.…

- ✪ "The problem with solar cells is that they're black, because they are designed to absorb light from the sun. But only 12 percent gets turned into electricity, and the rest is reradiated as heat – which contributes to global warming." – Steven Levitt & Stephen Dubner, *SuperFreakonomics* (2011)

- ✪ "The agnostics grumble that human activity accounts for just 2 percent of global carbon dioxide emissions, with the remainder generated by natural processes like plant decay." – Steven Levitt & Stephen Dubner, *SuperFreakonomics* (2011)

- ✪ "If we all switched to driving a Prius, it would only cut one half of a percent of what we would need to cut by mid-century." – Bjørn Lomborg

There are some undisputed truths, at least to the best of my knowledge. Thus, there is some scientific progress. Hopefully, this can lead to some dampening of emotions that environmental topics can elicit.…

- ✪ "So even if humankind immediately stopped burning all fossil fuel, the existing carbon dioxide would remain in the atmosphere for several generations." – Steven Levitt & Stephen Dubner, *SuperFreakonomics* (2011)

- ✪ "In the rich world, the environmental situation has improved dramatically. In the United States, the most important environmental indicator, particulate air pollution, has been cut by more than half since 1955, rivers and coastal waters have dramatically improved, and forests are increasing." – Bjørn Lomborg

OVERTIME....

The Solyndra Effect

There is the widespread perception that any 'green' investment delivers sub-par performance: a large investment toll to do a little good. If you try to argue that this is the not the case, Solyndra will likely be part of the rebuttal. Solyndra, a now defunct U.S. solar panel manufacturer, has become the face of government involvement in green energy. The company received a $573 million loan guarantee from the federal government, only to subsequently file for Chapter 11 bankruptcy in September 2011, displacing almost its entire workforce. Yet, as you have read, rigid ideologies aren't in your best interest. Don't let one belly-up company shape your entire thought process on green investments. Consider that total returns from 2006 through 2010 for companies participating in the Global Reporting Initiative (GRI) were 19.9 percent compared to 6.7 percent for the S&P 500 (equal weighted), according to Ernst & Young. The GRI is a globally recognized framework for the measurement of sustainability information. Yes, Solyndra was a disaster. Yes, there will be future green investments that are duds. However, the truth is always somewhere in the middle, and the GRI results illustrates that.

Solyndra will be an impediment to future government involvement in the 'green' arena. This may prove unfortunate, as many of these companies cannot get off the ground without government credits or subsidies. If anything, the government's role is a bit more unpredictable now, which creates its own set of risks. The Spanish solar market proves a telling example, as it was undermined by the abrupt curtailment of government subsidies. In the wake of the 2008 global credit crisis, the government implemented rather abrupt austerity measures. This policy shift contributed to a decline of the 2009 photovoltaic output to roughly one-fourth of 2008 levels.[74] The precipitous fall of the Spanish solar

---

74 Angel Gonzales and Keith Johnson, "Spain's Solar-Power Collapse Dims Subsidy Model," *The Wall Street Journal*, September 8, 2009.

market shows that unpredictable government involvement may be worse than no involvement at all.

Solyndra has not been a glowing endorsement for green investment, and it appears investors have taken notice. Global clean energy investment dropped almost 11 percent in 2012 to $269 billion. In the U.S., the drop was even more pronounced, as investment fell 37 percent to $35.6 billion. Yet, all is not lost. Global renewable capacity continued to expand in 2012 (up 17 percent to 91.1 newly installed gigawatts), which shows a greater yield on invested capital.[75] Fortunately, past investments in the space planted the seeds of industry innovations and greater efficiency that world still benefits from today.

---

75 Michael Davidson, "NREL Notes: Cleantech' s New Economics and the U.K.'s Electric Superbike," *Xconomy*, December 11, 2013.

RISK MANAGEMENT

The future is uncertain. This truism permeates all corners of the world around us and is the basis for investment risk. In other words, a certain future is not a risky one, as we can make decisions based on known outcomes. What is also clear is that level of risk you incur shapes your investment results. Yet, while we know these basic tenets, the concept of risk remains unsettled. In particular, how people define risk is different depending on who you ask and when. For instance, some will cite price volatility; others will say risk only surfaces if an investment fails to provide a desired return. Then there are the different drivers of risk, including leverage and illiquidity. Risk may be a chameleon, but it is a prerequisite to a return, and a necessary toll during your investment voyage….

- "To live without risk is to risk not living." – this and its variants are attributed to all sorts of people, including Pope Pius XII and Charles Lindbergh

- "You miss 100 percent of the shots you never take." – Wayne Gretzky, Hockey hall of famer

According to Roger Alcaly's 2003 *The New Economy*, even after including dividends, if an investor had purchased stocks right before the crash of 1929, it would have taken them 15 years to recover their value.

- "If no one ever took risks, Michelangelo would have painted the Sistine floor." – Neil Simon, American playwright and screenwriter

☞ "You've got to go out on a limb sometimes because that's where the fruit is." – Will Rogers, American cowboy and performer

Risk resides everywhere. There is even risk with holding money in a savings account (i.e. the interest rate might be below inflation and your purchasing power erodes). We do know where risk is more commonly found....

☞ "Some investments do have higher expected returns than others. Which ones? Well, by and large they're the ones that will do the worst in bad times." – William F. Sharpe, Nobel Laureate in Economics, as quoted in Money Magazine's July 2007 issue

Successful investing is often more a function of what you don't own as opposed to what you do own. In other words, look down before you look up. Consequently, your investment results will largely be determined by the efficacy of your risk management. Just think of the daunting math that awaits you after a material correction in performance. For instance, you need a 100 percent return to get back to where you started after a 50 percent loss. It's no wonder Vinny Mattone said, "[When you're down by half,] You're finished."[76]....

☞ "No matter how careful you are, the one risk no investor can ever eliminate is the risk of being wrong." – Benjamin Graham, *The Intelligent Investor* (1949)

☞ "Most investors are primarily oriented toward return, how much they can make, and pay little attention to risk, how much they

> Good risk management starts with conducting a *Premortem*, as psychologist Gary Klein called it. Figure out what can kill an investment (e.g. rich valuations, management transition, patent expiration) before you put your money to work.

---

76 As quoted in Roger Lowenstein, *When Genius Failed: The Rise and Fall of Long-Term Capital Management* (New York: Random House, 2000).

can lose." – Seth Klarman, *Margin of Safety: Risk-Averse Value Investing Strategies for the Thoughtful Investor* (1991)

☞ "Risk means more things can happen than will happen." – Elroy Dimson, professor at the London Business School

☞ "Traders come and go; risk managers are here to stay." – Nassim Taleb, *Fooled by Randomness* (2004)

☞ "The paradox exists because most investors think quality, as opposed to price, is the determinant of whether something's risky. But high quality assets can be risky and low quality assets can be safe. It's just a matter of the price paid for them." – Howard Marks, *The Most Important Thing: Uncommon Sense for the Thoughtful Investor* (2011)

☞ "In trading, like golf, it's how you play the bad shots that really matters." – Anonymous, as quoted in *Inside the House of Money* by Steven Drobny (2006)

☞ "Risk comes from not knowing what you're doing."- Warren Buffett

☞ "Riskier investments are those for which the outcome is less certain." – Howard Marks, *The Most Important Thing: Uncommon Sense for the Thoughtful Investor* (2011)

☞ "Riskier investments absolutely cannot be counted on to deliver higher returns. Why not? It's simple: if riskier investments reliably produced higher returns, they wouldn't be riskier." – Howard Marks

You can't manage what you can't measure. There is no foolproof way of gauging risk, but perhaps the most common convention is standard deviation[77]. It is a statistical measure of historic investment volatility. The higher the standard deviation, the more risky the investment is and vice versa. Standard deviation can also be thought of as a measure of future return predictability. In other words, the lower the standard deviation of an investment the more foreseeable the future returns should be. Unfortunately, standard deviation relies on past performance as inputs. Therefore, if the future deviates wildly from the past, then standard deviation may not be an accurate representation of coming volatility.

Value at risk (VAR) is another common risk gauge. VAR measures the amount of loss possible given a specified time frame with a given degree of confidence. It too is backward looking, along with reliance upon the notion of rational human behavior, which can be a bold assumption.

Risk, unlike uncertainty, can be measured. We can assign probabilities to events occurring and the more likely a dire outcome, the greater the degree of risk. The level of an asset's risk will ultimately shape its price....

Running a phantom portfolio without any cash on the line is one way to get to know thyself. You may not experience the full range of emotions as if you actually invested money, but it is as good a way as any to cut your teeth as an investor.

Moreover, don't be afraid to ask for input. Even Warren Buffett does, as he relies on Charlie Munger as a sounding board for ideas. Sometimes your emotions can taint your thoughts, so additional perspective can prove invaluable.

☞ "Uncertainty must be taken in a sense radically distinct from the familiar notion of Risk, from which it has never been properly separated . . . . The essential fact is that 'risk' means in some cases a quantity susceptible of measurement, while at other times it is something distinctly not of this character; and there

---

77 If you are looking to know the math behind standard deviation then the following tutorial might be a helpful starting point: http://www.ehow.com/video_4980169_calculate-standard-deviation.html?ref=Track2&utm_source=ask

are far-reaching and crucial differences in the bearings of the phenomena depending on which of the two is really present and operating . . . . It will appear that a measurable uncertainty, or 'risk' proper, as we shall use the term, is so far different from an unmeasurable one that it is not in effect an uncertainty at all." – Frank Knight, *Risk, Uncertainty, and Profit* (1964)

☞ "there are known knowns; there are things we know we know. We also know there are known unknowns; that is to say we know there are some things we do not know. But there are also unknown unknowns – he ones we don't know we don't know." – Donald Rumsfeld, press briefing on Iraq's alleged weapons of mass destruction (February 12th, 2002)

Tolerance to risk varies from person to person. Unfortunately, there is no mechanical formula that will magically tell first time investors their risk tolerance. Many try and some get pretty darn close, but without living through the sting associated with a material market correction that personal definition of risk will be inexact. You may be perfectly stoic, but that could change when the rest of the world is in a state of panic. It's kind of like driving in the snow, as us Northerners can appreciate. Despite how skilled you may be navigating a treacherous terrain you are still not immune from the knuckleheads who don't know what they are doing and could easily derail your voyage. It's no different with investments. Market corrections can send asset prices from inexpensive to illogically cheap by the selling of the unwitting and fickle. That can be emotionally trying to experience and risk tolerance will remain undefined until lived through.

All is not lost. Risk may be personal, but in many cases time horizon can and should be the controlling factor. Your investment time horizon is a fancy way of saying when you will need your money back. If you don't have any expenditures or liabilities then your time horizon will be correspondingly long. A long time horizon is an asset as it gives you the ability to tune out the market noise caused by all those bad drivers....

❦ "Yet each of us defines the long run with a different time span in mind, which means that yours will be appropriate for me only by coincidence." – Peter L. Bernstein, *"Is Investing For the Long Term Theory or Just Mumbo-Jumbo?" Journal of Post Keynesian Economics* (Spring 1993)

Your *ability* to take risk is more easily quantified than your *willingness*. This distinction makes the definition of risk unique to each investor. One way to gauge your willingness to take risk is through the anxiety it creates....

❦ "Sell down to the sleeping point." – commonly attributed to J.P. Morgan, but you can also credit it to Dickson Watts (1891)

❦ "If you want to dine well, go in for the first (i.e. high risk investment). If you want to sleep well, invest in the second (i.e. low risk investment)." – Baron Rothschild, "A Banker's Advice," *Citizen Patriot* (January 4th, 1896)

You need to know your risk tolerance before you start assembling a portfolio, not when you're in the middle of managing it. You don't want to figure out your tolerance for risk real-time. Letting emotions dictate investment decisions often leads to self-inflicted wounds. Accordingly, a critical pillar of risk management is to have a grasp of your weaknesses....

❦ "Know thyself." – commonly credited to Socrates

❦ "Denial ain't just a river in Egypt." – attributed to Mark Twain

❦ "Some people hit the gas at a yellow light, some people hit the brakes." - Anonymous

❦ "Insanity: doing the same thing over and over again and expecting different results." – commonly credited to Albert Einstein

❧ "It takes considerable knowledge just to realize the extent of your own ignorance." – Thomas Sowell, *A Childish Letter* (August 17th, 1998)

❧ "Above all, never fool yourself, and remember (as physicist Richard Feynman said) that you are the easiest person to fool." – Charlie Munger

❧ "After you burn your mouth on hot milk, you blow on your yogurt." – old Turkish proverb

❧ "The speculator's deadly enemies are: Ignorance, greed, fear and hope. All the statute books in the world and all the rule books on all the Exchanges of the earth cannot eliminate these from the human animal." – Edwin LeFevre, *Reminiscences of a Stock Operator* (1923)

❧ "The fault, dear investor, is not in our stars – and not in our stocks – but in ourselves." – Benjamin Graham, *The Intelligent Investor* (1949)

Awareness and deference to an asset's valuation may be the most effective risk management technique. Notably, be very leery of investing in the 'hot' manager or security, which is effectively 'buying high.' Further, good performance is a magnet for fund flows. A larger asset base may mean this same 'hot' manager may not be as nimble and stealth as he or she was in the past. That may not be the end of the world, but it needs to be considered….

❧ "Sooner or later, every great investor's edge is destined to unravel." – Sebastian Mallaby, *More Money Than God* (2010)

❧ "The investor of today does not profit from yesterday's growth." – Warren Buffett

∞ "Even Napoleon had his Watergate." – *St. Louis Post-Dispatch* columnist Dan O'Neill, parodying Yogi Berra

∞ "But reaching for 'star' managers and using past performance to identify which managers are likely to achieve superior future performance increase the odds of future disappointment because past performance – however compelling it may appear – cannot predict future performance." – Charles Ellis, "Murder on the Orient Express: The Mystery of Underperformance," *Financial Analysts Journal* (July/August 2012)

Try to invest with investment managers who demonstrate asset base discipline. These are ones who have turned away additional assets, or even returned them, when they feel they cannot deliver adequate performance with a more sizable portfolio. This is especially true for managers who dabble in the less liquid corners of the markets.

∞ "Size is the enemy of performance." – Wall Street adage

∞ "Mutual fund managers are trapped in this rather deadly vicious circle: the more successful they are, the more money flows into their mutual fund. Then, it is more difficult for them to beat the market averages or even to match their own past performance." – Ron Chernow

Another beneficial risk management tactic is to avoid being complacent. Complacency does follow a predictable pattern, as it increases as markets rise. This is a dangerous combination, as valuations lose their luster when markets ascend....

∞ "The received wisdom is that risk increases in the recession and falls in booms. In contrast, it may be more helpful to think of risk as increasing during upswings, as financial imbalances build up, and materializing in recessions." – Andrew Crockett, former head of the Bank for International Settlements (2000)

☞ "Investment risk comes primarily from too-high prices, and too-high prices often come from excessive optimism and inadequate skepticism and risk aversion." – Howard Marks, *The Most Important Thing: Uncommon Sense for the Thoughtful Investor* (2011)

When it comes to investing, you can trip all over yourself. There are fees, taxes, illiquidity, your emotions and all sorts of other landmines that can prove punitive. You should view these aforementioned items as risks, but ones that are often avoidable. While the market's direction can be an unknown at times, items like expenses and taxes (for the most part) are not. Thus, control what you can control. For instance, you set a really high bar when you pay a two-percent management fee for an actively domestic equity large cap fund (buying the likes of Chevron, Target, Johnson & Johnson, etc.), especially when there are passively managed alternatives that cost $1/20^{th}$ of it. That's a hefty incremental management fee in a space that is becomingly increasingly commoditized (recall the message in the 'A New Breed of Index' vignette). So, in this instance, the calculus behind paying an extra 1.9 percent or so doesn't quite compute. The higher cost fund might seem like it has a lot of razzle dazzle and will mint money, but you are really just inviting unnecessary risk in the form of higher fees. You don't have to pour the concrete for these performance speed bumps, and removing these seemingly little impediments will make your investment journey that much smoother....

☞ "If you take care of the small things, the big things take care of themselves. You can gain more control over your life by paying closer attention to the little things." – attributed to Emily Dickinson, 19th century American poet

Lastly, risk management may be of heightened importance in this day and age of unprecedented political and Central Bank activism....

๏ "Because in the New Normal you are more worried about the return of your capital, not return on your capital."[78] – Mohamed El-Erian

๏ "It is not the return on my investment that I am concerned about; it is the return of my investment." – Will Rogers

---

78   The New Normal is a phrase coined by PIMCO that describes an investing environment that will yield muted returns as compared to the past due to sub-trend economic growth, courtesy of increased government regulation and activism, more localism (globalization in reverse), and deleveraging.

OVERTIME....

Portfolio Moneyball

Billy Beane, the general manager of the Oakland Athletics, became a household name after being the focus of Michael Lewis's part business, part sports hit *Moneyball*. Beane was able to cobble together a Major League baseball team on a shoestring budget and transition them into a perennial playoff contender. Beane had to conceive a way to compete in a league that had no salary cap. In other words, you could buy a championship if your pockets were deep enough. That wasn't an option for the Athletics, so Beane had to defy the typical logic of the league. Beane's unconventional approach was to bring a never before seen brand of science to the game of baseball. He needed to make sure he got the most out of every dollar he spent in order to compete with other teams flush with cash. Beane's unique approach resulted in the Athletics winning more baseball games per dollar spent than any other Major League club.

Investors should strive for the same – doing a lot with a little. For instance, a 20 percent return with a standard deviation of 20 (risk reading) should be viewed differently than a 20 percent with a lower risk reading of 10. In my eyes, the latter portfolio is the superior one, as it clearly utilizes its risk budget much more effectively. Fortunately, there is a way to measure return per unit of risk utilized, courtesy of Nobel Laureate William Sharpe. Robust returns are great, but how you achieved those results is also a very important consideration. The *Sharpe Ratio* is an oft-cited gauge of risk-adjusted results, or a portfolio *Moneyball* gauge[79].

Risk comes in many varieties, and represents more than just price volatility. Here are a few types of risk:

---

79 The calculation for the Sharpe Ratio is as follows: (Return – Risk Free Rate) / Standard Deviation. The return for United States Treasury Bills (T-Bills) is commonly used as the Risk Free Rate input. With T-Bill rates so microscopic these days, you can just short-circuit the Sharpe formula by dividing investment return over investment volatility and arrive at close to the same result.

Concentration – Quite simply, concentration is the opposite of diversification (this will be further discussed shortly) or keeping your eggs in one basket. Concentration has two possible outcomes: wealth generation or wealth devastation….

- ☞ "It is paradoxical that wealth is often created through investment concentration, but maintained through diversification and careful management." – Brad Berggren, Parametric Portfolio Associates (2013)

- ☞ "Don't bunt. Aim out of the ballpark. Aim for the company of immortals." – David Ogilvy

Liquidity – Liquidity is often described in two ways: a) the amount an individual can spend or invest or b) the asset's ability to be sold without becoming impaired. For instance, your savings account is highly liquid, but your primary residence is very illiquid. Each investor's situation is different, but what's overarching is that both dimensions of liquidity need to be properly calibrated or else liquidity (or lack thereof) can be debilitating to a portfolio.

As an investor, liquidity needs to be properly managed. In particular, insufficient liquidity can force you into a corner as a forced seller. In these situations, the buyer sets the price. So, if your only asset was your primary residence and you desperately needed to sell to raise cash, there is a good chance you receive back something less than the appraised value of your home. You always want to have enough liquidity to last you through the grimmest stretches of the economic cycle. Think of yourself as a camel. You want to have enough

The *Current Ratio* can give you a sense for the general liquidity of a company, along with its ability to pay its short-term obligations. The math for the ratio is a division of short-term assets over short-term liabilities. The higher the result - the better. It has its blemishes, but it can give you a sense of if the well is going dry for a business.

liquidity to let you wander through the desert and can only count on an oasis to refill. Liquidity is a risk, but it can also be an invaluable asset. Liquidity allows you to buy from those feeble forced sellers, which as you might surmise, will often prove lucrative.

There is a cyclical, psychological element when it comes to embracing illiquidity: it is coveted at market troughs and despised at market peaks. Illiquid investments do have merit. The long-term track record for private equity, which is a about as illiquid as it gets, serves as prima facie evidence. Consider that the Cambridge Associates U.S. Private Equity Index has outperformed the S&P 500 by 5.9 percent annualized over the 15 year stretch ending in September 2013, which is a pretty meaty return differential. However, know that, while quite seductive, illiquidity can be combustible if added to a portfolio at the wrong time....

☞ "All markets look liquid during the bubble (massive uptrend), but it's the liquidity after the bubble ends that matters." – Colm O'Shea, as quoted in *Hedge Fund Market Wizards* by Jack Schwager (2012)

☞ "It is easier to get into something than to get out of it." – Donald Rumsfeld, *Rumsfeld Rules* (1974)

☞ "The market can stay irrational longer than you can stay solvent." – attributed to John Maynard Keynes

☞ "Sell when you can, not when you have to." - Anonymous

Another way to define liquidity is the amount of potential buyers and sellers there are in a given market. Yet, the prudent course of action would be to never count on potential trading partners being there when you need them to be. Thus, always have enough cash or cash-like investments to last you through periods of market turbulence.

The ability to be a liquidity provider and buy assets from motivated sellers will generally deliver lucrative returns. Thus, the thoughtful investor wants to pay attention to liquidity trends. For starters, liquidity is highly coveted and expensive when it is in short supply. This can take some emotional fortitude, as these moments when liquidity becomes scarce typically occur during times of market adversity. Yet, did you ever wonder why ATM's in remote locations charge such high surcharges? It is rather unpalatable considering they simply provide *your* money. In any event, they get away with it because they are the only game in town in terms of having ready cash and you begrudgingly pay it because you need it. You want to be that ATM machine, not the one taking money out. In other words, you want to be an investing loan shark and have a balance sheet that allows you mobilize liquidity to desperate souls and reap a handsome return as a result. There are other ways to capitalize, too. In particular, liquidity injections into an economy or capital markets, whether they are fiscal or monetary, can help lift asset prices....

- "Don't fight the Fed." – Wall Street maxim

- "That's where the money is." – Willie Sutton, bank-robber, quip regarding his motives

- And as long as the powers that be are trying to stimulate the economy....

- "As long as the music is playing, you've got to get up and dance." – Chuck Prince, Citigroup CEO (July 2007)

In order to reinforce the importance of liquidity, here are some cautionary tales....

- "Our liquidity is fine. As a matter of fact, it's better than fine. It's strong." – Kenneth Lay, former CEO of Enron (weeks before Enron's bankruptcy on December 2nd, 2001)

- "At the end of 2007, I didn't believe we had a liquidity problem . . . we had just completed a record year." – Richard Fuld, former

CEO of now bankrupt Lehman Brothers, testimony to House of Representatives (October 2008)

In parting....

☞ "In God we trust, all others must pay cash." – American proverb and name of a novel by Jean Shepherd

Leverage – Leverage, or the accumulation of debt, can be a double-edged sword. From an investment standpoint, skillful application of leverage can be used to enhance returns. However, imprudent use of leverage can lead to financial turmoil. Most importantly, leverage does not change the underlying prospects of the investment, just the degree of returns.

The theme throughout this book is there are two sides to every story, and leverage is no exception. Debt has value, as it serves as a lubricant to the economy and can serve to allocate capital to parts of the economy where it is needed. It's a bit of the American way to be quite frank. In fact, corporations derive a tax benefit from the interest on their debt issuance. This is economical capital, courtesy of the US Tax Code, that businesses can use for growth. Leverage can be capricious, but don't categorically dismiss its utility....

☞ "We'd be a poorer economy if everyone who wanted to purchase a home had to pay in cash, if every small-business owner seeking to expand either had to pay for that expansion out of his or her own pocket or take on extra, unwanted partners." – Paul Krugman, *End this Depression Now!* (2012)

The real danger with leverage is that it can force you to sell assets when it is least desirable. This evokes the Wall Street adage of, "sell what they can, not what they should."

☞ "With borrowed funds, a business can invest, gain leverage, and leverage is a pair of wings. Leverage is flight. Leverage is a way for small to be big and big to be huge, a glorious abstraction, the promise of tomorrow today, yes, a liberation from time, the resounding triumph of human will over dreary, chronology-shackled physical reality. To leverage is to be immortal." – Mohsin Hamid, *How to Get Filthy Rich in Rising Asia* (2013)

That said, debt, like most items in life, if used in excess, can be precarious. In other words, when debt finances over-consumption and cannot be paid back, it's a problem. Accordingly, a prudent approach to leverage may not be exciting, but may be the best path for investors and consumers....

- "Debt is like any other trap, easy enough to get into, but hard enough to get out of." – Henry Wheeler Shaw, 19th century American Humorist

- "When you combine ignorance and leverage, you get some pretty interesting results." – Warren Buffett

- "Neither a borrower nor a lender be; For loan oft loses both itself and friend, And borrowing dulls the edge of husbandry." – William Shakespeare, *The Tragedy of Hamlet, Prince of Denmark* (c. 1599-1602)

- "Annual income twenty pounds, annual expenditure nineteen pounds nineteen and six, result happiness. Annual income twenty pounds, annual expenditure twenty pounds nought and six, result misery." – Charles Dickens, *David Copperfield* (1850)

- "No man can calculate to escape ruin but he who owes no money; happy is he who has a little and is free from debt." – Philip Hone, New York City mayor from 1825-1826

- "Never spend your money before you have it." – Thomas Jefferson, letter to Thomas Jefferson Smith (February 21st, 1825)

☞ "Pay every debt, as if God wrote the bill." – Ralph Waldo Emerson, "Suum Cuique" (1841)

☞ "Every nonprofessional who operates on margin should recognize that he is ipso facto speculating." – Benjamin Graham, *The Intelligent Investor* (1949)

While you may use debt judiciously, you must be aware of the systemic or widespread application of leverage by others. Just because you're prudently leveraged or without debt does not mean the world around you is on solid footing. Gluttonous use of debt by the masses can lead to a coronary for the broader economy and capital markets, as we saw during the 2008 credit crisis. Know that complacency and leverage use are positively correlated. Confidence, which will grow in tandem with an economic expansion, leads to debt accumulation and an erosion of underwriting standards (i.e. loans requiring less collateral and predicated more on hope). If use of leverage is widespread and applied recklessly, don't be naïve enough to think that your portfolio will be immune....

The *Debt/Equity Ratio* is one way to gauge if a company is too highly leveraged. The threshold of what constitutes an unhealthy ratio varies by industry. Ideally, you own companies that can self-finance their growth and are not vulnerable to an unexpected rise in interest rates on their debt.

☞ "My belief is that because the system is now more stable, we'll make it less stable through more leverage, more risk taking." – Myron Scholes, *Risk Manager, The Wall Street Journal* (March 3rd, 2007)

☞ "I, however, place economy among the first and most important republican virtues, and public debt as the greatest of the dangers to be feared." – Thomas Jefferson, letter to William Plumer (July 21st, 1816)

Deleveraging, or the act of reducing debt to assets or income levels, is often a sensible act. In particular, you typically want to prioritize paying down or off your highest cost debt. However, there is some ugly math to consider with leverage. Debt is rather inelastic, at least when compared to publicly traded assets. So even if you pay down debt, your leverage ratios (assets are the numerator and debt is the denominator) might not improve. This is because even if leverage is reduced, a violent market move can send asset prices falling even further. For instance, from October 1929 to March 1933, while debtors frantically reduced the nominal value of their debt by 20 percent, asset prices fell even more, with the result being an increase of their remaining debt burden by 40 percent[80]....

Hyman Minsky's *Financial Instability Hypothesis* suggested that periods of economic stability lead to rising leverage, which subsequently leads to economic instability.

☞ "The very effect of individuals to lessen their burden of debts increase it, because of the mass effect of the stampede to liquidate. Then we have the great paradox ... the more debtors pay, the more they owe." – Irving Fisher, "The Debt-Deflation Theory of Great Depressions" (1933)

☞ "Liquidity allows for ready leverage, but it also creates the means for crises." – Richard Bookstaber, *A Demon of Our Own Design: Markets, Hedge Funds, and the Perils of Financial Innovation* (2008)

---

80 Nouriel Roubini and Stephen Mihm, *Crisis Economics: A Crash Course in the Future of Finance* (New York: Penguin, 2011).

DIVERSIFICATION

Diversification is the act of spreading your wealth amongst a variety of assets. For instance, owning only a handful of your favorite stocks may demonstrate courage in your convictions, but you would be leaving some diversification benefits on the table. Instead, those stocks should just be the starting point of your portfolio. Complement those best ideas with a medley of other assets such as foreign securities, bonds, and commodities. You want your portfolio to multitask, with different assets doing different things. Diversification espouses the notion of "the more the merrier," and, if done right, the upside is both enhanced return and reduced risk. How? Diversification earns its stripes in down markets, as the less money you lose in market corrections, the greater your participation in the subsequent rally. Diversification is commonly thought of as a 'free lunch,' which is as rare as it is beautiful in the investing game.

Not all assets are created equal when it comes to their diversification potential. You want assets that behave differently. Correlation, or lack thereof, is the cornerstone of diversification. When assets have high correlations, they trade indiscriminately and your diversification is limited, and the reverse is true as well. It may seem a somewhat curious concept that incorporating assets that behave differently can create stability, but the evidence shows that is the case. For example, solely owning both Coke and PepsiCo will not yield a great deal of diversification benefits, since both companies' fortunes are largely tied to the soft drink market. Coke and PepsiCo are highly correlated and, despite some of their snack product offerings, will likely not yield diversification's free lunch ability. Further, two domestic stocks of any kind aren't exactly going to maximize diversification capacity with their rather limited economic exposures. The more bang for your buck on the diversification front comes from owning a broad mix of asset classes, managers, styles, capitalizations, and geography that won't move in perfect unison....

⚭ "Tis the part of a wise man to keep himself today for tomorrow, and not venture all his eggs in one basket." – Miguel de Cervantes, *Don Quixote de la Mancha* (1605)

⚭ "It is better to be vaguely right than exactly wrong." – Carveth Read, *Logic, Deductive and Inductive* (1898)

Unfortunately, not all types of risk can be exorcised from a diversified portfolio. *Unsystematic Risk*, or company specific risk, can be diversified away through a thoughtfully constructed portfolio. On the other hand, an investor cannot fully immunize himself from *Systematic Risk*, or market-related risk, through diversification alone. It doesn't take much to reduce unsystematic risk. However, that doesn't mean your portfolio is invulnerable to the ebb and flow of the market. It just means that the chance of a single stock impairing your portfolio is quite limited....

⚭ "at least fifty equal-sized and well-diversified U.S. stocks (clearly, fifty oil stocks or fifty electric utilities would not produce an equivalent amount of risk reduction). With such a portfolio, the total risk is reduced by over 60 percent." – Burton G. Malkiel, *A Random Walk Down Wall Street* (1973)

Sometimes less may be more. There is a camp that doesn't think too highly of diversification. This constituent would prefer the label of 'di*worse*ification.' The mindset is predicated upon not diluting your investment of ideals of highest conviction, which can at times deliver stratospheric performance. Further, these diworseifiers are emboldened by tales of businessmen, like Henry Ford or Steve Jobs, who bet the farm on a single company and enjoyed subsequent success that propelled them to reverential status. Not to mention, there has to be some logical boundaries to the definition of 'uncorrelated asset'. It seems quite odd to add ill-fated, toxic waste-esque investments for the sake of diversification. Keep in mind that many of these opinions are from seasoned industry veterans. Concentration is not an approach for novices....

- "Diversification is a hedge for ignorance." – William J. O'Neill, Founder of *Investor's Business Daily*

- "We're non-diversified. We focus. Why not buy more of your best idea rather than your 60th best idea? How many companies can I really know well over time and focus on, on a daily basis?" – Bruce Berkowitz, Fairholme Funds

- "We much prefer owning a non-controlling but substantial portion of a wonderful business to owning 100 percent of a so-so business." – Warren Buffet, as quoted in "5 Ways Warren Buffett invests that you don't", Fidelity (March 14th, 2013)

- "I can't be involved in 50 or 75 things. That's a Noah's Ark way of investing – you end up with a zoo that way. I like to put meaningful amounts of money in a few things." – Warren Buffett (1987)

- "but the wise man saith 'Put all your eggs in one basket and then watch that basket.'" - Mark Twain, *Pudd'nhead Wilson* (1894)

Diversification, like many risk management techniques, is often coveted when it is least needed. Don't let complacency get the better of you. You want to buy insurance before your house catches on fire, not while it is burning down. It behooves one to be proactive and seek to diversify before the lack of it proves punitive.

Overtime....

Black Swans

Centuries ago the conventional wisdom was the swans only came in one variety – ones with white feathers. This train of thought was upended when Dutch explorer Willem de Vlamingh stumbled up on a black swan in Australia in 1697. Close to three centuries later, the black swan transcended zoology and entered the world of risk management. Nassim Taleb has become a mainstream name in risk management from his writings on the *Black Swan* event, which was first introduced in his 2004 book *Fooled by Randomness*. They have three defining traits: they're unpredictable, they have a massive impact, and ex post facto explanations are concocted that make the event appear less random and more predictable than it was. They don't have to be negative, as broad scale adoption of the internet meets the criteria. Yet, the avoiding of the black swan has become an obsession of risk managers.

The black swan concept is a bit surreal and had some doubters. How do you prevent something so catastrophic that you can hardly see coming? Enter the global credit crisis. It took a near economic catastrophe for Taleb's premise to gain broad scale legitimacy. The credit crisis surely fit the description of being a significant black swan. In large part, it was an unforeseen event, as much as most would hate to admit. Everyone in hindsight will allude that it was obvious, but there were few that actually did something about it.

> *Tail Risk*, which is Black Swan-esque, refers to the occurrence of extremely rare events. Technically speaking, these events reside on the outer boundaries of the normal distribution curve and are supposed to occur once every thousand years or more. Yet, these tail risk events tend to occur on an annual basis or even more frequently these days. When they do (frequently) occur, they pack quite the punch.

Only a few brazen investors, like John Paulson, profited from this and can make the credible claim that they read the tea leaves correctly. The pressing question is: what is the next black swan? Maybe the sovereign debt bubble will be the next. One thing is clear; when it comes, everyone will claim to have seen it coming.

BANKING/FINANCIAL SYSTEM

"A banker, it has been said jestingly, is a man who lends you an umbrella when the weather is good and takes it back when it rains."
– attributed to Robert Frost,
the American poet, amongst others

The banking system has a much-maligned history, at least as Frost would say. Shaping this mindset are the all-too-frequent banking crises, both in this country and across the globe. The internet is littered with literature dating back centuries about these various banking crises. These tales are almost like biblical parables that testify to the many ways that leverage, complacency, and reckless lending practices can rear their ugly heads and cause many a financial system to flirt with utter disaster. They also warn of the truth that financial system upheaval will happen again – a fact you can take to the bank.

The most recent turn of events in 2008 and 2009, when the financial system experienced what felt like a near apocalypse, was certainly one of the more severe episodes, but not without precedent. Once again, greed, which was thought to have been siphoned out of the industry, infected otherwise sound lending practices and turned some segments of Wall Street into high-risk casinos where the insured deposits of the everyday American were the common currency. The so-called Wall Street "fat cats" have shouldered their

> "Banks have done more injury to the religion, morality, tranquility, prosperity, and even wealth of a nation than they can have done or ever will do good." – John Adams, letter to John Taylor (March 12th 1819)

share of blame, while more than just a dash of jealousy fuels the populist outrage. Profits flooded the coffers of Wall Street, at least until the dam broke from being overwhelmed by a reckless amount of leverage. In fact, roughly 40 percent of all corporate profits were attributed to the financial sector in 2007 right before the credit bubble burst, according to data compiled by the Commerce Department. This number has since been cut in half, which more closely resembles their weighting in the S&P 500. This reduction is largely due to new regulation, namely the Dodd–Frank Wall Street Reform and Consumer Protection Act, which aims to have banks resemble sleepy, regulated utility companies, rather than hedge funds that have eyes bigger than their stomachs.

Bank profits and business tactics may be returning to normalcy, but another point of contention is that these banks were bailed out with taxpayer dollars. The severity of the global credit crisis necessitated government intervention, and the financial system was deemed critical to the wellbeing of the nation. It sounds counter-intuitive to save institutions that played a role in almost sending the United States to the economic dark ages. It's kind of like donating an organ to somebody who stabbed you. As frustrating as this was for some, there was a reason why they were bailed out. Banks are an under-appreciated and vital set of economic cogs. The banking system is analogous to the cardiovascular system; both reside beneath the surface and provide the critical lifeblood to keep the host functioning….

- "You can't have prosperity without a functioning financial system." – Paul Krugman, *End This Depression Now!* (2012)

- "Banks mean credit, and credit means power." – Charles W. Morse, famed early Wall Street baron and speculator in the early 20th century (1907)

- "If you want to get rich, go into finance or a related field. Finance is the technology for making things happen." – Robert Shiller

☞ "the ruin of these great banks would greatly impair the credit of all." – Walter Bagehot, *Lombard Street* (1873)

☞ "Banking is necessary; banks are not." - Bill Gates (1994)

☞ "The biggest mistake that could be made would be to allow significant banking institutions to fail . . . the sequential events that would follow, largely driven by psychology, cannot be quantified." – Gabriel Bornstein, managing director of Enclave Capital, LLC, as quoted in Bob Ivry's *The Seven Sins of Wall Street* (2014)

Financial institutions are the backbone of an economy, serving to facilitate broader commerce. Like it or not, banks and economies are joined at the hip. Unsurprisingly, there is a strong relationship between the maturity of the financial system and a country's economic stature. Case in point, the United States has long been an epicenter of finance....

☞ "Money always has a tendency to concentrate itself, and stocks, bonds, gold, rapidly accumulate at those points where the most considerable financial activity prevail. The greater the volume of floating wealth, the more conspicuous this peculiarity." – James Knowles Medbery, *Men and Mysteries of Wall Street* (1870)

The basic utility of banks is to collect deposits and make loans. As hinted at, this seemingly simple process is inherently fragile. For starters, it depends on depositors not asking for their money back all at once. There are also interest rate considerations. Deposits are liabilities to banks, and if interest rates spike it can adversely impact their earnings.

Perhaps it should be no surprise that most brick-and-mortar bank branches are well-maintained, with visually reassuring, upscale architecture. They try to instill confidence in other overt ways, too: who wouldn't want to bank with New Jersey's *Sturdy* Savings Bank. It's important for banks to instill peace-of-mind and demonstrate to its customers (depositors) that they have staying power and are not fly-by-night operations....

☞ "On occasion, however, banking can go very wrong, for the whole structure depends on depositors' not all wanting their funds at the same time." – Paul Krugman, *End this Depression Now!* (2012)

☞ "There has never been a single example in the history of finance where financing long-term liabilities . . . with short-term debt, ends well." – Mitch Stapley, Fifth Third Asset Management

Unveiled in December 2013, the Dodd-Frank financial reform legislation was designed to make banks look, well, boring again. The legislation has an approximate word count of 297,000. For comparison, the U.S. Constitution, excluding amendments but including signatures, only comes in at around 4,400 words.

☞ "If you owe your bank $100, that's your problem. If you owe them $100 million, that's the bank's problem." – commonly attributed to J. Paul Getty

In the lead-up to the credit crisis, many banks were run aggressively, with imprudent lending practices and excessive leverage. In the years preceding the global credit crisis, many once highly regarded Wall Street institutions were running very risky leverage ratios above 30:1. In particular, Bear Stearns had a leverage ratio of 33:1, which meant it only took a three percent decline in its balance sheet assets to turn insolvent. Rather predictably, Bear Stearns failed in March 2008.

The decision was made to rescue the banks (except for Lehman Brothers) in order to avert financial calamity. The sins of many banks were socialized, as the resulting bail out was taxpayer-financed. Further, cynics will tell you that this has fueled a *Moral Hazard,* which is an incentive to take corporate risks (financial and perhaps other systemically important non-financial institutions), as you know someone else will bear the burden of your losses. As such, this was a controversial tactic, as it created little disincentive for future bad behavior....

    * "The cardinal maxim is, that any aid to a present bad bank is the surest mode of preventing the establishment of a future good bank." – Walter Bagehot, *Lombard Street: A Description of the Money Market* (1873)

OVERTIME....

Not All Acronyms are Bad

The government's track record of financial system activism is not categorically bad. For starters, Troubled Asset Relief Program (TARP) helped stabilize the economy with minimal cost to the taxpayer. George Bush signed TARP into law on October 3rd, 2008, during the throes of the credit crisis. It authorized the U.S. Treasury to purchase or insure $700 billion of assets to stabilize the economy. While largely considered a bank bailout plan, it deployed capital into other segments of the economy. Notably, General Motors (automaker) and AIG (insurance company) were aid recipients. However, the AIG investment was considered a backdoor bailout to the banks. AIG's failure would have put in jeopardy the insurance (Credit Default Swaps, also known as CDS) banks had purchased to hedge some of their credit risks. On May 23rd, 2013 the Congressional Budget Office announced that the cost to the taxpayers for TARP was an estimated $21 billion (down $3 billion from their October 2012 estimate), with the loss largely attributed to assistance for AIG, the automotive industry, and grant programs to stem residential home foreclosures. Interestingly enough, the bank 'bailout' part of TARP was a positive for the taxpayer; as the CBO claims that, "transactions with financial institutions will, taken together, yield a net gain to the federal government."[81]

The actor Jimmy Stewart would have told you that insuring your savings is another helpful form of government assistance. The Federal Deposit Insurance Corporation (FDIC) insures all deposit accounts, including checking and savings accounts, up to $250,000 per depositor, per insured bank. Without this, 'bank runs,' or a mass request for deposits based on perceived weakness of the bank, would be more prevalent. *It's a Wonderful Life* provides a visual of the hysteria that surrounds a

---

81 "Report on the Troubled Asset Relief Program – May 2013," *Congressional Budget Office*, May 23, 2013.

bank run. In this classic scene, dozens of people descend upon their local bank that was perceived to be on life support. They want their checking and savings back immediately, but fortunately Stewart's character George Bailey is able to talk them out of it. The problem is that bank runs hasten that same bank's demise. Deposits are the lifeblood of commercial banks, and bank runs deprive them of it. They use these deposits to make loans that benefit homeowners, businesses, and the broader community. George Bailey knew that a healthy bank means a healthy economy. That's what makes FDIC insurance so important. It's a disincentive for depositor panic and gives banks a chance to live to fight another day.

Family/Generational Wealth

Have you been curious about why financial dynasties are rather uncommon? In fact, by the third generation, a general rule of thumb is roughly 70 percent of the wealth created is no longer controlled by descendants of the creator. The villain here is typically not the obvious ones, such as taxes or imprudent investments. Those certainly don't help. However, quite commonly the demise of the family fortune is due to non-financial factors. Sounds strange, but think about some of the classic examples, such as in-fighting, drugs issues, that crazy uncle, etc... The root problem is really a shaky or missing governance structure. Families should be run like well-tuned corporations, with an oversight body and clearly defined mission. There needs to be an effective feedback mechanism to voice problems and concerns before they manifest as the aforementioned examples. Too often, this is not the case and without this cohesive structure the odds are wealth will dissipate over the ensuing generations. This shouldn't be trivialized, as over the next 40 years Americans will reportedly transfer over 40 trillion dollars of financial assets to younger generations.…

- ☞ "Shirtsleeves to shirtsleeves in three generations." – American version of a Lancashire proverb

- ☞ "I'd hate to see any descendants of mine fall into the category of what I'd call 'idle rich' – a group I've never had much use for." – Sam Walton, *Sam Walton: Made in America* (1992)

⚘ "Wealth contains the seeds of its own destruction." – Malcolm Gladwell, *David and Goliath: Underdogs, Misfits, and the Art of Battling Giants* (2013)

⚘ "It is wonderful to think how men of very large estates not only spend their yearly income, but are often actually in want of money. It is clear, they have not value for what they spend." – Samuel Johnson

> John Paul Getty, the richest man on earth in 1966, is believed to have quipped that, "Money is like manure. You have to spread it around or it smells."

⚘ "I want to give my kids just enough so that they would feel that they could do anything, but not so much that they would feel like doing nothing". – Warren Buffett, *An Exclusive Hour with Warren Buffett and Bill and Melinda Gates*, Charlie Rose (2006)

⚘ "The question about the meaning and purpose of wealth should drive the thinking of individuals and families, and the resulting estate planning decisions and outcomes. Think about values first, products second." – Charles W. Collier, *Wealth in Families* (2001)

⚘ "A family's wealth consists primarily of its human capital (defined as all the individuals who make up the family) and its intellectual capital (defined as everything that each individual family member knows), and secondarily of its financial capital." – James E. Hughes Jr., *Family Wealth – Keeping it in the Family* (2004)

Great wealth carries with it great complexities and a disproportionate share of risk, as greed can rip a family apart. Once the wealth has been amassed, effective risk management is essential....

⚘ "It requires a great deal of boldness and a great deal of caution to make a great fortune; and when you have got it, it requires ten times as much wit to keep it." – Ralph Waldo Emerson, *Conduct of Life* (1860)

SAVINGS

S aving and instant gratification are at odds with one another. We need a refined sense of self-control to sacrifice for the future, as opposed to enjoying something in the present. This is true especially when it comes to saving for the unforeseen. We know with some level of certainty that we will need to save for college education and retirement and we can put some reasonable math to these future liabilities. However, it takes even more discipline to save in addition to these known amounts. Rainy day funds require sacrificing the near-term enjoyment for something that may never happen. The whole notion of building 'unforeseen' savings is quite analogous to an insurance policy. We aren't particularly thrilled to pay the premiums and only realize the true value on the remote occasion when something bad happens. Yet, we know that having some money tucked aside is an invaluable asset for these occasions when conjecture becomes reality.

"The American saver" is a bit of an oxymoron. The personal savings rate is half of what it was in the early 1980's and very few countries save less than Americans. We just like to spend, myself included. This innate spendthrift-ness has it pros and cons, but don't let the behavior of others overshadow the importance of saving.

You can track the US personal savings rate here: (http://research.stlouisfed.org/fred2/series/PSAVERT/).

Our innate impulses make savings difficult, but not insurmountable. Everyone is different, but typical guidance suggests you save 10 to 15 percent of your annual income, and have 11 times your annual salary set aside by retirement. Another helpful tip is to put some math to your future expenditures and sketch out a conservative financial plan. Shining some light on your future financial needs may help one to spend more prudently today. You can also set up automatic deductions to fund your savings account and you can rather effortlessly put into motion some fiscal discipline.

Saving is hard, but necessary. Savings help to soften the impact of known and unknown liabilities, but it is also a prerequisite for investing. You need to be able to mobilize capital to gain exposure to the markets. Thus, the more you consume, the less you can put to work in the asset classes covered in this book....

- ☞ "If you can't save enough, be really nice to your kids." – Dan Ariely, professor of psychology and behavioral economics at Duke university

- ☞ "A penny saved is two (pretax) pennies earned." – Andrew Tobias, American journalist

- ☞ "Start saving now, not later: time is money." – Burton G. Malkiel, American author and economist

- ☞ "Anything that we can do to raise personal savings is very much in the interest of this country." – Alan Greenspan, Senate hearing (March 15th, 2005)

- ☞ "No strategy can make up for inadequate savings or premature retirement." – Robert Arnott, American investor and author

Lastly, no conversation about savings is complete without mentioning the *Rule of 72*. This is a simple formula that tells you how long it will take for your savings to double. Just divide 72 by your expected rate of return. So if you anticipate an eight percent return (the general rule of thumb for what you will get in the equity markets over the long haul) then you will double your money in 10.3 years (72 divided by 10). I view that as quite the bounty for the patient saver, and I'm not alone. Albert Einstein is believed to have once remarked that the most powerful force in the universe was 'compound interest.'

OVERTIME....

Don't Think. Just Save.

Automatic enrollments for defined contribution retirement plans, like a 401(k), represent a financial innovation success story. Participation rates, and corresponding savings amounts, increase from roughly 50 percent to upwards of 90 percent when this very simplistic plan feature is put in place. Savers should take note. Setting up automatic withdrawals from your account can enforce some fiscal discipline on those having a hard time trying to save.

If you have young children, like me, the escalating costs of college tuition are a substantial and unnerving future liability. In fact, the long-term inflation rate for college costs is in the four to six percent range, which is higher than just about every day-to-day expense you encounter. It's a risky gambit to rely on the cost curve for higher education being fixed in the future. Therefore, saving should start as soon as possible. As such, you may want to consider starting a 529 Plan, which are a terrific vehicle to prepare for that looming college expenditure. You can set up an automatic recurring withdrawal to impose some self-control on your finances. These plans grow tax-deferred with no income tax bill when you make college payments. Also, contributions can be deductible at the state level. Note that the outstanding amount of student loan debt now exceeds credit card debt. While the tax benefits of 529 plans are nice, the real advantage is alleviating your future college graduates from a smothering amount of debt.

Investing Like a Pension Plan

If you have a big expenditure right around the corner, you don't want to be swinging for the fences with your savings. When it comes to investing your savings in anticipation of such an outflow there is a rather sophisticated technique you can utilize. *Liability Matching* is a concept used by many defined benefit (pension) plans, which are considered some of the better risk managers out there in the investing business. These pension portfolios have recurring, somewhat predictable cash needs (i.e. retiree payments). The idea is to tailor a portfolio around these liabilities, which can be accomplished in a few ways. For instance, if a sum certain benefit payment is due on February 1st, they will have purchased a bond that matures the same day for the same amount. This concept can be employed outside the pension plan realm. For instance, if you settle on a house on February 1st, make sure you have this amount due (liability) invested in something that will deliver a steady return without much volatility, like a short duration investment grade bond fund, between now and then. So when that payment needs to go out the door, you can have some peace of mind knowing that your savings will be there too. The moral of the story is that anyone can be an effective risk manager. Just mimic the ones who have it down to a science.

DEMOGRAPHICS

Demographics are collection of statistical data points that paint a picture of a population. They are not insider information that comes out of thin air to abruptly impact asset prices. Material changes in demographics, such as age, gender, or education, are surely slow to develop. However, they shouldn't be ignored, as they can leave a significant and enduring impact on a country. The lasting effects of demographic changes help shape a country's economic potential and investors need to pay attention.

Whether it's age, gender, workforce participation (research has shown that a rise in female workers tends to boost an economy), or literacy levels, demographics are economic clues.[82] These population characteristics help shine light on the productive capacity of a nation, which can dictate a country's economic future. In other words, you want a population that is engaged and innovative, as that will ignite a country's economic potential. It does take a little digging to understand if a country is innovative and engaged, but demographic data can lead you to the answer.

"In a curious way, age is simpler than youth, for it has so many fewer options." – Stanley Kunitz, two-time U.S. poet laureate for 1974 and 2000

The world is getting older, which is one of the more salient demographic themes. Soon, for the first time, there will be more people on

---

82 "The Last Three Decades of Women's Rising Hours of Work Added $1.7 Trillion to GDP in 2012," *Center for Economic and Policy Research*, April 15, 2014.

the planet over the age of sixty-five than under the age of five.[83] As you might infer, it's not just industrialized nations that are aging, like Japan (they sell more adult than youth diapers there), but also some emerging countries, like China. Be sensitive to countries with an aging demographic, as their populations may not be the economic locomotives they once were. Note that many of the great business innovators of the past generation, like Elon Musk or Steve Jobs, were, well, young when they launched their famed businesses (Tesla and Apple, respectively). The population pool that is most conducive to unleashing economic growth is brimming with energized, intelligent, entrepreneurial, and often young individuals.

Another consideration of an aging population is that retirees have a pattern of slowing their consumption and liquidating their savings, which can put downward pressures on asset pricing. Aging can also be very taxing on entitlement systems, which is leading to a lot of the ugly math with Social Security and Medicare. We all age. It's an inevitable part of life. However, we can avoid some investing mistakes by being aware of this demographic clue.

The *Demographic Dividend* is a period of accelerating economic growth due to a decrease in a country's population rate. The economic gains outweigh the population growth, which increases per capita income levels. Also, government expenditures decline, as less strain is placed on entitlement systems and infrastructure and societal goods are taxed less.

Another noticeable demographic theme is urbanization. For instance, the year 2009 marked the first time in human history when more people lived in urban rather than rural areas. Urbanization tends to lead to a pick-up in per-capita incomes for a given nation. This migration from rural to urban areas entails the build out of infrastructure, housing, etc., which has a positive spill-over effect into the broader economy.

---

83 Daniel Pink, *Drive: The Surprising Truth About What Motivates Us* (New York: Riverhead, 2009).

Demographics are more than just census numbers. They are a treasure trove of data points that can help shape an investment strategy. Further, they can have a profound impact on the world around us....

- ❧ "Demography is destiny." – attributed to Auguste Comte, 19th century French philosopher

- ❧ "People do predictable things as they age . . . . The average family borrows the most when the parents are age forty-one, typically the time of their largest home purchase. They spend the most at age forty-six . . . . People save the most at age fifty-four and have the highest net worth at age sixty-four." – Harry S. Dent, Jr., *The Demographic Cliff: How to Survive and Prosper during the Great Deflation of 2014-2019* (2014)

MISCELLANEOUS

Here are a hodge-podge of quotations and thoughts that don't fit neatly into a category, but should provide some value for the eloquent investor....

⚘ "If there is any one secret of success, it lies in the ability to get the other person's point of view and see things from that person's angle as well as from your own." – Henry Ford

⚘ "To study and not think is a waste. To think and not study is dangerous." – Confucius

⚘ "Listen first. Speak last." – Peter Drucker, *The Effective Executive* (1967)

⚘ "Nothing recedes like success." – Bryan Forbes, as quoted in the London *Observer* (December 19th, 1971)

⚘ "The search for a scapegoat is the easiest of all hunting expeditions." – Dwight Eisenhower

⚘ "Baseball is the only field of endeavor where a man can succeed three times out of ten and still be considered a good performer." – Ted Williams, baseball hall of famer

Last, but not least....

⚘ "The first one to mention price in a negotiation loses." – Thomas J. Raymond, Sr. (my Dad)

CONCLUDING REMARKS

Success in investments may produce shallow or transitory benefits. In other words, the high you get from buying that new, flashy sports car or speedboat will only last so long. In the end, the definition of success is personal and subject to varying perspectives and it can certainly have another dimension to it unrelated to wealth. So here are some more unusual and feel-good ways people have looked at success….

- ☞ "The success of most people . . . almost always depends upon the favour and good opinion of their neighbors and equals; and without a tolerably regular conduct these can very seldom be obtained." – Adam Smith, *The Theory of Moral Sentiments* (1759)

- ☞ "Giving is one of the most important and rewarding parts of your Total Money Makeover. Once you are completely debt-free, you have that much more money to spend, invest and give. Just remember that money given produces more joy than it could ever buy. Whatever you make, set aside 10 percent to give to those less fortunate than you. If you cannot live off 90 percent of what you make, what makes you think you can live off 100 percent?" - Dave Ramsey, author and motivational speaker

> Studies show that nations with the happiest people are not the ones with the highest per capita income. Further, research shows that there is little correlation between money and happiness beyond minimum financial thresholds.

☞ "If I had to give a definition of happiness, it would be this: happiness needs nothing but itself; it doesn't have to be validated."
– Herman Koch, *The Dinner* (2009)

☞ "What is the use of living, if it be not to strive for noble causes and to make this muddled world a better place for those who will live in it after we are gone?" – Winston Churchill, (October 10th, 1908)

☞ "Do not let your happiness depend on something you may lose."
– C.S. Lewis, *The Four Loves* (1958)

☞ "Lay not up for yourselves treasures upon earth, where moth and rust doth corrupt, and where thieves break through and steal" – Matthew 6:19, Oxford King James Version.

☞ "Money and time are the heaviest burdens of life, and the unhappiest of all mortals are those who have more of either than they know how to use." – Samuel Johnson, *The Idler* (1758)

☞ "He has achieved success
who has lived well,
laughed often, and loved much;
who has enjoyed the trust of
pure women,
the respect of intelligent men and
the love of little children;
who has filled his niche and accomplished his task;
who has left the world better than he found it
whether by an improved poppy,
a perfect poem or a rescued soul;
who has never lacked appreciation of Earth's beauty
or failed to express it;

who has always looked for the best in others and
given them the best he had;
whose life was an inspiration;
whose memory a benediction."
 —Bessie Anderson Stanley, "Success" (1904)

SELECT BIOGRAPHIES

Robert Arnott – Arnott has had a varied career, but now serves as the face of Research Affiliates based in Newport Beach, California. He is a prolific writer and researcher with more than 100 published articles to his credit. I personally tend to gravitate toward his works that have an overarching theme of embracing common sense. His works are academic in caliber with a tendency to preach that fees, taxes, and commissions are not an investor's friend.

Ben Bernanke – Bernanke passed the baton to Janet Yellen as head of the Federal Reserve in February 2014. His tenure was certainly interesting, as he presided during one of the most difficult economic periods in the history of this country. A self-proclaimed scholar on the Great Depression, Bernanke feared a repeat of that economic famine and this largely shaped his governing actions. He sanctioned never-before-seen asset purchases and a zero interest rate policy that has lasted for half a decade. Frankly, it worked, if averting an economic calamity was the primary objective. However, skeptics will say his legacy has yet to be finalized, as there still could be long-term repercussions from his aggressive maneuvers.

John 'Jack' Bogle – Bogle is a pioneer of passive investing and the index fund. Bogle founded The Vanguard Group in 1975, which has since amassed close to $2 trillion in assets under management. He still frequently makes media appearances and remains a staunch proponent of investment simplicity, as low-cost, straightforward solutions can work wonders.

Ironically, Jack's son runs a high turnover, actively managed domestic small cap fund. Despite Jack's warnings regarding exotic investments, the fund has performed reasonably well. Through the end of January 2014, the fund had a ten year annualized return of 8.2 percent, which compares to the Russell 2000 Small Cap Index of 8.3 percent (using the corresponding passive solution of the iShares ETF as a proxy for performance).

Warren Buffett – Ben Graham passed away in 1976, but his spirit still lives on with the Oracle of Omaha. Buffett will forever live in investment lore not only for his majestic investment performance via his Berkshire Hathaway holding company, but his talents as an effective messenger. He has the uncanny ability to make the complex easy to grasp, which is typically accomplished through metaphors and analogies. His shareholder memos and sporadic op-ed columns are must-reads and Berkshire Hathaway's annual shareholders meeting attract loyal followers from all corners of the country.

Buffett's refreshingly simple approach has imitators, but it has come curiously during an era of complexity. Turnover has achieved new heights, hedge funds have gained assets at a blistering pace, and mathematically oriented 'quant' funds claim they have cracked the code on future market movements. Buffett would argue less is more, but it now seems that his message too often falls on deaf ears.

Jim Chanos – Chanos came to fame after uncovering the flaws at Enron and subsequently shorting the stock. That trade was quite the coup for Chanos, as Enron filed for bankruptcy in 2001. He has more recently shifted his focus to China, which he felt is an overheated economy set for an economic correction. As you may surmise, Chanos and his firm Kynikos Associates are mainly on the hunt for shorting opportunities. He is a bit of forensic accountant and fraud detective, as he is always on the lookout for questionable and unsustainable financial situations. Further, he can effectively do his work from afar. He once responded to criticism of his lack of on-the-ground research for his bearish stance on China with, "Well hell, I didn't work at Enron either."

Chanos is a busy man. He frequently appears on television with his prognostications. He also served as a consultant for the movie *Wall Street: Money Never Sleeps.* He teaches a class at the Yale Business School, his alma mater, called "Financial Fraud throughout History: A Forensic Approach."

Peter Drucker – Drucker passed away in 2005, but left an indelible mark on American business as a purveyor of management ideologies. He is often referred to as "the father of modern management" and has legions of disciples. During his storied career he was a management consultant, educator (the Claremont Graduate University now bears his name), and prolific author with 41 books to his credit, including co-authoring a book on Japanese painting, of all things. Drucker also was a staunch believer in the non-profit sector and a skeptic of the value of macroeconomics.

Benjamin Graham – Considered the father of value investing. Graham, born Benjamin Grossbaum, has spawned a slew of disciples, including investment heavyweights such as Warren Buffett and Charles Brandes. He authored a half dozen books, with none more famous than *The Intelligent Investor* and *Security Analysis* (co-authored with David Dodd). Outside writing, he spent decades as a professor at the Columbia Business School in New York, in part evangelizing the value investors' credo of 'buying low.'

Alan Greenspan – 'The Maestro' was at the helm of the Federal Reserve for close to two decades (1987-2006). He was more of a monetary dove then a hawk with a quick trigger on monetary stimulus when there appeared economic fragility. This perceived safety net came to be known as the 'Greenspan put' and it should come as no surprise that the Dow Jones Industrial Average grew more than four-fold during his tenure.

Greenspan was an Ayn Rand disciple. He firmly believed, like Rand, that the market and economy was best left off to its own devices. Individuals would act in their own self-interest and this would be a governor for excesses. This train of thought came under attack after the global credit crisis, when unbridled greed took the economy to the brink of collapse.

Seth Klarman – Klarman in 1983 founded the Baupost Group, one of the larger and more successful hedge funds. In fact, he was recently ranked by Bloomberg as the fourth best performing hedge fund manager of all time, coming behind George Soros, Ray Dalio, and John Paulson. However, he may be better known for his mark on the literary field. *Margin of Safety: Risk-Averse Value Investing Strategies for the Thoughtful Investor*, the value investor's definitive road map, retails on Amazon for at least $1,600 for used versions. There is a scarcity element driving the price to such heights. Perhaps unsurprising, it has been rumored to be one of the most commonly stolen books from libraries across the country.

Howard Marks – Marks was one of the co-founders of Oaktree Capital Management, LLC. He has a very intensive, but pragmatic, investment style that aligns more with the value camp. He is also a masterful writer. His Oaktree memos are must-reads, as they are a unique combination of academic, thought-provoking, and reader-friendly.
His memos can be found here: (http://www.oaktreecapital.com/memo. aspx).

John Paulson – Paulson cut his teeth in the investment business as a merger arbitrager, which bets on the probability of M&A events materializing. He branched off on his own in 1994 to form Paulson & Co. He had a respectable but unheralded track record in the hedge fund arena for over a decade, but all that changed when he saw the opportunity of a lifetime. Paulson bet big that the real estate market was on the verge of collapse, which was certainly at odds with conventional wisdom. His personal bounty for being correct on this call is said to be close to $4 billion and shorting the housing market has been referred to as "the greatest trade ever."

Paulson has had some swings and misses since then. He wrongfully garnered some bad press for Goldman Sachs's manufacturing of real estate securities that went belly up. He also took a heavy stake in gold, which had a trying 2013. Don't count Paulson out, as his firm does not lack the resources for future success. Surrounded by Ivy League talent and an advisory panel that has included Alan Greenspan and A. Gary Shilling, Paulson's performance could very well perk back up.

Jim Rogers – Rogers made his initial impact on the investing business was as co-manager of the Quantum Fund with George Soros, which was reported to deliver an eye-catching 4200 percent return during Rogers and Soros's first ten years together. He has since moved on to other ventures. Notably, in 1998, he founded the Rogers International Commodity Index. He has authored several books over the last twenty plus years, including *Investment Biker: Around the World with Jim Rogers* and *A Bull in China: Investing Profitably in the World's Greatest Market.*

Rogers has a heralded record as an investor, author, and business-man. Yet, he may be best known now for his colorful and unabashed comments on politics, markets, and the economy. In particular, he holds nothing back in his negative assessment of the loose money policies of our Federal Reserve. He also is a staunch believer that Asia will take the baton from the United States as the future epicenter of the global economy. He is putting his money where his mouth is, as he is making sure his children can speak Mandarin.

George Soros – Perhaps the most impressive aspect of Soros's career is the starting point. His career journey embodies a true 'rags to riches' story. Soros was born in Hungary in 1930. The Nazis would occupy Hungary by his teenage years, which prompted him to immigrate to England in 1947. He would soon enroll in the London School of Economics, but the student would eventually become the teacher.

Soros is often referred to as 'The Man Who Broke the Bank of England'. The renowned trader once profited approximately $1 billion on a trade that ultimately drove England out of the European Union, by betting an estimated $10 billion that currency was artificially high and the Bank of England would have to back away from defending it. They did, and the legend of Soros was born. While a billion dollars isn't what it once was, it still was a remarkable feat for an investor to take on and defeat a Central Bank. Consequently, Soros's reported buy and sell activity always makes the press.

Jack Welch – Welch is another management guru and a man driven by success. His fame came from taking General Electric to new heights. During his role as chief executive, from 1981 through 2001, the stock's market capitalization grew 30-fold. Welch is certainly a bright mind, as he has a PhD in chemical engineering. These smarts were combined with an aggressive management philosophy. Notably, he would ritualistically lay off the bottom ten percent of his work force. He felt he was doing these displaced 'non-producers' a favor, as their talents were best suited for another profession.

ACKNOWLEDGEMENTS

Being a non-famous first-timer trying to break into the book biz is humbling, rewarding, and exciting, but certainly a trying experience. Without some words of encouragement and good counsel along the way, who knows if this book would have ever gotten finished. So it may seem like a big cliché, but thanks are due. First, I am indebted to my two consigliores. Erin Arvedlund got a lot of frantic calls when this voyage took some unexpected twists and turns. As a first-rate author who has been through this process, she provided invaluable insight. She also led me to my hired gun Deb Englander. Debbie challenged me to make this more than a quote book, which was more or less what it was when she first got her hands on the manuscript. She pushed me, and hopefully her nudging made this book a more enjoyable read.

Keith Whitaker and Kristen Doyle Highland also deserve a nod. Their support and counsel was so very vital. More specifically, Kristen led me to my copy editor – Morgan Wyeth Shnier. He gave this manuscript an invaluable facelift and was as good of a business partner as I could have asked for. I would vouch for this NYU product any time. Then there are those good corporate citizens out there who made the permissions process as painless as possible. There were a few who want the extra mile and my hat is off to you. I owe you one for sparing me some grief and aggravation. As is always the case, there are others who I am failing to mention that deserve some recognition. Sorry for not naming names, but understand that I am certainly grateful.

Then there is my wife – Kieren. She bared the brunt of fulfilling this dream of mine. She had to put in overtime to make sure the Raymond ship didn't sink. Mission accomplished, but not without going through some rough seas. She also played the role of editor-in-chief at times, and this book is better written because of her, if you ask me. It's not lost on me how much you helped. I hope this book makes you proud. It's for you, the G-man, and Owie.

PERMISSIONS

Core Principles

"Great investors . . . for sport." – David F. Swensen, chief investment officer of the Yale endowment, as quoted in Sebastian Mallaby's *More Money Than God* (2010). Used with permission from Penguin Group.

"Wishing will . . . bring riches." - Napoleon Hill, *Think and Grow Rich* (1937). Used with permission from Penguin Group.

"It's not supposed . . . easy is stupid." – Charlie Munger, Vice-Chairman of Berkshire Hathaway, Oaktree Capital Management, LLC, *It's All a Big Mistake* (June 20th, 2012). Used with permission from Oaktree Capital Management, LLC.

"I have . . . none, zero." – Charlie Munger, Berkshire Hathaway Annual Meeting (2003). Used with permission from Charlie Munger.

"And this . . . the world." – John Steinbeck, *East of Eden* (1952). Used with permission from Penguin Group.

"The person . . . their calling." - Napoleon Hill, *Think and Grow Rich* (1937). Used with permission from Penguin Group.

"He will . . . priced automobile." - Edwin LeFevre, *Reminiscences of a Stock Operator* (1923). Copyright © 2006. Used with permission from John Wiley & Sons, Inc. Any third party material is expressly excluded from this permission.

"Failure is . . . within reach." – Napoleon Hill, *Think and Grow Rich* (1937). Used with permission from Penguin Group.

"The Mistake . . . play line." - Edwin LeFevre, *Reminiscences of a Stock Operator* (1923). Copyright © 2006. Used with permission from John Wiley & Sons, Inc. Any third party material is expressly excluded from this permission.

Economics

"No one . . . so on." – Ruchir Sharma, *Breakout Nations: In Pursuit of the Next Economic Miracles* (2012). Used with permission from W.W. Norton & Company, Inc.

"The 'boom' . . . consumer desires." – Murray Rothbard, *America's Great Depression* (1963). Used with permission from Mises Institute.

"Being an . . . Austrian school." – Nouriel Roubini and Stephen Mihm, *Crisis Economics: A Crash Course in the Future of Finance* (2011). Used with permission from Penguin Group.

"Creative destruction. . . of capitalism." – Ruchir Sharma, *Breakout Nations: In Pursuit of the Next Economic Miracles* (2012). Used with permission from W.W. Norton & Company, Inc.

"In a depressed . . . to invest." – Paul Krugman, *End This Depression Now!* (2012). Used with permission from W.W. Norton & Company, Inc.

"If a country . . . financial circles." – Mark Skousen, *The Big Three in Economics: Adam Smith, Karl Marx, and John Maynard Keynes* (2007). Used with permission from M. E. Sharpe, Inc.

"There is . . . or China." – Kenneth Rogoff, *Technology and Inequality* (June 20th, 2011). Used with permission from Kenneth Rogoff.

"It is difficult . . . understanding it!" – Upton Sinclair, *I, Candidate for Governor: And How I Got Licked* (1935). Used with permission from University of California Press.

"Of all . . . most of the time?" – Howard Marks, *The Most Important Thing: Uncommon Sense for the Thoughtful Investor* (2011). Copyright © 2011. Used with permission from Columbia University Press.

"If you . . . his shirt." - Nassim Nicholas Taleb, *The Black Swan: The Impact of the Highly Improbable (2007)*. Used with permission from Random House.

"It is . . . the professionals." – Benjamin Graham, *World Commodities and World Currencies* (1944). Used with permission from Martino Publishing.

"If there . . . my attention." – Bob Kirby, as quoted in *Capital: The Story of Long-Term Investment Excellence by Charles Ellis* (2004). Copyright © 2004. Used with permission from John Wiley & Sons, Inc. Any third party material is expressly excluded from this permission.

Monetary Policy

"Since its . . . bubble economy." – Michael G. Pento, *The Coming Bond Market Collapse: How to Survive the Demise of the U.S. Debt Market* (2013). Copyright © 2013. Used with permission from John Wiley & Sons, Inc. Any third party material is expressly excluded from this permission.

"In the . . . their votes." – Ron Paul, *The Revolution: A Manifesto* (2008). Used with permission from Grand Central Publishing.

"How does . . . create stimulus?" – Colm O'Shea, as quoted in *Hedge Fund Market Wizards* by Jack Schwager (2012). Copyright © 2012. Used with permission from John Wiley & Sons, Inc. Any third party material is expressly excluded from this permission.

"The reason . . . higher demand." – Paul Krugman, *End This Depression Now!* (2012). Used with permission from W.W. Norton & Company, Inc.

"One myth . . . printing money." - Ben Bernanke, 60 Minutes interview (December 3rd, 2010). Used with permission from CBS News/60 Minutes.

"The money . . . Treasury securities." – Ben Bernanke, 60 Minutes Interview (December 3rd, 2010). Used with permission from CBS News/60 Minutes.

Politics

"we exist . . . our orbits." – Mohsin Hamid, *How to Get Filthy Rich in Rising Asia* (2013). Used with permission from Penguin Group.

"As business . . . profit-making." – Ludwig Von Mises. Used with permission from Liberty Fund, Inc.

"Civilization is . . . from men." - Ayn Rand, *The Fountainhead* (1943). Used with permission from Penguin Group.

"The state . . . and disaster." – Ludwig Von Mises, *Omnipotent Government: The Rise of the Total State and Total War* (1944). Used with permission from Liberty Fund, Inc.

"If he . . . heavier taxes." – Ayn Rand, *The Ayn Rand Letter*. Used with permission from the Ayn Rand Institute.

"Big government . . . enough authority." – W. James Antle III, *Devouring Freedom: Can Big Government Ever be Stopped?* (2013), Published by Regnery Publishing, Inc. Copyright 2013. All rights reserved. Reprinted by special permission of Regnery Publishing, Washington, DC.

Portfolio Construction

"A good . . . of contingencies." – Harry Markowitz, *Portfolio Selection: Efficient Diversification of Investments* (1959). Used with permission from John Wiley & Sons, Inc. Any third party material is expressly excluded from this permission.

"The will . . . is vital." – Joe Paterno, former head football coach at Penn State. Used with permission from Jay Paterno.

"Stock market . . . pay dividends." – Edwin LeFevre, *Reminiscences of a Stock Operator* (1923). Copyright © 2006. Used with permission from John Wiley & Sons, Inc. Any third party material is expressly excluded from this permission.

"If you . . . in stocks." – John Bogle. Used with permission from John Bogle.

"Trends can . . . incredible celerity." – Barton Biggs, *Diary of a Hedgehog* (2012). Copyright © 2012. Used with permission from John Wiley & Sons, Inc. Any third party material is expressly excluded from this permission.

Business Success

"Google did . . . it in the hands of people." – Khanjan Mehta, "Why Ideas Fail," *The Penn Stater*, pg. 26 (January/February 2014). Used with permission from The Penn Stater magazine.

"In the . . . you create." – David Ogilvy, considered the Father of Advertising. Used with permission from Ogilvy & Mather.

"If anybody . . . potential success!" – Jim Rogers, *A Gift to My Children: A Father's Lessons for Life and Investing* (2009). Used with permission from Random House.

"The best . . . invent it!" – Alan Kay, American computer scientist (1971). Used with permission from Alan Kay and Viewpoints Research Institute.

"Thomas Edison . . . light bulb." – Napoleon Hill, *Think and Grow Rich* (1937). Used with permission from Penguin Group.

"Small companies . . . interest them." – Jack Welch, Letter to Share Owners in 1992 General Electric Annual Report. Used with permission from General Electric.

"If you . . . breeds mediocrity." – Tom Rath and Barry Conchie, *Strengths Based Leadership* (2009). Used with permission from Gallup Press.

"Those who . . . their performance." – Peter Drucker, *The Five Most Important Questions You Will Ever Ask About Your Organization (2008).* Copyright © 2008. Used with permission

Equities

"…. that discounting…..be watching." – David Durand, *Growth Stocks and the Petersburg Paradox*, The Journal of Finance © 1957, American Finance Association. Used with permission from John Wiley & Sons, Inc. Any third party material is expressly excluded from this permission.

"Smart investing … people understand." – Howard Marks, Oaktree Capital Management, LLC. Used with permission from Oaktree Capital Management, LLC.

"Do not . . . 'just right'." – Napoleon Hill, *Think and Grow Rich* (1937). Used with permission from Penguin Group.

"Over the . . . too expensively."– Jim Leitner, Falcon Management, as quoted in *Inside the House of Money* by Steven Drobny (2006). Copyright © 2006. Used with permission from John Wiley & Sons, Inc. Any third party material is expressly excluded from this permission.

"Over the . . . a result." – Charlie Munger. Used with permission from Charlie Munger.

"There are . . . feedback loops." – Nassim Taleb, *Fooled by Randomness* (2004). Used with permission from Random House and Nicholas Taleb.

"There are . . . opposite direction." – Mohsin Hamid, *How to Get Filthy Rich in Rising Asia* (2013). Used with permission from Penguin Group.

"For purposes . . . least resistance." - Edwin LeFevre, *Reminiscences of a Stock Operator* (1923). Copyright © 2006. Used with permission from John Wiley & Sons, Inc. Any third party material is expressly excluded from this permission.

"I never . . . you anywhere." - Edwin LeFevre, *Reminiscences of a Stock Operator* (1923). Copyright © 2006. Used with permission from John Wiley & Sons, Inc. Any third party material is expressly excluded from this permission.

"A trend . . . end…?" – Sir Alec Cairncross, Chief Economic Advisor to the British Government in 1960, as quoted in Barton Biggs's *Hedgehogging* (2008). Copyright © 2008. Used with permission from John Wiley & Sons, Inc. Any third party material is expressly excluded from this permission.

"According to the 2003 study . . . as stated by Robert Arnott." – Research Affiliates, LLC. Used with permission from Research Affiliates, LLC.

"If we . . . social insurance." – Robert Shiller, *Irrational Exuberance* (2005). Copyright © 2005. Used with permission from Princeton University Press.

Fixed Income

"A pure equity . . . the enterprise." – Stephen Schwarz and Daniel Lathrope, *Fundamentals of Corporate Taxation* (2012). Used with permission from Stephen Schwarz and Daniel Lathrope.

"High-yield . . . are refinanced." – Wilbur Ross, "Q&A with Wilbur Ross," *The Deal* (August 31st, 2012). Used with permission from *The Deal*.

"After all . . . with interest." – Michael G. Pento, *The Coming Bond Market Collapse: How to Survive the Demise of the U.S. Debt Market* (2013). Copyright © 2013. Used with permission from John Wiley & Sons, Inc. Any third party material is expressly excluded from this permission.

"[Friedrich Hayek . . . cause them." – Biography of Friedrich Hayek, from *The Concise Encyclopedia of Economics* (2008). Source: Library of Economics and Liberty. (http://www.econlib.org/library/Enc/bios/Hayek.html)

Cash

"This is perhaps . . . of all assets." – James Montier, *A Value Investor's Perspective on Tail Risk Protection: An Ode to the Joy of Cash* (June 2011). Used with permission from Grantham Mayo van Otterloo.

Real Estate

"Commercial real . . . and jobs come out." – Johnny Isakson, United States Senator (January 13th, 2010). *U.S. Sen. Johnny Isakson, R-GA, discusses real estate, health care with Examiner (Part 2)*. Used with permission from The Examiner.

Gold & Currencies

"Since the . . . suggest otherwise." – Robert Murphy, *Fiat Money and the Euro Crisis*, Mises Institute (October 10th, 2011). Used with permission from the Mises Institute.

"There's fool's . . . worthless dollars." – Jarod Kintz, *This Book Has No Title* (2012). Used with permission from Jarod Kintz.

"There is . . . other outcomes." – Mike Hewitt, "The Fate of Paper Money," *DollarDaze.org* (January 7th, 2009). Used with permission from Mike Hewitt.

Alternative Investments

"The top . . . $350 million." – Simon Lack, *The Hedge Fund Mirage: The Illusion of Big Money and Why It's Too Good to Be True* (2012). Copyright © 2012. Used with permission

Commodities

"Passive investing . . . the average." – David Stein, Parametric Portfolio Associates (2003). Used with permission from Parametric Portfolio Associates.

"Fiduciaries should . . . actively managed funds." – Michael C. Keenan, *The Elephant in the Living Room,* Financial Advisor Magazine (May 2008). Used with permission from Financial Advisors magazine.

"Unfortunately, this . . . even decades." – Robert Shiller, *Irrational Exuberance* (2005). Copyright © 2005. Used with permission from Princeton University Press.

"A random walk . . . be predicted." – Burton G. Malkiel, *A Random Walk Down Wall Street* (1973). Used with permission from W.W. Norton & Company, Inc.

"In relatively calm mark . . . in their dynamics." – Andrew Lo, *The Volatility of Volatility,* CFA Institute Magazine, pg. 33 (Sept/Oct 2013). Used with permission from the CFA Institute.

"While markets . . . aggregate market." – Robert Shiller, as quoted in *Crisis Economics* by Nouriel Roubini and Stephen Mihm (2011). Used with permission from Penguin Group.

Inflation

"For just . . . Thanks, inflation!" – Jarod Kintz, *This Book Has No Title* (2012). Used with permission from Jarod Kintz.

"Inflation is . . . the poor." – Michael G. Pento, *The Coming Bond Market Collapse: How to Survive the Demise of the U.S. Debt Market* (2013). Copyright © 2013. Used with permission from John Wiley & Sons, Inc. Any third party material is expressly excluded from this permission.

"Mere inflation . . . is not." – Henry Hazlitt, *Economics in One Lesson: The Shortest and Surest Way to Understand Basic Economics* (1946). Used with permission from Random House.

"As Japan . . . corporate profits." – Barton Biggs, *Diary of a Hedgehog* (2012). Copyright © 2012. Used with permission from John Wiley & Sons, Inc. Any third party material is expressly excluded from this permission.

"People associate . . . economic stagnation." – Michael G. Pento, *The Bond Market Collapse: How to Survive the Demise of the U.S. Debt Market* (2013). Copyright © 2013. Used with permission from John Wiley & Sons, Inc. Any third party material is expressly excluded from this permission.

"When inflation . . . ratios fall." – Barton Biggs, *Diary of a Hedgehog* (2012). Copyright © 2012. Used with permission from John Wiley & Sons, Inc. Any third party material is expressly excluded from this permission.

Illustrated below . . . 4.2 trillion. Source: Gene Smiley, *Rethinking the Great Depression* (2002). Used with permission from Ivan R. Dee publishing.

Behavioral Finance

"All people are . . . don't have them." - Peter Hatemi, "Are We Born Biased?," *The Penn Stater*, pg. 39 (September/October 2013). Used with permission from The Penn Stater magazine.

"People in . . . clear advantage." – John Henry, American businessman and owner of the Boston Red Sox, as quoted in Michael Lewis, *Moneyball: The Art of Winning an Unfair Game* (2004). Used with permission from W.W. Norton & Company, Inc.

"No matter . . . things up." – Howard Marks, *The Most Important Thing: Uncommon Sense for the Thoughtful Investor* (2011). Copyright © 2011. Used with permission from Columbia University Press.

"A large body . . . especially *recent* ones." – Robert Arnott & Denis Chaves, Research Affiliates, LLC, *Mind the (Expectations) Gap: Demographic Trends and GDP* (June 2013). Used with permission from Research Affiliates, LLC.

"When you . . . to sell." – John Neff, *John Neff on Investing* (2001). Copyright © 2001. Used with permission from John Wiley & Sons, Inc. Any third party material is expressly excluded from this permission.

"When things . . . ever so." – Howard Marks, *The Most Important Thing: Uncommon Sense for the Thoughtful Investor* (2011). Copyright © 2011. Used with permission from Columbia University Press.

"You can . . . same time." – Joe Rosenberg, *The Best Opportunities in a Half-Century*, *Barron's* (December 3rd, 2011). Reprinted with permission of *Barron's* Copyright © 2013 Dow Jones & Company, Inc. All Rights Reserved Worldwide. License number 3407181371755.

"Generally speaking . . . be correct." – George Soros, *The New Paradigm for Financial Markets: The Credit Crisis of 2008 and What It Means* (2008). Copyright © 2008. Reprinted by permission of PublicAffairs, a member of The Perseus Books Group.

"Fortunately or . . . the decline." – Barton Biggs, *Diary of a Hedgehog* (2012). Copyright © 2012. Used with permission from John Wiley & Sons, Inc. Any third party material is expressly excluded from this permission.

"In investing . . . rarely profitable." - Robert Arnott, Research Affiliates, LLC, Pension Fund Investment Management (1997). Used with permission from Research Affiliates, LLC.

"Human biases . . . not disconfirmation." – Jim Leitner, Falcon Management, as quoted in *Inside the House of Money* by Steven Drobny (2006). Copyright © 2006. Used with permission from John Wiley & Sons, Inc. Any third party material is expressly excluded from this permission.

"When you . . . more accurate." – Nassim Taleb, *The Black Swan: The Impact of the Highly Improbable* (2007). Used with permission from Random House.

"Opinions are . . . on earth." – Napoleon Hill, *Think and Grow Rich* (1937). Used with permission from Penguin Group.

"Many portfolio . . . their investors." – Allan H. Meltzer, American economist and professor at Carnegie Mellon University (August 2007). Used with permission from Allan H. Meltzer.

"It has . . . right one." - Nassim Taleb, *The Black Swan: The Impact of the Highly Improbable* (2007). Used with permission from Random House.

"By far . . . for professionals." – Jeremy Grantham (2012). Used with permission from Grantham Mayo van Otterloo.

"You will . . . not in control." – Antonio Damasio, professor of neuroscience. Used with permission from Antonio Damasio.

"Unlike dice . . . future generally." – Roger Lowenstein, *When Genius Failed* (2000). Used with permission from Random House.

Bubbles, Manias, and the Inevitable Crash

"the term . . . their valuations." – Cliff Asness, *My Top 10 Peeves*, Financial Analysts Journal, Volume 70, Number 1, ©2014, CFA Institute. Used with permission from the CFA Institute.

"It is . . . create bubbles." – Barton Biggs, *Diary of a Hedgehog* (2012). Copyright © 2012. Used with permission from John Wiley & Sons, Inc. Any third party material is expressly excluded from this permission.

"I define . . . gambler's excitement." – Robert Shiller, *Irrational Exuberance* (2005). Copyright © 2005. Used with permission from Princeton University Press.

"all three . . . in question." – Michael G. Pento, *The Coming Bond Market Collapse: How to Survive the Demise of the U.S. Debt Market* (2013). Copyright © 2013. Used with permission from John Wiley & Sons, Inc. Any third party material is expressly excluded from this permission.

"To be a great . . . speculating on bubbles." – Paul Strebel, chair of the Board of Directors at IMD, the Lausanne-based business school. Used with permission from Paul Strebel.

"The big . . . on paper." – Edwin LeFevre, *Reminiscences of a Stock Operator* (1923). Copyright © 2006. Used with permission from John Wiley & Sons, Inc. Any third party material is expressly excluded from this permission.

"Whatever the . . . a bang." – John Kenneth Galbraith, *A Short History of Financial Euphoria* (1990). Used with permission from Penguin Group.

The Sovereign Debt Bubble

"Boom-bust . . . equity leveraging." – George Soros, *The New Paradigm for Financial Markets: The Credit Crisis of 2008 and What It Means* (2008). Copyright © 2008. Reprinted by permission of PublicAffairs, a member of The Perseus Books Group.

"All crises . . . of payment." – John Kenneth Galbraith, *A Short History of Financial Euphoria* (1990). Used with permission from Penguin Group.

"There is . . . no exception." – Michael G. Pento, *The Coming Bond Market Collapse: How to Survive the Demise of the U.S. Debt Market* (2013). Copyright © 2013. Used with permission from John Wiley & Sons, Inc. Any third party material is expressly excluded from this permission.

"The United . . . nineteenth century." – Dani Rodrik, *The Globalization Paradox: Democracy and the Future of the World Economy* (2012). Used with permission from W.W. Norton & Company, Inc.

"Both the . . . all happened." – Paul Krugman, *End This Depression Now!* (2012). Used with permission from W.W. Norton & Company, Inc.

Taxes

"American tax . . . is incorrect." – Dave Barry, Pulitzer Prize winning author and columnist. Used with permission from Dave Barry.

Globalization

"No one . . . and Eve." – James Wolfensohn, economist and former president of The World Bank (August 1st, 2001). Used with permission from The World Bank.

"There globalization . . . and lose." – Med Jones, CEO Quarterly Magazine, Global Economic Outlook 2011, (January 3ʳᵈ, 2011). Used with permission from CEO Q Magazine.

"Never before . . . standard of living." – Martin Wolf, *Why Globalization Works* (2004). Used with permission from Martin Wolf and Yale University Press.

"It's worth . . . nation's people." – *Japan as Number Three: Beijing's rise, Tokyo's fall and the Wealth of Nations, The Wall Street Journal* (August 17ᵗʰ, 2010). Reprinted with permission of *The Wall Street Journal* Copyright © 2013 Dow Jones & Company, Inc. All Rights Reserved Worldwide. License number 3412471438294.

"Globalization is . . . of capitalism." – Dani Rodrik, *The Globalization Paradox: Democracy and the Future of the World Economy* (2012). Used with permission from W.W. Norton & Company, Inc.

"Wouldn't it . . . to work?" – Dani Rodrik, *The Globalization Paradox: Democracy and the Future of the World Economy (*2012). Used with permission from W.W. Norton & Company, Inc.

"Trade agreements . . . the treaty." – Michael G. Pento, *The Coming Bond Market Collapse: How to Survive the Demise of the U.S. Debt Market* (2013). Copyright © 2013. Used with permission from John Wiley & Sons, Inc. Any third party material is expressly excluded from this permission.

"The inevitable . . . economic growth." – Dani Rodrik, *The Globalization Paradox: Democracy and the Future of the World Economy* (2012). Used with permission from W.W. Norton & Company, Inc.

"If financial . . . somewhere else." – George Soros, *The New Paradigm for Financial Markets: The Credit Crisis of 2008 and What It Means* (2008). Copyright © 2008. Reprinted by permission of PublicAffairs, a member of The Perseus Books Group.

"some groups . . . people lose." – Dani Rodrik, *The Globalization Paradox: Democracy and the Future of the World Economy* (2012). Used with permission from W.W. Norton & Company, Inc.

"Outsourcing and . . . $1.12 to $1.14." – Larry Elder, *Lou Dobbs to outsourcing: Drop dead*, WND.com Commentary (March 10ᵗʰ, 2005). Used with permission from WND.

"frontier markets . . . to play." - Ben Levishon, *Braving the Frontier Markets, Barron's* (February 9ᵗʰ, 2013). Reprinted with permission of *Barron's* Copyright © 2013 Dow Jones & Company, Inc. All Rights Reserved Worldwide. License number 3407180517204.

"At the . . . about 80:1." – Dani Rodrik, *The Globalization Paradox: Democracy and the Future of the World Economy* (2012). Used with permission from W.W. Norton & Company, Inc.

"All successful . . . rotten door." – Excerpt from *The Age of Uncertainty* by John Kenneth Galbraith. Copyright © 1977 by John Kenneth Galbraith. Reprinted by permission of Houghton Mifflin Harcourt Publishing Company. All rights reserved.

"Economically considered . . . bad business." – Ludwig Von Mises, *Nation, State, and Economy* (1919). Used with permission from Liberty Fund, Inc.

China

"Just think . . . the world." – Burton G. Malkiel and Patricia Taylor, *From Wall Street to the Great Wall: How Investors Can Profit from China's Booming Economy* (2008). Used with permission from W.W. Norton & Company, Inc.

"China is . . . growth momentum." – Ruchir Sharma, *Breakout Nations: In Pursuit of the Next Economic Miracles* (2012). Used with permission from W.W. Norton & Company, Inc.

"China's economy . . . sustained level." – Wells Fargo Wealth Management, Global Perspectives Weekly (July 18th, 2013). Used with permission from Wells Fargo Bank, N.A.

"The aging . . . raise wages." – Ruchir Sharma, *Breakout Nations: In Pursuit of the Next Economic Miracles* (2012). Used with permission from W.W. Norton & Company, Inc.

Impact Investing

"I believe . . . their product." – Mats Lederhausen, Investor and former McDonald's executive, as quoted in Daniel Pink's *Drive* (2009)

"Pursuit of . . . a purpose." – Antony Bugg-Levine and Jed Emerson, *Impact Investing* (2011). Copyright © 2011. Used with permission from John Wiley & Sons, Inc. Any third party material is expressly excluded from this permission.

"Not all . . . prosperity." – Michael Porter and Mark Kramer, *The Big Idea: Creating Shared Value* (January/February 2011). Used with permission from Harvard Business Review.

"The environment . . . is silent." – John Mackey, Rajendra S. Sisodia, and Bill George, *Conscious Capitalism* (2013). Used with permission from Harvard Business Press Books.

"When governments . . . and miss." - W. James Antle III, *Devouring Freedom: Can Big Government Ever be Stopped?* (2013). Published by Regnery Publishing, Inc. Copyright 2013. All rights reserved. Reprinted by special permission of Regnery Publishing, Washington, DC.

"But no . . . economic development." – Antony Bugg-Levine and Jed Emerson, *Impact Investing* (2011). Copyright © 2011. Used with permission from John Wiley & Sons, Inc. Any third party material is expressly excluded from this permission.

"Listen, global . . . 150 years." - Bjørn Lomborg, author of *The Skeptical Environmentalist*. Used with permission from Bjørn Lomborg.

"European Union . . . by 2100." - Bjørn Lomborg. Used with permission from Bjørn Lomborg.

"In the rich . . . are increasing." - Bjørn Lomborg. Used with permission from Bjørn Lomborg.

"If we . . . mid-century." - Bjørn Lomborg. Used with permission from Bjørn Lomborg.

Risk Management

Vinny Mattone said," You're finished." As quoted in Roger Lowenstein's *When Genius Failed* (2000). Used with permission from Random House.

"Risk means . . . will happen." – Elroy Dimson, professor at the London Business School. Used with permission from Professor Elroy Dimson.

"Traders come . . . to stay." – Nassim Taleb, *Fooled by Randomness* (2004). Used with permission from Random House and Nicholas Taleb.

"The paradox . . . for them." – Howard Marks, *The Most Important Thing: Uncommon Sense for the Thoughtful Investor* (2011). Copyright © 2011. Used with permission from Columbia University Press.

"In trading . . . really matters." – Anonymous, as quoted in *Inside the House of Money* by Steven Drobny (2006). Copyright © 2006. Used with permission from John Wiley & Sons, Inc. Any third party material is expressly excluded from this permission.

"Riskier investments . . . less certain." – Howard Marks, *The Most Important Thing: Uncommon Sense for the Thoughtful Investor* (2011). Copyright © 2011. Used with permission from Columbia University Press.

"Riskier investments . . . be riskier." – Howard Marks, Oaktree Capital Management, LLC, *Risk* (January 19th, 2006). Used with permission from Oaktree Capital Management, LLC.

"It is . . . careful management." – Brad Berggren, Parametric Portfolio Associates (2013). Used with permission from Parametric Portfolio Associates.

"Don't bunt . . . of immortals." – David Ogilvy. Used with permission from Ogilvy & Mather.

"All markets . . . that matters." – Colm O'Shea, as quoted in *Hedge Fund Market Wizards* by Jack Schwager (2012). Copyright © 2012. Used with permission from John Wiley & Sons, Inc. Any third party material is expressly excluded from this permission.

"Uncertainty . . . at all." – Frank Knight, *Risk, Uncertainty, and Profit* (1964). Source: Library of Economics and Liberty. (http://www.econlib.org/library/Knight/knRUP.html.)

"Yet each . . . by coincidence." – Peter L. Bernstein, "Is Investing For the Long Term Theory or Just Mumbo-Jumbo?," *Journal of Post Keynesian Economics* (Spring 1993), Vol. 15, No. 3. Used with permission from M.E. Sharpe, Inc.

"Above all . . . to fool." – Charlie Munger. Used with permission from Charlie Munger.

"The speculator's . . . human animal." – Edwin LeFevre, *Reminiscences of a Stock Operator* (1923). Copyright © 2006. Used with permission from John Wiley & Sons, Inc. Any third party material is expressly excluded from this permission.

"Sooner or . . . to unravel." – Sebastian Mallaby, *More Money Than God* (2010). Used with permission from Penguin Group.

"But reaching . . . performance." – Charles Ellis, *Murder on the Orient Express: The Mystery of Underperformance*, Financial Analysts Journal, CFA Institute (July/August 2012). Used with permission from the CFA Institute.

"Investment risk . . . risk aversion." – Howard Marks, *The Most Important Thing: Uncommon Sense for the Thoughtful Investor* (2011). Copyright © 2011. Used with permission from Columbia University Press.

"We'd be. . . unwanted partners." – Paul Krugman, *End this Depression Now!* (2012). Used with permission from W.W. Norton & Company, Inc.

"With borrowed . . . be immortal." – Mohsin Hamid, *How to Get Filthy Rich in Rising Asia* (2013). Used with permission from Penguin Group.

Diversification

"at least . . . 60 percent." – Burton G. Malkiel, *A Random Walk Down Wall Street* (1973). Used with permission from W.W. Norton & Company, Inc.

"We much . . . so business." – Warren Buffet, "5 ways Warren Buffett invests that you don't," *Fidelity* (March 14th, 2013). Used with permission from Fidelity.

Banking/Financial System

"You can't . . . financial system." – Paul Krugman, *End This Depression Now!* (2012). Used with permission from W.W. Norton & Company, Inc.

"The biggest . . . be quantified." – Gabriel Bornstein, managing director of Enclave Capital, LLC, as quoted in Bob Ivry's *The Seven Sins of Wall Street* (2014). Copyright © 2014. Reprinted by permission of PublicAffairs, a member of The Perseus Books Group.

"On occasion . . . same time." – Paul Krugman, *End This Depression Now!* (2012). Used with permission from W.W. Norton & Company, Inc.

Family/Generational Wealth

"I'd hate . . . use for." – Sam Walton, *Sam Walton: Made in America* (1992). Used with permission from Random House.

"The question . . . products second." – Charles W. Collier, *Wealth in Families* (2001). Used with permission from Charles W. Collier.

Savings

"If you . . . your kids." – Dan Ariely. Used with permission from Dan Ariely.

"A penny . . . pennies earned." – Andrew Tobias. Used with permission from Andrew Tobias.

"Start saving . . . is money." – Burton G. Malkiel. Used with permission from Burton G. Malkiel.

"No strategy . . . premature retirement." – Robert Arnott, Research Affiliates, LLC, "The Glidepath Illusion" (September 2012) (http://www.researchaffiliates.com/Our%20 Ideas/Insights/Fundamentals/Pages/F_2012_Sep_The_Glidepath_Illusion.aspx). Used with permission from Research Affiliates, LLC.

Demographics

"In a . . . fewer options." – Stanley Kunitz, former U.S. poet laureate, as quoted in Daniel Pink's *Drive* (2009). Used with permission from Penguin Group.

"People do . . . sixty-four." – Harry S. Dent, Jr., *The Demographic Cliff: How to Survive and Prosper during the Great Deflation of 2014-2019* (2014). Use with permission from Penguin Group.

Concluding Remarks

"Giving is . . . 100 percent?" – Dave Ramsey. Used with permission from Dave Ramsey.

"If I . . . be validated." – Herman Koch, *The Dinner* (2009). Used with permission from Random House.

Praise for
The Eloquent Investor

"The Eloquent Investor has something for someone that is currently an active investor or someone that is thinking about getting started. Many of the quotes are what we have heard over the years and now you can enjoy these and many others, which causes you to think about the meaning and how it relates to your own experience."

– Bill Wallach, CEO, ILC Dover, LP

"An encyclopedia of words of wisdom for financial services professionals. A fantastic resource to use when conversing with clients about private wealth management."

– David Nanigian, Ph.D.,
Associate Professor of Investments at The American College

"A one-stop guide for business advice and investment strategy from the world's most successful people, a must read for any business owner."

– Kevin O'Malley, co-owner, Indie Brewing Company

"Tom Raymond was one of my finest students in the Graduate Tax Program at Villanova University. He brings the same high level of intelligence, clarity and practicality to this book."

– Prof. Christopher Woehrle, JD, LL.M (Tax),
The Guardian Deppe Chair in Pensions and
Retirement Planning & Adjunct Professor of Taxation,
Villanova Law School

"Brimming with wisdom and wit. Full of practical knowledge for the business school student or experienced professional."
– Cynthia Axelrod, CFA,
Assistant Professor at Temple University's Fox School of Business

About the Author

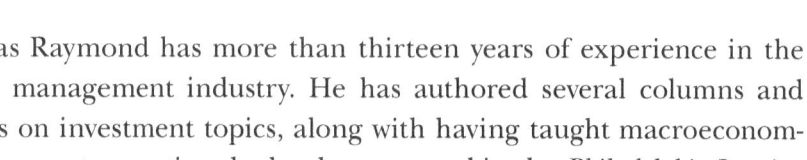

Thomas Raymond has more than thirteen years of experience in the wealth management industry. He has authored several columns and reports on investment topics, along with having taught macroeconomics. Apropos to mention, he has been quoted in the *Philadelphia Inquirer* and *The Wall Street Journal*. He was born, raised, and now resides in suburban Philadelphia with his wife and two boys. He has an undergraduate degree from Penn State, University Park campus, along with graduate degrees from Drexel and Villanova, and is a CFA charter holder to boot.

www.ingramcontent.com/pod-product-compliance
Lightning Source LLC
Chambersburg PA
CBHW030418290526
45786CB00001B/27